Deaf 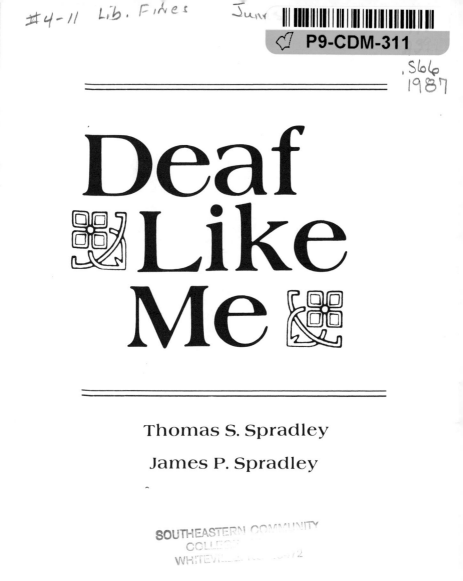 Like Me

Thomas S. Spradley

James P. Spradley

GALLAUDET UNIVERSITY PRESS

WASHINGTON, D.C.

Gallaudet University Press, Washington, DC 20002
© 1987 by Thomas S. Spradley and James P. Spradley
Epilogue © 1985 by Lynn L. Spradley

Hardcover edition published 1979 by Random House, Inc., New
York, NY 10022, and simultaneously in Canada by Random House
of Canada, Limited, Toronto.

Papercover edition published 1985 by Gallaudet University Press,
Washington, DC 20002, under agreement with Random House, Inc.

12 11 10 09 08 07   16 15 14 13 12 11

Manufactured in the United States of America.

Grateful acknowledgment is made to the following for permission to
reprint previously published materials:

 University of Illinois Press: Excerpts from *If You Have a Deaf
Child,* originally published in 1949 by the University of Illinois Press.
 Dr. McCay Vernon: Excerpts from "The Failure of the
Education of the Deaf," by Dr. McCay Vernon.
 The New Republic: Excerpts from "Dumb Children," by James
Ridgeway, originally published in *The New Republic* (August 2, 1969).
 John Tracy Clinic: Excerpts from the John Tracy Clinic
Correspondence Course for Parents of Preschool Deaf Children.

Library of Congress Cataloging-in-Publication Data

Spradley, Thomas S.
 Deaf like me.
 1. Children, Deaf. 2. Deaf—Means of communication. 3.
Children, Deaf—Family relationships. I. Spradley, James P. II. Title.
HV2391.S66 1985 362.4'2'088054 85-4468
ISBN 0-930323-11-4 (pbk.)

In memory of Jim

Jim Spradley had two rare gifts, perfected by good and faithful use: He could understand the lives of others—their fears and hopes—and see the whole texture of the world through their eyes. And he could put it all down so that the reader understood too.

—*William C. Stokoe, Jr.*

One

Louise screamed and sat bolt upright in a cold sweat.

"Wake up!" I whispered hoarsely and reached across to her in the darkness. "It's okay. It's okay. You must have been dreaming."

I could feel the tenseness in her shoulders begin to relax. Fully awake now, she shivered, then began to sob uncontrollably. We lay back down and I held her close.

"What's wrong?" I asked.

Louise didn't answer for several minutes. Then, between sobs, came the rush of questions. "Oh, Tom! Why does our baby have to suffer? Why me? I don't want to have a handicapped child. I just know it'll be blind. It's so senseless and cruel. Why does it have to happen? Why? Isn't there anything we can do?"

I didn't try to answer right away. I lay still, searching for words of reassurance.

"We don't know for *sure* that anything is wrong." I spoke as calmly as I could. "Even if you *did* have German measles, the baby could still be completely normal. Don't you remember what Dr. Bales said?"

I could hear the clock on our dresser ticking. I stared into the blackness and wondered if Bruce, our three-and-a-half-year-old, asleep in the next room, had heard us. I listened for noises from the students who lived upstairs, but all seemed quiet.

It was early November 1964, and Louise was five months pregnant. She had awakened in the night several times in recent weeks. Troubled. Anxious. Afraid. We talked often about the dangerous possibilities and struggled to dismiss our fears. We both felt helpless. But for Louise, as her body changed to ac-

1

commode the new life, it became such an intimate, personal experience that all my assurances could not completely dispel the foreboding.

It had begun more than six months earlier.

I had just finished my first year of teaching mathematics at Wheaton College in the Chicago suburb of Wheaton, Illinois, and we planned to travel until classes started again in September.

We loaded our 1960 Volvo with suitcases, sleeping bags and camping equipment, said good-bye to our friends, and headed north for Highway 90 and a carefree summer.

"Where are we going?" Bruce asked, squirming with excitement in the crowded back seat.

"To Minnesota," Louise told him, and she described the dormitories in which we would live for the next few weeks. I had received a summer stipend to attend a National Science Foundation institute for college math teachers at Carleton College in Northfield, Minnesota.

"Will we see Grandma and Grandpa there?" he asked.

"No," I said. "After Minnesota we're going on to California. They live in Los Angeles, where you were born." He had asked the same questions dozens of times before.

In less than an hour the Chicago skyline disappeared and we passed mile after mile of newly planted cornfields in southern Wisconsin. Late in the afternoon we arrived in Northfield and quickly found our way to Carleton College. I checked in, met the staff of the institute, and talked to some of the other students. We moved into two small rooms in the dormitory, an old ivy-covered brick building where we would spend the next five weeks. Louise and I started unpacking while Bruce went in search of other children on our floor.

The first weeks of the summer institute went by too quickly. Daily math classes each morning. Breakfast, lunch and dinner came cafeteria style in the basement of our dormitory. Louise painted, took long walks and looked after Bruce. I studied with several students each afternoon, but by dinnertime everyone had reached his limit of mathematics. The hot humid evenings drove us outside; five or six families would sit on the cool lawn or front steps of the dorm and tell stories of life at the various colleges from which they came. With sundown came thick clouds of mosquitoes that sent us back inside. Weekends we explored the Minnesota countryside.

One morning near the end of the first week Bruce went down the hall to play with his friends. In minutes he returned looking quite dejected. "Johnny and Billy are sick and can't play."

"You'll just have to find some of the other kids," Louise said matter-of-factly. The dormitories swarmed with children and most went to a college-directed summer activities program. We knew it wouldn't take Bruce long to make up for the loss of his two friends.

Later that morning their mother told Louise, "They have a rash. I think it must be the three-day measles because they don't seem too sick. But I thought I'd better keep them in for a day or two."

We hardly gave it a second thought. I went to class. Louise set up her easel outside and spent the morning painting. Later in the day Bruce found two older boys and joined them for a hike around the campus lake, a favorite place to hunt for frogs and feed the ducks.

One morning a week and a half later Bruce woke up complaining, "I don't feel good, Mom!" There was a bright-red rash on his chest and stomach, tiny spots coalescing here and there into larger blotches.

"I think I'll take his temperature," Louise said as I was shaving. Several minutes later she called from Bruce's room, "It's a little above normal. Probably better have him checked." We hurried down to the basement cafeteria for a quick breakfast and to bring some juice back for Bruce, who had stayed in bed. Louise saw Johnny and Billy's mother and asked for the name of the doctor she had called. It didn't seem serious. We only wanted to be sure.

I came back to the dormitory after my morning classes. "What did the doctor say?" I asked.

"It looks like rubella; that's what they call German measles. He said there's a lot of it going around."

"That's not serious, is it?"

"No, but he asked if I was pregnant. I told him I wasn't sure but that we had wanted another child. If I am pregnant, it could only be a few days. He said to come back and see him if it turns out I'm pregnant because rubella sometimes causes congenital defects in babies."

"Congenital defects?" I tried to hide the concern in my voice. "Like what? Did he say?"

The doctor hadn't explained exactly what he meant. Louise hadn't asked. That night we talked about the possibility that she was pregnant and wondered silently what might happen. When Bruce was born Louise had often said, "I don't care if it's a boy or girl as long as it's healthy." Now we tried not to think about the risk of congenital defects.

In two or three days Bruce was charging around our two rooms begging to go out. His rash had almost disappeared. But somehow the texture of the summer had changed for Louise and me. She lost interest in painting. Sometimes while I was working through a problem in finite algebra, a sense of dread would unexpectedly well up within me. When we were having dinner with the other families we laughed and talked as before, but beneath the surface of our lives we felt anxious and confused.

"I sure hope I'm not pregnant," Louise said at least three or four times a day. Two weeks dragged by. Each day she checked for any sign of a rash.

"How are you feeling today?" I routinely asked and we both knew what I meant. No symptoms of rubella, no signs of pregnancy.

Two more weeks and the summer institute ended. We said goodbye to the staff and to our many new friends. We headed north on Highway 35 to Minneapolis and St. Paul, the North Woods and Canada. When we settled into the long drive Louise remarked, as if to close a brief chapter in our lives, "Well, I'm sure I would have come down with a rash in a couple of weeks if I was going to get it. Maybe I had German measles in childhood. They say you can get it only once."

We picked up the Trans-Canadian Highway in Ontario and headed for the West Coast, camping along the way. As we left Banff National Park high on the eastern slope of the Canadian Rockies, Louise complained of an upset stomach. "I might go to my old doctor when we get back to L.A. and see if I'm pregnant," she added almost as an afterthought.

We decided not to pitch our tent that night and slept instead in a lonely motel on the Fraser River in British Columbia. Louise was restless, tossing, turning. Long after midnight I woke with a start.

"I'm covered with a rash!" Louise cried out. We tried not to wake Bruce, turned on a light and searched in vain for the small red blotches she had seen in her dream. Nothing. We drifted back to sleep.

One week later, as the parched brown hills of the Tehachapis gave way to the suburbs of Los Angeles, a rush of memories flooded us both. We had grown up here and married in the Eagle Rock Baptist church. We reminisced and watched the signs and picked our way through the maze of familiar freeways from San Fernando to North Hollywood to Glendale, and finally along Colorado Boulevard to Eagle Rock, where our parents still lived.

Louise had missed a period and we suspected she might be pregnant. But somehow the whole matter seemed less important now; we decided to wait until we returned to Illinois, where Louise could see her regular doctor. Eagerly we fell into the excitement of looking up friends, visiting places rich with childhood memories and talking with relatives.

Louise first noticed it on Saturday afternoon. She held up her arms and cried out in disbelief, "Tom! I've got a rash!"

Like hundreds of miniature volcanoes, the crimson eruptions had spread evenly over the inside of her arms. We looked at each other. All the uncertainty and fear that had slowly dissolved suddenly took form and came rushing back into our lives. For several minutes Louise looked at her arms as if she expected these

5

purplish red spots that had chased her imagination across the continent to suddenly disappear.

I looked up Dr. Anderson's number, dialed it for Louise and handed her the phone. The receptionist put her through.

"Hello, Dr. Anderson, I'm Louise Spradley. I used to be your patient when we lived in L.A. about a year ago. I'm living in Illinois now but I'm back here on vacation."

Dr. Anderson remembered and Louise described her symptoms, then answered his questions. Yes, she might be pregnant. No, she didn't know if she had ever had German measles. Yes, she had been exposed to rubella but it had been almost a month before. No, the rash had only appeared on her arms.

"You'd better come in first thing Monday morning," Dr. Anderson told her. "There's a real epidemic of rubella this year and it can cause defects like brain damage, blindness, deafness and heart problems in the unborn baby. But it only happens in about twenty percent of the babies. And that's only if the mother had rubella in the first three months of pregnancy, so don't start worrying until we know for sure."

"If it is German measles," I heard Louise ask, her voice trembling slightly, "what are the chances of having an abortion?"

"Not in California," Dr. Anderson replied. "I don't know about Illinois, but there are three doctors on trial right now for performing abortions on women who had rubella."

"Okay. I'll see you then on Monday morning." Louise hung up the phone and collapsed in tears.

Monday morning we parked at the clinic and entered through a rear door. "Just in case you have rubella," Dr. Anderson had explained; "I don't want you to infect anyone in the waiting room." Louise went into an examination room and I waited in Dr. Anderson's office.

"Well, your wife is pregnant. We've verified that," Dr. Anderson said to me as he and Louise returned and sat down. "I'm not so sure about the rash," he added thoughtfully as he inspected Louise's arms. He felt for swollen glands at the back of her neck.

"It could be rubella, but I don't think so. I'll tell you what—to be on the safe side, I'll give you a shot of gamma globulin that carries the rubella antibody. If this rash is something else, the shot may still keep you from getting rubella. And in any case, it may protect the fetus."

We walked out the back door of the clinic almost as uncertain as when we entered. A few days later we drove back to Illinois, the events of the past week having settled over our lives like a dark cloud. Louise was pregnant; we knew that for sure. Rubella, on the other hand, had remained as elusive as ever. If the rash was something else, we did not need to worry. But how could we be certain? And could we be sure the shot of gamma globulin would protect the baby?

We made a doctor's appointment the day we arrived in Wheaton. Before classes began at the college, on a humid, overcast day, we went to see Dr. Bales, our family physician. A kindly man in his mid-thirties, he listened attentively as we recounted the events of the summer. He told us about the defects caused by rubella, then added quickly, "I don't think you need to worry, the pediatrician you saw in California certainly sees a lot more German measles than most doctors. His diagnosis was probably right. And even if you did have rubella, the chances are still good that your baby will be completely normal."

"What about getting an abortion?" Louise asked hesitantly. "Is there any place I could go for one?"

"No, not a chance," he said, dismissing her question with finality. "Not in Illinois. It's against the law. It just isn't possible and I don't know of any place else where you could get one."

We left his office in what had begun to seem like a perpetual state of uncertainty. Puzzled and confused, we now started to wonder if there were any answers.

Indian summer soon brightened our days and renewed our spirits. The leaves on the elm and maple trees that shaded the campus lawn across the street from our house turned from green to gold, then drifted slowly to the ground. We looked forward to Thanksgiving and the brief holiday from classes. We were living downstairs in a large house that belonged to the college. The Ferris House, as it was called, housed sixteen students upstairs and we served as house parents. Several of the students could not travel home and we invited them to join us for a traditional turkey dinner.

On Tuesday of that week Louise went downtown to shop. Almost willing to believe that the odds were on our side, she walked with confidence through the brisk November air. For the moment, the expansive sky reflected her inner feelings. In the distance she noticed another young mother with four children walking down the street toward her.

"Look at the puppies, Mom!" Bruce tugged at her hand. They stopped to admire four collie pups in a pet-store window, then continued walking. The group she had noticed earlier was now quite close. As if a bolt of lightning had suddenly illuminated a hidden landscape, Louise saw the youngest of the children. Protruding from each tiny ear was an enormous plastic earpiece. Unsightly cords ran down to a small box held in a holster strapped to her chest.

Horror-stricken, Louise turned abruptly into the nearest store until the children and their mother had passed. Fighting back the tears, she walked back to the car and drove home. For several weeks the sight of that little girl haunted her thoughts.

Winter came early and stayed late. Temperatures seemed to drop lower, winds blew harder, snows piled higher, muddy drifts lasted longer, buds and leaves came slower. But by every indication our baby was developing normally. Louise gained just enough weight each month. We felt the first tiny kick on time. I can still see Bruce, his hand on Louise's stomach, his eyes wide with wonder at the movement inside. The baby's heartbeat came on schedule; when Dr. Bales heard it he said, "It sounds healthy." The baby moved into position without difficulty. The last act of our long drama drew to a close.

"I think you're about ready to deliver," Dr. Bales told Louise at her final checkup in early April. But a week went by. Most of the students at Wheaton College left for the Easter recess. A strange silence hung in the air. Several times I awoke in the dead of night, traced out the route to the hospital, then fell asleep again before getting there.

Louise was tugging at my arm. "I'm having some contractions."

"Three-thirty." It was Good Friday morning.

I called my brother Joe, who also taught at Wheaton College; he and his wife, Marilyn, had offered to take care of Bruce.

"Are they getting stronger?" I asked Louise as we pulled away from my brother's house.

"A little, but I'm okay."

The brick houses on Gary Road ended abruptly and I turned west on Jewell Road. We drove by recently plowed fields and I stepped on the accelerator. I could see the octagonal stop sign at the County Farm Road ahead, but the darkness in both directions told me no cars were approaching. I sped through the intersection without slowing down.

"Let's hope it's not a false alarm," I said, reaching out to squeeze Louise's hand.

"It sure doesn't feel like it. And if it is, I'm not coming home till I have this baby!" I caught a trace of her smile, then the next contraction came and I could sense the pain had increased.

We both fell silent as the gray outline of the Community Hospital in the tiny town of Winfield came into view. Our months of uncertainty, the intolerable waiting, was about to end. Neither of us could talk about what was really uppermost on our minds. I helped Louise out of the car. Within an hour a nurse took her into the delivery room.

I walked to the empty waiting room, sat down and absent-mindedly picked up the nearest magazine on the table beside my chair. I began leafing through it, an old issue of *Today's Health*, at the same time wondering how painful the final contractions would become, hoping it wouldn't take all night. The large print at the top of one page caught my eye: TODAY'S HEALTH NEWS. I looked down the page for subtitles of interest:

Chest Injuries
Water Allergy
Healthier Babies
German Measles Hazard!

I began to devour the last news item:

Laboratory test now can determine whether a pregnant woman exposed to German measles actually contracted the disease. It is important to know this because the virus infection can cause mental retardation or other defects in her baby. A therapeutic abortion may be advisable if she really had become infected. Mild symptoms can be missed, but the tests can give the answer, Dr. Stanley A. Plotkin of Philadelphia writes in the *AMA Journal.*

Lab tests! Mental retardation! A therapeutic abortion! Stunned and angry, I could feel the blood rising in my neck. Why hadn't our doctors told us of these possibilities? The months of worry and fear flashed before me.

Perhaps the test was too new. I turned to the front of the magazine, searching for the date. January 1965. And this was April 16, 1965! The piece must have been written at least a month before it was published, and Dr. Plotkin's statement had appeared in the AMA Journal before that! How long could it take for such tests to become available? I read the paragraph again.

I paced up and down the long hallway of the obstetrics wing of the hospital. Why hadn't we known about the tests? Would we ever know if Louise had had German measles? Would the baby be normal? What should I tell Louise? Should I ask Dr. Bales about the tests?

It was too late. In a short time we would know more than any test could have told us. I was still thinking about the news item when a nurse appeared in the doorway. "You can come down to the delivery room now, Mr. Spradley. You have a healthy baby girl.''

A great sense of relief swept over me. As I followed the nurse down the hospital corridor I glanced down at my watch. It was six-forty.

I met Dr. Bales outside the delivery room. His blue eyes beamed with pride. ''You've got a fine baby daughter,'' he said. ''Your wife's doing fine too.''

I felt an instant of uneasiness. Even though he exuded confidence and authority, I wondered if he knew something more but wouldn't tell me.

''Is there any sign of problems caused by rubella?'' I asked hesitantly.

''No. You don't need to worry. Your daughter is a fine healthy specimen.'' He smiled broadly. ''It's only a small percentage of babies that are affected by rubella, and if anything was wrong, it would have been easy to tell. Like a missing finger or toe. You have a perfectly normal baby girl. You can go home and get some rest.''

''Here's your daughter!'' A nurse had pushed through the swinging door of the delivery room. Wrapped in a white hospital blanket, her eyes shut, Lynn looked crinkly and pink and very tiny.

I went in to see Louise. ''A missing finger or toe.'' The words still rang in my ears. Was that all we had worried about for these many long months? Or had Dr. Bales meant that something lacking would have been the clue to look for more serious defects? I didn't know.

Louise smiled weakly. I squeezed her hand, and before I could say anything she asked, ''What did the doctor tell you about Lynn?''

''He said she's all right. Nothing wrong. He checked her and she's normal. Isn't that a relief?''

Louise squeezed my hand in silent agreement and closed her eyes.

Later she recalled that moments after Lynn was born Dr. Bales said, "It's a girl."

"Can she see?" Louise asked.

The nurse turned quizzically to Dr. Bales. "Why in the world does she want to know that?"

Two

"A perfectly normal baby girl!"

I felt so elated I wanted to shout it to everyone I saw as I drove home from the hospital. I stopped at my brother's house.

"It's a girl. And perfectly normal!" Joe and Marilyn had shared our fears of German measles; now they shared the joy and relief as they asked about Louise. Bruce woke up while we ate breakfast and I told him.

"I've got a sister too!" he said proudly to Danny, his cousin. And then he begged, "Can I come to the hospital and see Mom and my baby sister?"

"It's a girl. And perfectly normal." I said it again and again that morning as I called Louise's parents, my parents and several close friends in Wheaton who knew about our encounter with German measles.

Yet that evening when I went back to see Louise I knew that neither of us had discarded our fears completely. We hardly dared let ourselves believe the good news.

"Is she really okay?" Louise asked Dr. Bales each morning when he made his rounds. We half expected he would discover some hidden abnormality, but each day brought new assurances of Lynn's perfect condition.

I studied Lynn through the nursery window. I scrutinized her features. I watched her wave her little arms and kick her spindly legs. I observed her sleeping and crying. Whenever she was brought in for feeding, Louise searched for any clues that might reveal a defect. But Lynn looked like all the other healthy babies in the nursery and appeared as normal as Bruce at his age. She cried lustily, ate eagerly and slept peacefully.

I remember the day they came home from the hospital. Bruce sat in the front seat between Louise and me, talking to Lynn as if she understood every word. "Hi, Lynn. You're gonna live at my house. And we have lots of students upstairs. You can ride my trike." He placed one of his fingers in her tiny hand and squealed with delight when she held on. "When will she talk?" he asked.

"She has to learn," Louise explained. "Babies can't talk when they're born, but Lynn will learn. When she's two years old she'll be jabbering just like you did."

"Did Dr. Bales say anything more about Lynn today?" I asked Louise.

"He said that Lynn had a discharge exam this morning by a pediatrician. The doctors are sure she is okay. No sign of any problem. Either I didn't have German measles or it's just a miracle."

"Did he say what kinds of things the pediatrician checked?"

"Yes, he checked her skin, the size and shape of her head, her reflexes. He looked in her eyes and ears with special instruments, examined her mouth, her throat, everything. Dr. Bales told me that they listened to her heart and lungs and they are completely normal. There were other things, but I can't remember all of them. And everything was fine. Not a trace of a problem."

We arrived home in high spirits. Our resident students came to gaze and listen to Bruce extol the potential of his new baby sister. "And she can't talk yet but she's gonna learn to talk just like me when she's two," he exclaimed.

The students pooled their resources and purchased a month of diaper service for Lynn, undoubtedly one of the best gifts we received that spring.

During Lynn's first week at home Bruce watched with fascination as she drank from her bottle or squeezed his fingers in her tiny hand. Then, growing accustomed to having a baby in the house, he went back to playing with neighborhood children most of the time. The remaining weeks of the spring semester flew by and we all watched in amazement as Lynn grew more responsive each day. And then I was giving final exams and the disconcerting events of the previous summer seemed like ancient history.

On the Fourth of July, a bright sun filled the cloudless sky, evaporating the beads of moisture that sparkled across our lawn. I lifted the buggy down the three steps of our front porch; Louise laid Lynn on her back, tucking a blanket loosely around her legs. We all laughed as Bruce reached his hands far over his head, hoping to be the first to propel her carriage down the street. The parade would start in less than an hour but we had plenty of time.

Louise's mom and dad walked beside us. They had arrived at O'Hare International Airport on a hot, humid afternoon several days earlier.

"Oh, let me hold her," Mom had said as soon as we loaded their bags into the car. With the experienced eye of a grandmother she admired Lynn. "She is so healthy and looks so good," Mom said. Then she spoke directly to Lynn as if she could understand every word: "You're all right, aren't you? Such a good baby!" And Lynn had responded enthusiastically, smiling and wriggling in all directions at once. Nothing more had been said about the matter.

Five blocks from home on Main Street we found a place in the shade of a tall elm tree. A large crowd had gathered to see the local celebration and we could already hear the noise of a high school band in the distance. Louise and her mother talked about Lynn, who lay awake in the buggy between them. Bruce kept up a steady stream of chatter with his grandfather, talking about his friend Billy, the swing he wanted to hang from the tree in our front yard, the tree house planned by neighborhood kids.

The noise from unseen bands grew louder, the lead car came into view, a new Chevrolet convertible with the Grand Marshal sitting in the back. "Bruce! Look what's coming!" I called. He turned to look. The Grand Marshal waved to Bruce as the car glided slowly by in front of us.

"Look at that funny man, Grandpa!" Bruce laughed and pointed to a clown. Lynn seemed to listen contentedly in her buggy; she showed no concern for the resounding clang and clatter around her. A line of antique cars crawled by, decorated with streamers. The Wheaton Lions Club display, constructed on the back of a flatbed truck, moved slowly by, then came another band; a clown carrying an enormous bag tossed pieces of candy to outstretched hands on both sides of the street. Everywhere people smiled and waved. The deep-blue sky matched the carefree, holiday atmosphere.

By eleven-fifteen the parade was nearly over and we could hear the grand finale getting closer. Bruce grew excited. His grandfather hoisted him high onto his shoulders for a better view. We could see them now, the first of at least fifteen fire engines that brought up the end of the parade. With sirens at full blast they rolled slowly down the street. Engine Company 14 led the way, a giant hook-and-ladder rig, its bright fenders freshly polished, long ladders clinging to its sides. A fireman in a black helmet waved to us from far atop, where he controlled the rear steering mechanism. Then came a pumper, loaded with gleaming nozzles and coils of flattened hose. Bruce alternately waved to the men on the trucks and covered his ears to protect them from the shrieking sirens. They were deafening. I could no longer hear Louise's father beside me or my own shouts to Bruce.

Only a few seconds had passed when it occurred to me that Lynn might be terrified by the pealing dissonance that sent a current of excitement through the crowd. When I saw that she lay awake, quiet, undisturbed, gazing up into the elm tree overhead as if no one else were present, I relaxed, glad the sirens hadn't frightened her.

Then some instinct made me look closer. She did not flinch or turn; there was not the slightest movement or reaction to suggest that she even heard these sounds that vibrated in the air with such force. She could have been lying alone in her quiet bedroom enjoying the stillness of a summer day. A strange feeling crept up my spine as one by one the screaming trucks rolled by. The last hook and ladder moved off down Main Street and all I could think of was Dr. Bales reassurance: ". . . if anything was wrong,

it would have been easy to tell. Like a missing finger or toe.''
My thoughts flashed back over the last three months searching
for some clue we might have missed. Was it possible for a birth
defect to develop and lie hidden for months?

The crowd began to break up, small groups of people coalescing out of the mass, mothers and fathers holding firmly to
small children, all moving off to cars or turning to walk to nearby
homes. I wheeled Lynn's buggy around and watched her as we
started back, the blaring sounds of sirens and unanswered questions still ringing in my ears.

"How you doin' up there?" Louise's father was busy talking
to Bruce, who still rode his shoulders. Bruce surveyed the dis-
sipating crowd like a young prince looking down on his subjects.
I decided not to say anything about Lynn and the fire engines.

I thought back to the hundreds of times she must have heard
us. Whenever Lynn was awake, Louise and I talked and laughed
and sang to her. It didn't seem to matter that she could not
understand; there was plenty of time for that. From the start we
had spontaneously included her in our conversations. And Bruce
talked to Lynn as much as we did. He would stand beside her
crib endlessly describing his activities whether we were present
or not. And Lynn had responded to the sound of our voices. She
had rewarded us with her first smile only three weeks earlier
when Louise was changing her diaper and talking to her.

We had never wondered about Lynn's hearing but we had
worried about her eyes. "Tom, do you really think she can see
us?" Louise had asked at first. In early June we had checked to
see if she could follow moving objects, to calm our last lingering
doubts about rubella. Then, as Lynn began to focus, to turn and
look when we came into the room or spoke to her, we reassured
ourselves. "Look, she's turning her head to watch the teddy
bear," I had said one day when we were testing her vision. At
those times, too, it seemed clear that sounds were part of her
experience. If she was looking away from us and I shook her
rattle, often as not she would turn to look at it. Yes, we had been
sure Lynn was developing normally.

That evening, as dusk began to fill the eastern sky, we drove to the Cantigny War Memorial on Winfield Road, not far from the hospital where Lynn was born. The tanks and guns adjacent to the parking area had often fired Bruce's imagination with visions of some distant battlefield and sounds of exploding shells. Now he raced ahead and climbed up on the nearest dark-green half-track, which pulled a huge artillery piece behind it. Streams of people poured into the park from all directions; they laid out blankets, opened up lawn chairs and settled in to wait for the spectacular Fourth of July fireworks.

The warm evening grew dark; a soft breeze brought the smell of smoke bombs and sparklers. The stars came out one by one. We visited with Mom and Dad. Lynn soon fell asleep, lying on the blanket between Louise and me. The sense of anticipation grew and we could hear people in the groups around us asking, "When are they going to start?"

Without warning, the first explosion shook the air and a cheer went up from the waiting crowd. A rocket flashed its arching stream of fire across the heavens. Almost instantly hundreds of fireflies lit up in a simultaneous response from the grass and trees around us. But while the others watched the sky, Louise and I couldn't take our eyes off Lynn. Louise also had detected Lynn's calmness at the parade.

Barooom! The roar of the next explosion jolted the night air; you could *feel* it as well as *hear* it. I detected a slight twitch; the muscles in Lynn's hands tightened momentarily and then relaxed. The noise had startled her! I glanced at Louise; she had seen it too. But after the small spasm, not another muscle moved. Unawakened, her breathing came in the steady rhythm of peaceful slumber. I thought of touching her to see if that might arouse her, but held back as the next volley turned into a fountain of color floating slowly earthward like a thousand tiny parachutes of blue and green and orange. Then followed one explosion after another, each accompanied by brilliant color. But Lynn slept until the end, only waking as we gathered our belongings and headed for the car.

A few days later, after Louise's parents had left, we talked about what had happened.

"I'm not sure whether she heard those fire engines at all," I said. "She sure didn't show it."

"Yes, but she flinched ever so slightly when the first explosions came at Cantigny," Louise added, a note of perplexity in her voice.

"Maybe she just ignored the sirens. Maybe they were *too* loud."

"But, Tom, don't you think a baby with normal hearing would wake up crying? Those fireworks were deafening."

"I just don't know. Maybe Lynn is just a sound sleeper."

Then Louise, whose apprehension had never completely vanished, recalled other observations. "Most of the time when I go in with her bottle she turns her head and watches me coming; I've just assumed she always heard me. If I hold her bottle up or shake it in front of her, she starts sucking and waving her arms.

"But yesterday when I started to go into her room, about ten while you and Bruce were out, I noticed she was awake. So I just stood there and watched her staring at the string of toys hanging across her crib. She looked so happy and contented. I stayed real quiet for about a minute until I knew she hadn't seen me. 'Lynn. Lynn,' I called quietly before she looked in my direction. It was as if I wasn't there! She just kept looking at the string of toys. I stayed still, didn't move a bit, and called again, louder this time, 'Lynn, here's your bottle.' But she didn't turn her head or respond in any way.

"Finally I called her name as loud as I could and when she didn't look, I went to her crib. Right away she turned to look at me! She smiled and waved her arms—it was almost like she had been playing a game with me. When I walked out of there I had the strangest feeling in the pit of my stomach, like something dreadful was about to happen and I couldn't stop it. I think she may be *deaf*!"

DEAF! The word hit me with unexpected force, as if someone had hurled an iron bar through a plate-glass window, shattering the protective screen of explanations I had erected for Lynn's perplexing lack of response to sound. And then, as if welded to other ideas through some long past association, the words tumbled through my mind.

DEAF-AND-DUMB!

DEAF-MUTE!

The words came uninvited, set off like a chain reaction. I didn't know anything about deafness.

Louise remembered an uncle who couldn't hear very well; people had to shout at him as he bent his ear in their direction. Most of the time he sat quietly on the edge of conversations.

My thoughts went back to Bethel Temple, a large Pentecostal church in downtown Los Angeles, and a Sunday morning I hadn't recalled for more than twenty years. I couldn't have been more than seven or eight, sitting with my elder brothers on the long hardback pews. That morning, as usual, I expected the hour and a half to drag by while I drew pictures, whispered, fell asleep momentarily, or sat hoping for some small disaster that would bring the long church service to an end.

Up front, not far from us, I could see someone standing, facing the people, making gestures. Mom whispered when I pointed, ''Those are some deaf people visiting this morning and that lady is telling them what the preacher is saying.'' I sat entranced, spellbound by the intricate patterns her hands painted in the air. Up and down, now jabbing, twisting, curling; clenched fists, open hands waving, fingers pointing, palms touching and sliding across each other, arms crossing, darting here and there. And always with such speed and smoothness that it seemed to pull me along.

I sat through the entire service that morning, forgetting to ask Dad if I could be excused early, and when it ended, instead of racing for the door, I lingered and watched the people in the front rows get up to leave. Their hands and bodies came alive. Smiling, nodding, pointing, heads tilting, their facial expressions became silent gestures that kept time with their hands. It was difficult to separate their hands from their faces; they changed together in a kind of hidden rhythm. Somehow, behind all these grotesque and beautiful movements I sensed there was another world, one that our family had never seen, could not be part of. For days afterward I thought about these people, wondered who they were, where they went. Eventually I had forgotten about them. But now the memory returned.

"Maybe we're worrying too much," I said to Louise. "Jumping to conclusions too fast. Let's go check her now."

Together we went to her room and peered in quietly. Her tiny arms moved back and forth as if she wanted to grasp the rattle that hung just beyond her reach. Slowly we edged into her room; hardly daring to breathe, we watched for a long moment.

"Lynn!" Louise called softly.

Her head turned toward us and she broke into a delighted smile of recognition as if she had been waiting for us to come and call her name. Incredulous, Louise and I looked at each other, a mixture of surprise and relief written on both our faces. We burst out laughing at the same time.

"She certainly seems to have heard that," I said.

"She sure did," Louise replied. "I guess maybe she just felt like ignoring the sounds she heard some of those other times."

August turned hot and humid. One afternoon the air became oppressive, and light-gray clouds settled over us. Louise and I were stretched out on lawn chairs in the backyard while Bruce splashed in the shallow water of his plastic pool. Shortly after two it grew darker and the clouds took on a greenish cast.

"Looks like a storm coming up," I said to Louise.

Rain spattered across the yard as we folded up the lawn chairs. Then the first crack of thunder exploded directly overhead and shook the house.

"You'd better get Lynn," I said to Louise.

In a few seconds Louise came back into the kitchen carrying Lynn wrapped in a blanket. The way she looked at Lynn told me it had happened again. "Tom, she hadn't moved," Louise said. "She was sound asleep—and all this thunder."

Before I could say anything, an announcer, who sounded calm but serious, interrupted the music on the radio: "There is a tornado warning for all the western suburbs of Chicago, including Du Page County, in effect until four P.M." The kitchen light went off, along with the radio, then both came back on after a few seconds. I got a flashlight and a transistor radio, and we all huddled in the basement for the next hour while the wind and rain beat against the house with hurricane force. Every time the thunder shook the house I couldn't help watching Lynn, who had awakened briefly but fallen asleep again. The mystery lay unsolved, pushed to the back of our minds. By five o'clock the storm had passed, the sky had cleared, and the air felt clean and normal again when we went outside to check for fallen branches.

One day in the middle of August, Lynn temporarily set our fears to rest. We sat in the backyard trying to keep cool; Lynn, dressed only in a diaper, looked up at the world from her place on a blanket spread out at our feet. Louise picked her up and talked to her, laughing and throwing her head back and forth. Lynn suddenly laughed out loud!

"Listen to her!" Louise cried out in delight. Lynn laughed again, and again, as we both sat entranced. Like the sudden parting of dark storm clouds to allow the sun to break through, that small happy sound of laughter brought new hope. If she could laugh out loud, we thought, surely she must be able to hear.

Three

In the months that followed, Lynn smiled and laughed and cooed; she sat up on time and began babbling just the way Bruce had done. With each new development our hopes soared; for days we *knew* she heard us. Then she ignored our voices, and all the old doubts came rushing back and our spirits dropped.

In November, when Lynn was seven months old, she started banging her head and rolling her eyes. It began soon after she learned to sit by herself in her crib.

"Tom!" Louise called one day. "What is Lynn doing?" She sounded horrified and I quickly joined her in the bedroom. Propped against the end of her crib, Lynn was shaking her head back and forth, banging it against the wooden end. Each time her head struck the wood, the crib worked its way a few more inches across the floor. Then she stopped and rolled up her eyes, almost as if she wanted to see the underside of her eyelids. The pupils disappeared completely and left only the whites of her eyes exposed.

"Something must be wrong, Tom! Could she be retarded? Do you think it could be brain damage?"

I quickly picked up Lynn and her eyes moved down; she smiled and looked pleased with herself. I fought back the fears even as I tried to sound confident. "I don't think it's anything to worry about. Just because Lynn doesn't act exactly as Bruce did, we can't jump to conclusions all the time. Kids are all different."

But all through December and into January our hopes and suspicions chased one another in a vicious circle. Like detectives, we worked overtime, trying to catch the truth about Lynn. The head banging and eye rolling continued, as did her game of "Now

I hear you, now I don't.'' Sometimes we felt depressed; then we made overconfident declarations that Lynn *must* be O.K., and our hopes lifted for a few days. Round and round we went. For me it was enough to wonder if she could hear; the possibility of brain damage was almost unthinkable.

In January, Louise took Lynn in for her nine-month checkup. Louise sat in the examination room and watched Dr. Bales test Lynn's reflexes and listen to her heart.

"She's a good baby and we find her really responsive,'' Louise said. "Last summer, on the Fourth of July, we noticed that she didn't seem to hear the loud sirens or the fireworks. For the last six months we've tested her in dozens of different ways—coming up behind her, making loud noises, creeping into her bedroom when she's asleep and calling her name. Sometimes we think she can hear us; other times it seems like she can't.''

Dr. Bales listened patiently, reached again for a small instrument with a light that shone through a tiny funnel at the top. He bent over Lynn and looked through it into her ears again, taking at least a minute to scrutinize the details of each small opening.

Then he told Louise, "Well, there's nothing wrong with her ears as far as I can tell. Sometimes small babies just ignore sounds. Why don't you wait until Lynn is sleeping, then make a loud noise and watch for the slightest reaction from her. I really don't think there's anything for you to worry about. In any event, it's not possible to make a conclusive test until she is a few years older.''

They discussed Lynn's head banging and eye rolling. "Nothing to worry about, it's something some infants do. Just let me know if it persists.''

As Louise left his office she couldn't help but feel a trace of embarrassment. Did Dr. Bales think we were merely overanxious parents? Had we read too much into Lynn's erratic responses to sounds? Perhaps knowing about rubella influenced us to see things that didn't exist.

But now we both felt reassured. Louise had expressed our doubts and gained a professional opinion at the same time. Within a few weeks Lynn's head banging decreased. By late February it had disappeared entirely and her eye rolling had turned into a coy game. She turned her head away from us, looked down at the floor, and then slowly peeked at us out of the corner of her eye until we laughed. Then she would break into a wide smile and start the game over again.

We diligently administered the sleeping tests. Sometimes Lynn passed, sometimes she failed; most of the time we couldn't tell whether she had passed or failed. When she fell asleep for her afternoon nap, Louise sometimes vacuumed the entire bedroom and Lynn slept peacefully through it all. On several occasions we crept into the bedroom together and popped an inflated paper bag near Lynn's head. She flinched visibly but did not wake up. If we touched her, she woke up easily.

"But she's always been a sound sleeper," I argued after these tests, and Louise agreed. We both knew that Bruce also slept soundly. More than once, when he had fallen asleep during a noisy television program, I had lifted him off the couch and carried him to bed. He never woke up.

More amazing yet, the train had never aroused him at night. When we first arrived in Wheaton it was dark when we moved into the Ferris House; we didn't realize that the commuter train to Chicago passed less than fifty yards behind our yard. We had unpacked some of our things and went to bed exhausted. Sometime around two in the morning we were jolted from our sleep by what sounded like a locomotive going through our bedroom. Bruce remained sound asleep. Never once in three years did he awaken to the roar of that nightly engine or the clackety-clack of iron wheels against the tracks. Was Lynn, at ten months, supposed to be more sensitive to sound in her sleep than Bruce had been?

Lynn did continue to respond to many sounds. In the afternoon she sometimes looked in my direction when I came in the front door from work.

"I really think she hears you come in," Louise commented more than once.

One afternoon in March I arrived home as usual but opened the front door quietly. I peered into the kitchen to see if Lynn had looked in my direction. She was watching Louise knead dough for bread. Almost without thinking, I slammed the door to see if I could get her attention. Startled, she looked up instantly, her head searching in every direction but mine for the sound or the vibration she felt.

Louise heard me open the door again but sensed another experiment was under way; she did not look up or say anything. I slipped back outside, went around to the rear of the house, stealthily crept in and closed the back door softly behind me. I could now approach Lynn unseen. I tiptoed up behind her.

"Lynn." I spoke quietly and in an even tone.

She did not move. Had she seen me out of the corner of her eye and decided to play this game of "I know you're there, Daddy, but I'm not going to look"?

"Lynn."

I spoke louder this time, still careful not to make any movement. Nothing. Not a shift in her gaze, not a muscle twitch, not a hint of interest or awareness. I did not want to give myself away by any movement or vibration. Not by the slightest stirring of my breath or even a shadow cast within her range of vision.

"*Lynn!*"

The room echoed with the reverberation of my voice. Lynn instantly looked up at Louise, a faintly quizzical expression on her face. Then, completely ignoring me, she looked back at the cup and spoon that had occupied her attention on the tray. Louise and I looked at each other, baffled, perplexed, not wanting to accept the evidence we both had witnessed. Half a minute dragged by and then, gently, without speaking, I touched Lynn's shoulder. She whirled around instantly and broke into an eager smile.

I looked at Louise and read the test results in her expression. Neither of us said what we both knew. *Lynn could not hear*. At least not like Bruce had heard at this age and not like other children we had observed. Yet it seemed so elusive. Almost invisible. She experienced no pain or discomfort. No bleeding.

If only we had known someone to talk to, someone who had known a deaf baby. Was Lynn one in a million? Were there other parents somewhere who had struggled with these same perplexing questions? We didn't even know where to start looking for such parents.

In April we noticed something peculiar about Lynn's voice. From the day she was born she used her voice to cry, and then later to coo and laugh. By the time she had reached four or five months she responded to our voices with soft "aaaaahhh's" and "ooooohhh's." At six months she started to babble, and slowly this turned into a kind of meaningless baby talk—"gagaga," "bababa," "ninini," "mumumu," "dododo," "tatata"—short strings of consonants and vowels that sounded identical to the noises Bruce had made at that age.

In recent months we had noticed that she babbled less and less—unlike Bruce, who had talked in nonsense syllables for minutes at a time. We tried in vain to coax her. We wanted her to make more sound, not less. We talked to her far more than we had ever talked to Bruce at the same age.

A few days before Lynn's first birthday Louise was sitting on the couch after dinner reading to Bruce from his favorite book, *Skin Diving*. Although only five, Bruce was obsessed with scuba diving. Louise was holding Lynn, who seemed to thoroughly enjoy the pictures and the sound of Louise's animated voice. Louise read aloud about the hand signals used for communicating under water: "going up," "going down," "I am okay," "I need air," "time." Louise closed the book and the three of them played happily together. Lynn became quite animated and laughed delightedly as Bruce smiled and frowned and made grotesque faces.

"Ma ma ma ma ma," Louise said to Lynn as she had done many times before. I was reading on the other side of the room when Louise called to me without looking up. "Tom, come and look at Lynn, I think she's trying to say her first word!" I joined them and watched. Whenever Louise said "ma ma," Lynn would come right back with a silent but perfectly mouthed "ma ma." We coaxed her and said it louder, enunciating each syllable.

"Ma ma," her lips formed clearly, but still with no sound. Again and again we tried, but she would only make the tiny mouth gestures, lips tightly together, then opened wide. No "mmmm," no vowel sound, not even a whisper accompanied her movements. A few weeks later she mouthed "da da" clearly, distinctly, silently.

Then, just before school ended in June, a similar thing happened when Louise and I sat down to watch the early news on our portable TV, which sat on a round coffee table in the living room. Lynn hardly ever watched the picture except when it magically came on or disappeared—that fascinated her. Now she crawled over to the TV set, pulled herself up beside it, reached for the on-off switch and tried to turn it. Her little hands could not quite manage the required coordination.

"No! No!" I said emphatically, shaking my head. I picked her up and put her on the floor beside us. Walter Cronkite finished talking about a growing conflict between warring factions in Vietnam, and a commercial came on. Lynn reached for the switch; we waited for a minute to see if she could master the task she had set her mind to. Then, as Cronkite appeared again, she turned and looked at us with her hand still on the switch, an impish grin on her face.

"No! No!" She distinctly formed the words with rounded lips and shook her head slowly back and forth. Only her voice was missing.

A few days later, during another TV program, she pulled herself up and fumbled with one of the knobs until the picture faded away. She whirled around to look at us, pleased with her achievement, a puzzled grin on her face. In the next instant her hand went out toward us, palm turned up, in the gesture Louise always used when Lynn had finished all the food in her dish.

"All gone!" she mouthed at the same instant. But no sound joined her words.

I looked at Louise in amazement. "She just said two words

and she understands what they mean!" I burst out excitedly. "But why doesn't she use her voice?"

"I guess she's never heard it," Louise replied in a quiet, straightforward way.

It took a few seconds for her words to sink in. Then, like some timed device, their meaning exploded in my mind. She doesn't know about her own voice! She can't *make* sounds because she can't *hear* sounds. For the first time the full connection between hearing and talking came together like powerful magnets.

I thought about the months and months of learning she had missed. No chance to locate the sources of sound. No opportunity to make the fine discriminations between different kinds of noises or to distinguish one voice from another. How easily Bruce had learned to connect sound with faces, sound with lip movements, sound with the quick darting motions of our tongues. And finally to connect sound with his own voice.

With Lynn, we had completely taken for granted our reliance on sound. What had she missed? I wanted to rush back in time, to live through her first year again, this time not wondering if she could hear.

Even in the nursery at Winfield Community Hospital, sound must have been nonexistent for her. She could not hear the lusty, piercing cries that filled the room. Amid the din of other crying babies, she had rested quietly in the stillness, unaware that a chorus of untrained voices filled the air. Her own periodic cries of hunger and discomfort had never reached her ears; nurses talked to her with inaudible voices.

All through those months of testing and wondering, we wanted Lynn to hear *us*. We never thought about the more important question: "Can she hear *herself*?" If she heard *our* voices, and much of the time we believed she did, we *assumed* she heard her own voice.

We didn't fully understand why Lynn could mouth and gesture "all gone" but not say these same two words. In time we became aware that something strange was taking place: *Lynn was becoming an expert mimic of everything but our voices*. She copied our facial expressions. She imitated our lip movements. She used our unconscious gestures. As her babbling became more infrequent, then disappeared altogether, she became a curious combination of animated smiles, frowns, nods, shrugs, grimaces, questioning looks and a myriad of silent hand gestures.

For Bruce, the random sounds of babbling had enabled him to make the connection between *hearing sounds* and *making sounds*. He experienced this kind of feedback as naturally as breathing. Lying in his crib, he had experimented with his tongue, his lips, his breath and his voice. Tentatively, as the months passed, he drew a simple but profound conclusion: "Those sounds come from me! I make the noises I hear!"

Once Bruce had made this essential connection, he could start to control the sounds he made and to imitate the sounds we made. He progressed quickly from his early nonsensical jargon to single words, then to two-word sentences, and after that, with almost no assistance from us, to a jabbering question box. By the age of four or five he had become fluent in the language we spoke.

But Lynn missed out on this first lesson of human speech. She would have no chance to forge this link in the chain so naturally. The first stage of language learning passed before we knew anything about it. It was as if Lynn had climbed the first step on the stairway to language, stood for a while, then stepped quietly down while we continued to wonder if she was really deaf.

A sense of urgency now pervaded our lives, but still, I felt hesitant and unsure of what to do. More than once our anxiety turned into arguments. Our tempers flared. I would blame Louise for jumping to conclusions and she would accuse me of denying the obvious—that Lynn couldn't hear.

"Why don't *you* come with me and talk to Dr. Bales?" Louise would ask angrily.

"What good would that do? He can't tell me anything he can't tell you!" For some reason I did not want to face Dr. Bales, to push for conclusive answers.

Louise finally returned to Dr. Bales with additional evidence about Lynn's lack of hearing. She arrived home in tears. "I don't think he takes me seriously," she began as her mood turned into anger. "He says Lynn is just too young to tell anything for sure. Tom, I wish *you* had gone with me. Maybe he would listen to you." Then she broke into tears again.

We were both silent for a long time as we tried to sort out our emotions. Finally Louise said in a quiet voice, "I think I'll call Kathy Andrews. At least we can compare Lynn with Debbie."

Louise had shared the same hospital room with Kathy when Lynn was born. Kathy's daughter Debbie was only a few hours older than Lynn. An easygoing person, Kathy had impressed Louise as a mother who possessed an extraordinary amount of common sense with children. Kathy also knew the whole story about our experience with rubella. Louise hadn't talked to her since coming home from the hospital, but they quickly renewed their friendship over the phone.

"It doesn't sound to me like you're overreacting at all," Kathy said emphatically. "There might be nothing wrong with Lynn, but I wouldn't take your doctor's word for it. He may know a lot about kids but he doesn't know everything! Sometimes they just don't want to admit they don't know something. Why, I had to change pediatricians myself because I didn't think one of them examined my kids thoroughly. If I were you, I'd ask to see a specialist. If he doesn't think that's necessary, go find one yourselves."

Dr. Bales referred us to an ear specialist, an otologist, he called him. The earliest appointment we could make was two weeks later, in the middle of July.

The drive to Chicago took only half an hour. We found the small red brick medical building on the corner of Oakland Street, not far from the first of several white frame houses. I checked the list of names near the front door. "George Williams, M.D., Ear, Nose and Throat Specialist." We gave the receptionist our names and sat down in the corner to wait.

I looked around the waiting room at the chrome chairs with well-worn cushions. Copies of *Today's Health* lay scattered on a small table. The empty chairs seemed to stare back at us and

I wondered how many other parents had come with the same unanswered questions. We hoped that Dr. Williams could give us a clear answer about Lynn's lack of hearing and tell us about the latest methods to treat her problem.

"Mr. and Mrs. Spradley?" A nurse spoke to us from the doorway on the far side of the waiting room. "Dr. Williams will see your baby now."

I smiled hopefully at Louise as I lifted Lynn from her lap and turned to follow the nurse.

A small efficient-looking man, Dr. Williams smiled momentarily, his eyes shifting back and forth. "Sit down here and hold your baby in your lap," he said to me. He than proceeded to check her throat and ears. He fumbled in his white laboratory coat, as if searching for something, and then reached for a tuning fork on a nearby shelf. He tapped the fork and when Lynn looked at Louise, he moved it close to her left ear, at the same time watching her face for any response. He tapped it again and repeated the same procedure with her right ear. I watched Dr. Williams' face for some sign, but his expression told us nothing.

After the tuning fork came the now-familiar funnel-shaped instrument. Lynn squirmed when the cold metal went into her ear but quickly settled into a quiet, relaxed position. Dr. Williams peered intently through the lighted instrument into Lynn's left ear. Louise and I watched his every movement, wondering what he saw, what he might recommend. He moved the funnel to Lynn's right ear and looked again, squinting to shut out the light from his other eye. He straightened up, clicked off the light in the shiny instrument and returned it to its place on the shelf.

Turning to us, he said, "Well . . . ah, well, there is nothing wrong with her ears. Ah . . . ah . . . if she is deaf, then it must be the nerve and there is nothing I can do about that. You'd better take her to the audiologist at Children's Memorial Hospital. Maybe she can use a hearing aid and they can test her hearing response to sound better than I can."

Before we could recover from the brevity of his exam, the uncertainty of his diagnosis or the finality of his words, he had left the room. We looked at each other, stunned and angry. I wanted to jump up and follow him out of the examination room, to plead with him for advice, to ask questions. Instead I looked at Louise and fought back the sense of helplessness that welled up within me. We had come with such a mixture of anxieties and hopes that we both felt at a loss for words. Was this all the help a specialist could offer?

We drove home trying desperately to sort out our emotions, to find perspective. We were positive Lynn was deaf. We had not gone to this specialist in fear he would discover something we didn't already know. We needed confirmation. We needed advice. We needed to talk to someone who knew something about deafness. Our disappointment came from that strange helpless feeling of not knowing what to do. We had hoped for guidance. What could we do to start helping Lynn *now*?

The next morning, while I taught my summer school classes at the college, Louise called the audiologist at Children's Hospital. It was impossible to schedule a hearing test for at least three months. October 23 was the earliest opening. Louise started to explain. This was not just a routine checkup to allay our suspicions. We had been to two doctors already and we felt sure that our daughter was deaf. We needed help *now*. She might need a hearing aid. We wanted to know about her deafness and how to begin helping her.

"I'm sorry," came the voice from some office at the hospital, "you'll have to wait until October. We can send you some material on deafness that will help answer your questions."

Louise took the appointment. Upset and troubled by the delays, she called her mother, who told Louise about a world-famous clinic near the University of Southern California that specialized in research and treatment of deaf children. "If I can get an appointment for Lynn," she asked, "could you and Tom come to California for your vacation when summer school ends?"

Five weeks later we pulled out of our driveway and started the long drive to California.

Four

Wednesday dawned bright and clear, a typical September morning for Eagle Rock. I picked up Lynn and went out to start the car. We had an appointment at the John Tracy Clinic for ten-thirty.

I looked up at the familiar chaparral-covered ridge. Louise had grown up in this small community, which lies strung out along the foothills between Glendale and Pasadena. After we were married we had lived there for four years while I went to college and started teaching.

Louise and her mother climbed into the car; we drove through Highland Park toward the Pasadena Freeway, passing the house where I'd grown up. I could still recall vividly my eight brothers and sisters getting up early in the morning, catching breakfasts at different times, and all going off to different schools. I could hardly remember a time when someone wasn't going to some college or university. One June all nine of us graduated at the same time from as many schools. Dad proudly showed the clipping from the Highland Park *News Herald* to everyone he met.

The value of education was nourished by reminders that one could miss the opportunity. Mom had finished all her high school requirements in the little town of Wilmington, California, but when the principal refused to allow an early graduation, she quit school at sixteen and married Dad. Earlier, he had enrolled at the University of Washington. After one quarter he transferred to the College of Pacific in Santa Clara to play basketball, then dropped out a year later and went to work, a decision he seemed to regret for the rest of his life.

We had always taken for granted that Bruce and Lynn's opportunities for education would expand beyond what Louise and I had known, just as ours had seemed greater than our parents'. Now, fully expecting the specialists at the John Tracy Clinic to verify our suspicions that Lynn was deaf, we were wondering what to do to prepare Lynn for school. We always talked to Bruce about things that interest small children; after all, it was through words that he had begun to discover the meaning of the world around him.

We located the John Tracy Clinic on West Adams Boulevard, a two-story beige stucco building. It sat back from the street, almost hidden behind a high brick wall and hedge that separated the sidewalk from the parking area. Jacaranda trees lined the driveway to the parking lot. We pushed open the tall glass doors and entered the reception area.

"I'm Tom Spradley," I said. "We have an appointment for our daughter, Lynn." I nodded toward Lynn, who smiled at the receptionist.

"Oh, yes. We've been expecting you. Please follow me this way."

The receptionist walked toward a door that led us down a hallway to a small room, where we were introduced to Dr. Murphy, a staff psychologist. She wore rimless glasses, a blue suit, and appeared to be about forty-five. Speaking in an easy, friendly manner, she offered us chairs and said how glad she was that Lynn's grandmother had also come. I began to relax.

"How old is Lynn?" she asked in a way that included all of us in the conversation.

"A little over sixteen months," Louise replied.

"How long have you suspected she might be deaf?"

"Well, we first noticed that she didn't respond to sound when she was about three months old. I think I suspected it even a little earlier."

"That's quite early," Dr. Murphy said, nodding thoughtfully. "Have you had her hearing tested anywhere else?"

"No," I said. "In fact, we came to L.A. for our vacation in

order to bring her to the John Tracy Clinic. An otologist in Chicago examined her and he said there was nothing wrong with her outer ear or the middle ear. I guess that could mean nerve deafness?''

"I'm not going to test Lynn's hearing; that will be done down the hall by the audiologist. I want to give her some tasks that will help assess her physical and mental development.''

We talked easily about Lynn, about our fears and hopes, about rubella and the months of confusion we had experienced. Dr. Murphy listened, asked questions, smiled, nodded, asked more questions. She said she had seen hundreds of other parents who had gone through the same experience.

I put Lynn in a small high-armed chair. Dr. Murphy placed a board across the arms to form a tabletop. She sat down opposite Lynn and placed three green and yellow blocks on the makeshift table. Lynn immediately stacked them up, looked up at me for an instant, and then, with a pleased expression on her face, knocked the pile over.

"Has she started walking yet?" Dr. Murphy asked.

"No," Louise said, "but she crawls a lot and can walk if she holds on to a chair or our hands.''

I watched Dr. Murphy carefully as she worked. She smiled warmly at Lynn, took away the blocks and replaced them with a board, inset with triangular, round and square pieces of wood. She had an air of assurance, a calmness about her that seemed to say, "This is a normal procedure; Lynn is a normal child.''

"What about dressing? Does she help put her clothes on?''

"Yes, some—she tries to pull her socks on and manages partway. She watches when I pick up a shirt and raises her hands so I can put it over her head. She even tries to pull on pants and can get them started.''

The wooden shapes disappeared and in their place Dr. Murphy presented Lynn with a bottle, not more than two inches tall, with a narrow mouth; she placed a small red bead next to the bottle and then sat still to watch. Lynn's eyes sparkled with interest, following Dr. Murphy's every move. She reached immediately for the bead, picked it up, turned it over slowly between the thumb and forefinger of her right hand. As an impish grin spread over her face, she dropped the tiny treasure into the bottle and looked up at Dr. Murphy as if to say, "Well, what's next?"

"She's a little small for her age," Dr. Murphy said in a tone of voice that told us she had finished the tests. "I think her physical development is a little slow, but otherwise she is a very normal little girl. With special training she'll be able to learn as well as any child. Now I'll take you to the audiologist who will test her hearing."

I looked at Louise, whose raised eyebrows told me, "Well, it's good to know that!" We had been right all along. Lynn was just too alert, responsive and quick to be retarded.

As I picked up Lynn and started to follow Dr. Murphy to the audiologist, I felt a new appreciation for the John Tracy Clinic. We were finally getting some answers. Those people know what they're doing, I thought to myself. It began to seem as if the long drive to California might turn out better than either of us had hoped. Only the day before, I had called to confirm our appointment and had been surprised to discover that all the services of the clinic were free for parents of deaf children—the tests, the consultations, even a correspondence course about raising a deaf child.

We had read about the clinic in *If You Have a Deaf Child*, a book sent to us by Children's Hospital before we left Wheaton. Louise Tracy's story about her deaf son had impressed us the most. Years after she discovered his deafness she recalled what happened:

When our son, Johnny, was about ten months old, he was taking a nap one afternoon out on the sleeping porch and he was sleeping very late. I decided to wake him. It was about four o'clock. I started out to the sleeping porch and I suppose I was humming along, as mothers do, saying something about it being time to wake up now. I remember very distinctly that I slammed the screen door... you remember things like that sometimes. Yes, I slammed the screen door after me. Still Johnny didn't wake up. I stopped beside his crib. I said, "Johnny, time to wake up," and I saw he wasn't waking. I went still closer and said it again and again until I fairly shouted in his ear, "Johnny, wake up!" Then finally, very gently, I touched him. His eyes flew open and he looked up at me.

I knew he was deaf.

Louise and Spencer Tracy learned that John had nerve deafness, that nothing could be done to restore his hearing. Their first doctor also said there wasn't much either of them could do; when John reached the age of six or seven, they could send him away to a state school for the deaf where they had special teachers.

Louise Tracy took John to a specialist in New York who told her something that became the cornerstone of her life work: "Your child can learn to lip-read. He can learn to talk. He can go through a university. He can do almost anything that a hearing person can do, but *you* have a job! It can be a very interesting job. It is up to you."

In the years that followed, as Louise Tracy painstakingly worked to teach her own son, she also became convinced that other parents of deaf children needed assistance. In September 1942 she organized a nursery school for mothers and their deaf children; they met in a small cottage on the campus of the University of Southern California. The next year the John Tracy Clinic incorporated, and Spencer Tracy and Walt Disney, among others, became the first board members. The clinic grew over the years, developed its own correspondence course, added staff, and in 1952 moved into the modern facilities where the psychologist had just tested Lynn.

As we walked into the small room where the audiologist would evaluate Lynn's hearing, we knew only these sketchy facts about the history that surrounded us. We couldn't fully appreciate the philosophy of the John Tracy Clinic or its implications for Lynn. We couldn't begin to grasp the impact it would have on our lives.

Before the day had ended, we felt as if we had taken the first step of a long journey; it would take us years to understand the course we would travel.

The room, about ten feet square, appeared larger because one wall contained a rectangular two-way mirror into a smaller control room containing electronic equipment. A low kidney-shaped table occupied the center of the room; blocks, a miniature car, several plastic numbers and a wooden train with a removable engineer were scattered on the table.

"Hello! I'm Mrs. Caldwell, one of the audiologists here at John Tracy." Friendly lines crinkled around her eyes as she spoke. We introduced ourselves and she motioned for us to sit down. I helped Lynn into a child's chair at the table and sat down beside her; Louise took a seat on the opposite side of the table, and her mother watched from the control room. A speaker protruded from each of the other walls about four feet from the floor.

Mrs. Caldwell sat down on the other side of Lynn and asked us when we first suspected that she might have a hearing impairment. We told her about the Fourth of July parade and the months of testing to see if Lynn heard our voices.

"I see from the psychological tests that she has normal intelligence and no other problems." Mrs. Caldwell was looking down at some notes in the manila folder that Dr. Murphy had given to her. "I want to test Lynn's hearing; first I'll use some ordinary sounds and then some pure tones with the audiometer. That will help us find out how much hearing she does have. See if you can get her to play with these toys, and I'll start the test."

Lynn had already pulled the wooden train closer and was attempting to extricate the engineer from his place at the front. Mrs. Caldwell stood up and walked in back of Lynn. She moved slowly, almost cautiously. She picked up two rattles, held the small rattle in one hand, the larger in the other hand. At a distance of about five feet she shook the small rattle for a moment, then stopped.

Lynn did not look up.

The larger rattle went into sudden, vigorous motion, filling the room with a clackety noise.

No response.

She moved closer and shook the smaller rattle again, this time holding it about twelve inches from Lynn's unsuspecting ear.

Lynn did not turn, look up or react in any way; she reached calmly for a bright red number eight as if she couldn't be bothered with these sounds when she could play with new toys. I glanced at Louise across the table and she seemed to be thinking, We've done similar tests before; now she's getting the same results.

Mrs. Caldwell shook the larger rattle again, moving it rapidly back and forth near Lynn's left ear.

No response.

As she set down the rattles, she seemed unconcerned; the calm smile remained on her face. She selected a stick with three bells attached to the end. Stepping back from Lynn, she shook the bells. They jingled loudly, a high ringing sound that seemed quickly absorbed by the carpet that covered the floor. Lynn tried to stack two blocks on top of the number eight without success; the bells jingled again, this time close beside her head.

No response.

A single bell followed, ringing out a deeper, clearer tone. I watched intently, hoping to see her turn, look up, even flinch; instead she held up a block for her mother to see. Mrs. Caldwell started a small music box, let it play for a moment, moved it closer and closer to the back of Lynn's head, her eyes concentrating all the while on the still, small child in front of her. I thought I detected a puzzled expression on her face, a slight wrinkling near the center of her forehead, but her smile still seemed to say she was unconcerned. She picked up a toy horn shaped like a fish and blew a single, high blast.

No response.

She moved closer, blew again, careful to point the fish toward the floor so that the rush of air would not disturb Lynn.

No response.

Only three or four minutes had passed. It seemed like an hour.

After each noise the silent intervals became heavier. The muscles in my neck and shoulders grew taut.

"I want to use these other noisemakers, they have lower tones," Mrs. Caldwell said as she walked into Lynn's range of vision and picked up a toy drum and a castanet. I thought I detected a low sigh from Louise. She unfolded her arms and let her hands drop loosely into her lap. Lynn looked up, spied the drum and reached out for it.

"Here, Lynn, look at these blocks," I said, piling up two of them in front of her.

Mrs. Caldwell waited a few seconds, then thumped the drum with four quick beats using the knuckles of her right hand. A low, booming noise vibrated the room. At the same instant Lynn flinched. A tiny movement, a barely visible twitch of muscles. Louise had seen it too.

Moving closer, Mrs. Caldwell again produced a series of low tones from the drum, like the thunder of a crashing surf on a cold, windy day. Lynn looked up instantly. The throbbing vibrations had reached her, caught her attention. She looked at me for a moment, then at Louise. Searching no further for the sound, she went back to playing with the blocks.

Mrs. Caldwell had easily seen this response, but now the puzzled expression on her face, her narrowed eyes, the lines in her forehead had replaced the confident smile. The castanet created a harsh clacking sound that bounced back and forth between the walls.

Lynn remained still, encased in silence.

The clacking sound came again, like a flock of noisy crows, this time a few inches from her ear, and again she flinched visibly.

I looked at Mrs. Caldwell. I tried to read her face. I searched for some clue to the conclusions she seemed to be forming. The pattern of lines on her forehead and the shape of her mouth suggested a slight but unmistakable look of disappointment. It was intensified by Lynn's coy smile, her pink dress set off by a pink bow in her hair, her delicate features.

In the long months of our struggle to accept the fact of Lynn's deafness, we had started asking more specific questions about the extent of her hearing loss. Was it a complete loss? Could she hear anything at all? If she had some ability to hear sounds, how much could she hear? Then, the moment we began to pin down the elusive handicap called deafness, it had broken into a dozen different kinds and degrees of hearing loss. When we read *If You Have a Deaf Child*, the first great division became quickly apparent: *hearing children* vs. *deaf children*. A hearing child can imitate your sounds and learn your language easily; a deaf child can't imitate your sounds. A hearing child can learn quickly to follow your directions. A deaf child will find even the smallest instruction difficult to understand.

But then another idea emerged from what we read. *Deafness is not a single phenomenon.* In place of the forest I began to see the trees: dozens of species, subspecies and varieties of deafness. The array of forms often seemed interchangeable. "If your child is *hard-of-hearing* . . ."; "If your child is *profoundly deaf* . . ."; "If your child is *severely deaf* . . ."; "If your child has *usable hearing* . . ." Scattered everywhere throughout the book the words appeared without definition.

Truly deaf
Hard-of-hearing
Totally deaf
Hearing-impaired
Severely deaf
Profound hearing loss
Reduced hearing
Hearing-handicapped
Mild hearing loss
Profoundly deaf

Now, at the John Tracy Clinic we hoped to find out how much hearing Lynn did have.

"I'm going into the control room," Mrs. Caldwell said, pointing toward the mirror. "You will hear short bursts of pure tone over the speakers from the audiometer. I'll watch Lynn from in there. I'll do a single tone several times, a little louder each time.''

As the door closed behind Mrs. Caldwell I puzzled over the difficulty of establishing the *presence of deafness*. And the even greater difficulty of measuring the different *degrees of deafness*.

A high, sharp whistle broke the silence of the audiology testing room. Its clear, pure tone lasted about three seconds. The air went silent. Unaware, Lynn played with the miniature replica of a car, bumping it into the blocks. The whistle came again, splitting the air with greater intensity.

No response.

The moment of stillness was interrupted by another and louder blast that filled the room. Intently I watched Lynn, hoping she would hear, look up at the speakers, react in some way to the sound.

No response.

The tone changed. Slightly lower, it now came through like a high tenor voice without any trace of vibrato. Silence. The same tone, now louder. Silence. The final tone made me want to cover my ears, to shut out some of the sound. But any movement would catch Lynn's attention.

No response.

Step by step the audiometer came steadily down the scale. One after the other the pure tones collided against Lynn's eardrums. I fastened my attention more securely on Lynn. A soft, low tone flowed like liquid from each of the speakers.

Lynn did not react.

It filled the air a second time, its volume suddenly expanded.

Lynn appeared uninterested.

Mrs. Caldwell turned the dial up still higher and the pure, clear sound rushed at us with such force that I could almost feel a vibration run up my spine. It was as if the sound had come down the walls from the speakers, raced through the floor and flowed up through the legs of my chair.

Lynn looked up momentarily at her mother, then went back to her play. Had she heard? I wasn't sure.

On the final and lowest series of tones she waited until the loudest one, then looked up and turned her head a full 180 degrees as if searching for the invisible presence that had joined us in the small room.

Mrs. Caldwell came out of the control room, plugged a telephone jack into an outlet near the viewing window and placed a small box with a dial on the table. In her hands was a large single earphone that she held over Lynn's left ear, making her tiny head look even smaller. Lynn looked apprehensive for an instant, tried to see what Mrs. Caldwell was doing and reached for the earphone at the same moment that I heard a clear tone inside it. I couldn't tell whether Lynn responded to the tone or to the presence of this strange object against her ear. Mrs. Caldwell moved the earphone to Lynn's other ear, turned the dial quickly, then removed the tangle of cords from the table and returned the equipment to the control room. I looked at Louise and shrugged my shoulders, unable to make any interpretation of this brief earphone test.

Mrs. Caldwell came back into the room and sat down in silence. Louise's mother sat down next to Louise. Half a minute went by as Mrs. Caldwell studied the folder in front of her and we studied the lines of concern and puzzlement in her face. Finally she looked up at us, a tentative smile on her lips, and motioned for Louise and her mother to pull their chairs closer to the table.

"Everyone has a little hearing," she said slowly. Her words came in a carefully controlled sequence. She hesitated, then placed the folder on the low table. "Even the most profoundly deaf person has a little hearing, and with training almost all deaf children can learn to use whatever hearing they have. Lynn does have a hearing loss," she said, then quickly added, "but it's an *educable loss*."

Before Louise or I could ask any questions, Mrs. Caldwell had shifted her attention to the folder on the table. She reached inside and brought out a single sheet of paper with a graph on it and placed it so we could all see. The graph's horizontal scale displayed sound frequencies in cycles per second starting at 125 cycles and going up to 8,000 cycles.

"The speech range is here," Mrs. Caldwell said, pointing with her pencil, "between 250 and 4,000 cycles per second, but the most important speech sounds are between 300 and 3,000."

The graph's vertical scale, showing hearing levels, increased by jumps of 10 from 0 decibels at the top to 100 decibels at the bottom.

"The threshold of hearing in the middle of the speech range is near zero decibels for the normal ear," Mrs. Caldwell continued. "You can see that in the middle of the speech range it took more than 100 decibels of sound pressure to get a response from Lynn. "That's more than a loud shout at a distance of one foot. As you can see, Lynn's loss at 250 cycles is 90 decibels. At 500 cycles per second, her loss is 95 decibels. At 1,000 cycles she has a loss of 100 decibels or more. That means she doesn't respond to 100 decibels at this frequency. The same is true at 2,000 and 4,000 cycles. Lynn appears to have a severe hearing impairment."

I looked blankly at the audiogram, trying to untangle the lines on the graph. A severe hearing impairment? How much hearing did that imply? How much deafness? The penciled line on the graph descended quickly as it moved across the page in front of me, indicating with mathematical precision what we wanted to know. A severe hearing impairment. A loss of 90 decibels.

Mrs. Caldwell hadn't said she was totally deaf; only a severe hearing impairment. Perhaps impairments could be restored. Or a powerful hearing aid might bring that jagged line on Lynn's audiogram closer to normal. Perhaps a severe hearing impairment wasn't as bad as we had thought. Even as Mrs. Caldwell spoke the words came with a hint of reassurance. And whatever the audiogram was saying to us, we had a more important concern.

"What can we do to help her now?" I asked, looking up from the audiogram at Mrs. Caldwell.

"First of all, remember that at Lynn's age hearing tests are not always reliable. As she grows older and more aware of sounds she should be retested. I think you will find that she will respond to many sounds that she did not respond to today. For now, all we can say is that she appears to be functioning as a child with a severe, if not profound, hearing loss. We may notice a big difference when Lynn begins using a hearing aid.''

That sounded encouraging. I glanced at Louise, then back at the audiogram for an instant. It no longer seemed so foreboding, so final. The uncertainty of test results and the myriad classifications of hearing loss suddenly began to lose their importance. Here was something we could hang on to.

Mrs. Caldwell's voice had become slightly louder, more authoritative. ''The most important thing is to treat her like a *normal* child. Talk to her all the time just as if she can hear you. When you talk, look at her and try to make sure she can see you. Talk as often as you can. Whenever you are with Lynn, talk about the things around you, about what she is doing, what you are doing, what you see, what she sees. You can't talk too much.

''Lynn is a very observant little girl. She follows what is going on because she has learned to make excellent use of situational cues as a means of understanding. I noticed that she imitated my mouth movements several times during the testing and she even made a few vowel-type sounds. I'd say she is at a beginning-language level.

''But I want to caution you about one thing. Since Lynn is so observant, she will imitate every gesture you make. I notice she uses some gestures to be understood. That's okay, but don't gesture back to her. You don't want her to rely on gestures. If she does that, she will not want to learn to use her voice.''

''Treat her just like a normal child.'' ''Talk to her just as if she can hear you.'' I turned the words over slowly in my mind as Mrs. Caldwell spoke. Part of me kept asking, ''But isn't there something more? She can't hear us!''

Deep within, another part of me had already begun to grasp this small reassurance. Lynn could be normal. Treat her that way and she will learn. Talk to her and she will talk. Hope had already begun to grow, and before we left the clinic it had turned into quiet determination. She didn't have to be different. She could grow and learn and talk. Lynn could be treated as if she was normal. Like Bruce. Like the child we had hoped for.

"She's only seventeen months," I heard Mrs. Caldwell saying, "and our correspondence course doesn't really start until the deaf child is two years old. But we will send you material that will give you some ideas in the meantime. When Lynn is two we can start you on the correspondence course and that will give you specific ways to teach Lynn and help her lip-read and talk."

Louise shifted in her chair, lifted Lynn from her lap and rested her against her shoulder.

"Before we left Chicago," she began hesitantly, "we made an appointment at Children's Memorial Hospital—the audiology clinic. They couldn't see us until late in October. Should we go ahead and have her tested again?"

"I think it would be a good idea. It will confirm what tests we have done here, and they will be able to tell you what kind of hearing aid you can get for Lynn."

We left the audiology testing room talking casually with Mrs. Caldwell. We walked slowly down the hallway to the reception room. We thanked her for what she had done. Yes, it had helped. She smiled at Lynn, and then, as we made ready to leave, she gave one last reminder. "Now, be sure to talk to her. In time she will understand what you say and also learn to use her voice."

Five

A few days later we said good-bye to our families and left for Illinois.

Much of the trip home we didn't think about Lynn's future. At other times, driving across the hot desert of California or watching mile after mile of monotonous cornfields in Iowa, each of us found our thoughts going back to Lynn's deafness. We talked about the John Tracy Clinic, about teaching Lynn to talk, about hearing aids, about the extent of her hearing loss, about what the audiologist had said, about all the pieces of the puzzle we now needed to fit together.

We did know that Lynn had some usable hearing. Her hearing loss of 90 or 100 decibels didn't seem to bother Lynn. She was a bright, cheerful baby. She understood us most of the time and communicated almost as well as Bruce had done at eighteen months. And we could treat her like a normal child.

We kept coming back to the fact that rubella hadn't destroyed all of Lynn's hearing. With our own eyes we had seen her respond to low sounds in the audiology testing room. We had been told her loss was "educable." Some tiny bit of hearing remained. All the books and pamphlets we read called it "residual hearing." In some way that we didn't understand, this residual hearing could grow, improve, develop. Lynn could actually be taught to hear.

"Perhaps it's like my painting," Louise had said. "At first I only saw the stark contrasts of blue and yellow and red; the more I painted and took classes, the more I could see—all the different shades of yellow, and other subtle differences when I mixed colors. With more training I noticed how different textures created things I hadn't seen before. I guess I just learned to see better and Lynn can learn to hear better.''

It was while we were driving along Interstate 15, across the Mojave Desert, somewhere between Barstow and Las Vegas, that we talked about hearing aids, how soon we could purchase one for Lynn, how she would adjust to wearing it, what it would cost.

''Just how much do you think hearing aids will really help Lynn?'' Louise asked.

''It could mean a *lot* of difference,'' I said. ''Let me read to you what a Northwestern University professor says.'' I looked down at the papers and pamphlets on deafness scattered in my lap and found the one I had read earlier. '' 'All clinical workers and teachers know of children who were once thought to be totally deaf, or at least too deaf to profit from the use of a hearing aid, who later proved to have a lot of useful hearing.' '' I looked up from the page as Louise pulled out into the passing lane, steadily gained on a moving van, and then eased back to the right side of the highway. A thin, empty strip of pavement stretched ahead as far as I could see.

''This professor,'' I went on, ''says it's always a gamble with hearing aids because it's hard to tell whether a child will learn to use his hearing. But he also says it is *always* worth the gamble. I think what it means is that we'll have to work with Lynn when she gets her hearing aid. To teach her how to use it. To develop her hearing. From what this says, I think there's a good chance she'll eventually be able to hear a lot we say.''

But even if a hearing aid did not improve Lynn's hearing, if for some reason she still couldn't hear our voices, we determined she would grow up normally. At the clinic we had been introduced to a few basic principles for teaching deaf children. We felt confident that as we learned more of this specialized field, Lynn would show steady progress. She would not have to resort to gestures or writing things on paper. Whatever sacrifice it meant, it would be worth it.

I came across a passage by Mrs. Spencer Tracy that clearly laid out the challenge.

The hearing baby learns to speak through hearing. That's the way all of us hearing people learn to understand and to speak. But the need for communication is so great within us that if we can't get it one way, we'll get it another. If we hear, we will get it through our ears. The deaf child can learn to understand what is said to him by reading the lip movements of others and eventually can learn to talk through imitating these movements which he sees and the vibrations which he feels on his teachers face.

Of course, he also can learn to express himself by hand movements and to understand by reading the hand movements of others. It is up to the parents. In the *home* it is decided whether that child will become oral. You know that being oral means being able to use speech and lip-reading, without having to use signs or finger spelling. Naturally we want our children to become oral if possible. So talk, talk, talk.

It was easy to see the logic in her challenge. Even on the trip home we became aware of how much Lynn had already come to depend on gestures.

Late on the second afternoon we turned off State 12 in southern Utah to a campground in Bryce Canyon National Park. We set up camp and within fifteen minutes smoke from our fire drifted up into the trees. We poured boiling water into mugs of instant coffee and sat down to wait for the meat and spaghetti sauce to finish cooking. Bruce had turned a hanging branch into an imaginary horse by straddling it and bouncing off the ground. Lynn sat contentedly in Louise's lap. For the moment we pushed our concerns about her to the backs of our minds.

Then Lynn pointed in a way that we knew meant "I want to get down." Louise first held Lynn's hand out toward the flames so she could feel the radiant heat. "Hot! Hot!" she said, looking directly at Lynn.

Lynn watched Louise's lips, looked at the fire for an instant, then turned her eyes to me. I repeated the warning. "Hot! Hot!"

Lynn's look of interest changed to a smile, her hand came up and she made the quick motion of touching an invisible coffee cup with her index finger and instantly withdrawing it.

"Look at that!" I exclaimed. "She knows what we mean!"

One morning earlier in the summer Bruce had come dashing into the kitchen, climbed up on the chair next to Louise, reached out to investigate the contents of a cup on the table and burned his hand on steaming coffee. That night at dinner Louise took Lynn's tiny hand, pressed it against the side of an uncomfortably warm coffee cup, then pulled it quickly away and said, "Hot! Hot!" As Lynn absorbed this brief lesson I reached out and touched the same cup with my index finger, pulled it back quickly and said emphatically, "*Hot! Hot!*"

Without hesitating, Lynn imitated my movements, punctuating this new expression with the same worried look on her face. After that, this gesture accompanied our voices to call attention to hot food.

Lynn looked back at the campfire and touched the air again with her tiny index finger, then pulled her hand quickly back. Her very quickness with gestures suddenly seemed like a handicap in itself, an ominous cloud over our hopes that she would quickly learn to talk.

I caught Lynn's eyes, and making sure she saw my lips, I spoke again, distinctly, without any gestures. "*Hot! Hot!*"

She looked confused. I pointed to the fire, waited until she turned back to look at my face, then formed the words slowly, clearly. A look of recognition spread across her face and her hand came up again to make the distinct, touching gesture for "hot."

Had she read my lips? Or was it only an old association between hot food and a gesture that now included a hot fire? It would take us years to find the answer to these questions or appreciate how our spoken words disappeared so quickly inside our mouths.

Even when we spoke a simple word like "hot" Lynn only saw a slight movement. My mouth opened, that was clear. But she could not see the rush of air that created the "h" sound; she could not see my vibrating vocal cords which made the vowel "o" that Louise and I so easily heard; she could not see my concealed tongue dart to the top of my mouth to form the "t."

How different our simple hand gesture for "hot." From start to finish it was easy to see, easy to understand, easy to imitate. We both realized why everything we read on deafness stressed that we should avoid using gestures. How easily we could let hand movements become a substitute for speech and lip reading. In fact, without knowing it, we communicated with gestures most of the time. Lynn had picked up our gestures without effort. She had incorporated them into an effective communication system with all of us.

She waved "bye bye" when I left for school, probably the first word she had learned to recognize and use. She shook her head "no no" sometimes in great defiance, other times with a twinkle in her eye to tease us. "All gone" had been part of her vocabulary of gestures for months, the quick turning up of an open palm. She understood "come here"—the quick curling of an index finger toward ourselves. Without knowing it, we had all begun to speak with our eyes and faces. We easily understood when her expression said "I'm confused," "I'm angry," "I'm teasing you" or "I won't." We pointed constantly; we shrugged our shoulders; we raised our eyebrows in visible question marks; we nodded our heads or shook them in various forms of negatives; we yawned and pantomimed sleep. We had literally created a silent language.

What would happen if we made a conscious effort to develop this means of communication? This thought had crossed our minds before. By accident we had given Lynn gestures for "hot" and "all gone"; now she "spoke" these words with her hands as easily as we spoke them with our voices. If we worked at it, we could probably teach her a useful vocabulary of gestures. Perhaps we could even find some way to learn the special sign language that deaf people use among themselves.

But even as we considered these possibilities we rejected them.

We could never settle for second best. Lynn needed to learn to talk. The audiologist at the John Tracy Clinic had warned us: "You don't want her to rely on gestures; if she does, she will not want to learn to use her voice." And we knew that if we depended on gestures to communicate it would constantly call attention to Lynn's handicap. It would mark her as deaf. It could even isolate her from us into the world of other deaf people who could not speak.

We finished dinner in the dark, roasted marshmallows over the last coals and then went to sleep, the four of us snuggled securely together in our two-man tent. Long after I could hear the rhythms of steady breathing from Lynn, Bruce and Louise, I lay awake and thought about Lynn and the whole problem of communication. Earlier in the day I had read an article by a language specialist at the Illinois School for the Deaf who said that because deaf children can't hear, they lose the power to communicate. That statement had seemed strange when I read it. Now, I knew it wasn't true, at least not for Lynn. Had the author meant to say, "They lose the power to communicate *with speech sounds*"? I fell asleep determined to follow the Tracy Clinic's recommendation not to gesture.

In the days and weeks that followed, we tried to talk to Lynn at every opportunity. We spoke in short sentences, repeated words over and over, and named the things she played with. We talked about whatever we were doing, making a not-always-successful effort to be sure Lynn saw our lips. It was a tedious job and I often found it easier to say nothing, to hide behind a book or to plan the next day's assignments for school. With Louise the flow of words was often slowed or stopped by preoccupations or sheer tiredness. Then Lynn's silent, inquisitive smile would remind us that she might never learn to speak unless we talked and talked.

The need to talk and our own forgetfulness became a source of friction between us. We both felt guilty about not talking enough and at times I would become angry with Louise, blaming her for what I saw as insufficient talk. We would find ourselves embroiled in arguments, confused, and upset. But slowly we learned to accept the fact that neither of us could do the impossible and fill every waking moment with conversation for Lynn. Over and over again we had to renew our efforts to make the ordinary situations a chance for Lynn to see our moving lips—mealtime, bedtime, bathtime, riding in the car, playing games, reading stories. Although we tried to include Bruce, there were times when he felt left out because we focused so much attention on Lynn. When this happened, one of us would try to take extra time to talk and play with him. We tried to explain: "Someday Lynn will begin to understand what all of us are saying. It may take a long time but we all need to talk to her as much as we can. Someday she'll learn to talk like you, even though she can't hear."

I remember the day we arrived back in Wheaton, a warm Thursday morning. Bruce and Lynn both grew excited as they recognized familiar landmarks. I turned onto Seminary Street and drove slowly past our house, pointing it out to Bruce and Lynn.

"That's our *old* house," Louise said, turning so Lynn could see her mouth. "We can visit it, but we don't live there anymore."

A few blocks away I parked in front of 421 Emerald, an old but well-preserved two-story frame house, gray with white trim. A wide porch ran across the front, its heavy roof supported by four widely spaced, rectangular columns. Near the middle of the spacious yard stood an aging elm that cast a cool blanket of shade from the house to the street. We had packed our belongings before our trip to California and left them stacked in the living room.

"This is our new home," I said as we went up the walk, looking at Lynn, her arms tightly wrapped around Louise's neck.

"It has a big porch."

"This is a porch where you can play."

"Front door. This is the front door."

"Here are my keys." I held them up for Lynn to see, then unlocked the door and we all went in. A faint musty odor hung in the air and Louise rolled up the shades in the living room and raised two windows. I looked around at the stacks of boxes and other belongings.

"Boxes," Louise said, looking at Lynn. "These are our boxes." She patted the nearest stack of brown cardboard containers I had retrieved from behind a nearby grocery store.

"This was Davy Brandt's house," Bruce said, looking at Lynn. "I've been here lots of times."

A year before, I had helped Dave Brandt move his furniture from a smaller college apartment into the roomy downstairs of this house, which we took over when Dave left to go to the University of Oklahoma. Dave had graduated from Wheaton, completed his M.A. degree, then returned to teach physics. We arrived at the same time as novice instructors. We had shared an office on the second floor of Blanchard Hall. A heavyset man with brownish red hair, Dave's lively sense of humor and rapport with his students taught me a great deal without his ever knowing it.

Louise frequently went shopping with Melva Brandt and exchanged baby-sitting with her during the day. The Brandts were among the first to learn about Lynn; they offered understanding and encouragement. We climbed the stairway to the rooms which would soon reverberate with the noise of ten seniors. We went into each room, Bruce running ahead to see what new mysteries he could discover.

"Bedroom."

"This is a bedroom," Louise said and Lynn watched from her perch on my arm.

"Mattress. This is a mattress." We went into the next room.

"Bathroom," Louise commented. "Bathroom."

"Here's the bathtub," I said.

"Water," Louise said, turning on the water in the sink. I held Lynn closer and she put her hand under the running stream.

We came back downstairs into the living room and walked over to the window. Louise continued to talk.

"Window . . . This is a window . . . Look! You can see Blanchard Hall through the trees." She pointed out the closed window. Without speaking, we looked out at the old bulding for several minutes. Then the silence was broken, except for Lynn, by the creaking of the oak floor beneath our feet.

By the time of our appointment with the audiologist at Children's Memorial Hospital in late October, Louise and I both noticed that our talking had not gone unrewarded. Lynn now watched our mouths most of the time when we spoke. She listened with her eyes and had moved one step closer to talking.

"All gone." "No no." "Bye bye." "Hot." She clearly mouthed these words and someday, we knew, she would add her voice.

The students had returned for the fall semester; our seniors had settled into a predictable routine. The day of our appointment I canceled my afternoon calculus class and right after lunch we left for Chicago. I thought I could find the hospital easily. Driving north on State Street, I couldn't decide where to turn; I slowed down and peered up the cross street when suddenly a pulsating red light jumped out at me from the rear-view mirror.

"Oh, no! All we need is a ticket now," I said to Louise as I pulled over.

A tall policeman, his freckled face contrasting sharply with his dark-blue uniform, came to my window. I reached for my driver's license.

"What's the trouble? You lost?" he asked in a friendly voice.

"I guess so," I answered sheepishly, only partly relieved. I quickly added, "We've got to find Children's Hospital for our daughter here." Lynn smiled innocently at the officer from Louise's lap.

"Follow me!" Without another word he turned on his heel and climbed back into his black-and-white car. I waited as he pulled out into the traffic, red light still flashing. I followed quickly. As other cars slowed down, we picked up speed behind our escort. Within three or four minutes he waved us off and we turned into the parking lot next to the hospital.

Mothers, kids and a few fathers filled the chairs in the long, narrow waiting room of the audiology clinic. After a half-hour wait we were ushered down a hallway to the audiologist's office. Mrs. Jenson introduced herself. She was younger than I had expected.

"Aren't you a cutie!" she said to Lynn. She motioned for us to sit down, then settled into a red swivel chair, her back to a large desk strewn with papers and folders. Mrs. Jenson asked about Lynn. Did we have other children? Where did we live? Had we ever had Lynn's hearing tested?

"When did you first suspect Lynn might have a hearing impairment?"

"At about three months," Louise told her. "But our doctor said you couldn't really tell until she was about two years old."

Mrs. Jenson shook her head slowly, her mouth tightly closed, her lips forming a thin straight line. "I hear that from so many parents," she said, a note of impatience in her voice. "And the whole future of a hearing-impaired child like Lynn depends so much on early detection. You can't start teaching a child to lip-read too soon."

Lynn squirmed in Louise's lap and looked around the office; Mrs. Jenson leaned forward slightly in her chair.

"Most people, including most physicians," she said, emphasizing each word, "just don't understand audiology or the importance of early detection. You're lucky that Lynn is only eighteen months old. Why, I see some children over three years old—and that's for their first hearing test! Some doctor has told the parents to wait, that there is no way to tell until the child is older, that the child is probably just ignoring sounds. Canada and Australia and England are all so far ahead of the United States when it comes to programs for early detection of hearing impairments."

As she spoke her hands came up in wide, sweeping gestures that seemed to underline the critical necessity of starting early with deaf children.

I carried Lynn into a small carpeted room that had a two-way mirror in the door. Among the few toys scattered on a low table in the center of the room, I noticed a telegraph key. Across the table near a mirror was a little clown with a striped shirt, baggy green pants, a painted face and an oversized red nose. We sat down and Mrs. Jenson spoke to us through the two wall speakers.

"I want to try to condition Lynn to respond to sounds. That way we can get a better idea of what she hears. Watch her closely, and if she seems to hear any of the tones, take her hand and press that key on the table. It will light up the clown's nose. Then remove her hand so she doesn't touch the key until she hears another sound."

I watched Lynn all through a series of high tones. As the intensity increased on the second blast of a mid-range tone, Lynn unexpectedly looked around. Immediately I picked up her hand, pressed the telegraph key and watched her wide-eyed surprise at the clown's illuminated nose. I quickly removed her hand, the nose blinked off and I gave her the wooden car. She pushed it back and forth on the table, never taking her eyes off the clown.

Mrs. Jenson sent the same tone piercing into the room three more times; together Lynn and I pressed the key; she was delighted when the clown's nose came to life. We did the same for the loudest blast of the next tone and the one after that. Then, as a still lower tone came from the speakers, Lynn reached for the key without my assistance, clamped down on it vigorously, then looked up at me, her eyes glowing with pride. I nodded enthusiastically, then we waited for the next tone.

For ten minutes Lynn demonstrated her skill in this game. The audiologist filled the testing room again and again, first with lower tones, then skipped up and down the scale. Pleased with her new power, Lynn repeatedly turned the clown's nose to glowing red, but only after the very loud, low tones.

"You can come back into the office now." Mrs. Jenson's clear voice came over the speakers.

I sat down next to Louise. Mrs. Jenson held out the now-familiar audiogram for us to see.

"Lynn is still a baby," she began slowly, speaking more hesitantly now. "In another year, the same test might show she hears even more. But Lynn *can* hear. She responded to a 250 cycle tone when I increased it to 65 decibels; that's close to middle C on the piano.''

That Lynn could hear at all was encouraging. We lost sight of the fact that this tone fell below the normal speech range; and it didn't seem important when Mrs. Jenson mentioned that in the speech range Lynn only responded to a volume of 100 decibels or more.

Lynn *had* heard sounds at only 65 decibels! We clung to this new finding. At the John Tracy Clinic she hadn't heard anything under 90 decibels. Perhaps this indicated improvement, that she already had begun to learn how to use her residual hearing. And future tests might show even further improvements.

"Lynn should have another test when she is two years old," Mrs. Jenson said. "After that test she can be fitted with a prescription hearing aid.''

"Is it really necessary to wait another six months for a hearing aid?'' I asked, sounding impatient without meaning to.

"An effective hearing aid must be prescribed specifically for Lynn," she said. "By two years she will be old enough to help us get a more accurate picture. It's best to wait till then, but in the meantime you can use an auditory trainer with Lynn.''

"What's an *auditory trainer*?" Louise asked; we were both pleasantly surprised to discover there was at least something we could do while we waited.

"It's an electronic device especially constructed for teaching very young children to use their residual hearing. It consists of a microphone, amplifier and headphones. And you can use it to help Lynn recognize the sound of your voices, to connect your lip movements with your voice sounds.'' Mrs. Jenson said she would write to the Chicago Hearing Society; we might borrow a trainer from it until we purchased Lynn's hearing aid.

An auditory trainer, with its larger amplifier and more efficient earphones, could pick up voices and amplify them to well over 100 decibels. We could control the amplification and adjust the training unit to the special needs of communicating with Lynn.

"It is important to use the auditory trainer every day," Mrs. Jenson said as we left. "It's an excellent way to prepare Lynn for using her own hearing aid."

I called the people at the Chicago Hearing Society as soon as we arrived home. I told them a letter would come from the audiologist at Children's Memorial Hospital. We wanted to borrow an auditory trainer as soon as possible. To our great disappointment, all the trainers were in use; they couldn't loan us one until sometime in December.

Every day that passed seemed like another lost opportunity. We chafed at the delay but continued to talk to Lynn, filling our home with conversations she could see.

Six

Treat her like a normal child.

We followed that advice without difficulty. Lynn didn't appear handicapped; her deafness was invisible. She communicated without words and we understood her most of the time. She watched us when we spoke. We talked to her as if she could hear as well as Bruce. As the leaves turned from gold to red in the crisp autumn air, our optimism increased.

In every way Lynn appeared so normal we sometimes had to remind ourselves she lived in a world of silence. She had started to walk. She played happily with Bruce. She enjoyed other children. She cried and laughed the way Bruce had done at her age.

Perhaps we found it easy to see Lynn as normal because she kept showing us that she wasn't handicapped. She had grown increasingly animated; her face and hands came alive with expressiveness even as her voice faded. Lynn loved books. She would pull one from the shelf, whichever was currently at the top of her rating list, find Louise, motion to the couch or a chair in the living room, climb into her lap and wait for her to open the book. Over and over again, she loved to go through the familiar pages. She pointed to the faces of children she knew. She laughed at the antics of dogs and cats. She imitated wagons and airplanes with hand motions. She pointed and looked up eagerly, searching Louise's mouth and face for the familiar words.

Many times I came home from school in the late afternoon to find Lynn and Bruce playing on the front porch. Other children often joined them. They had transformed it into a fort, a dungeon, a pirate ship, a bowling alley. They draped old blankets over chairs and boxes to make tentlike hideaways, then carried their afternoon snacks into these make-believe worlds. Lynn often saw me first. An excited smile lit up her face; she waved and then in an instant she raced to the stairs. With a sudden about-face, she dropped to her knees, bumped down the stairs in rapid succession, made another about-face, then dashed across the lawn toward me.

"Hi, Lynn!" I scooped her into my arms. Her silence didn't seem to matter.

She pointed insistently toward the elm tree and I knew what she wanted. The week after we moved in, I had fastened a single thick rope to one of the branches and tied a bulky knot at the bottom. Bruce could make a running leap, land on the knot and propel himself in a wide arc; Lynn could not manage the swing by herself. I lifted her onto the rope, her tiny legs wrapped securely around the knot, and she clung tightly as I pushed her high into the air. Her eyes grew wide with excitement and a touch of fear; her delighted smile begged to go higher. As I pushed her back and forth she would look up into the dizzying heights of the elm, its black branches standing out starkly against the red and yellow leaves of early fall. She closed her eyes tightly, as if in that brief moment of darkness she could enjoy more completely the sensations of rising and falling. I finally lifted her off the rope amid protests and gestures that begged for more.

"Not now. Later. I want to go in and see Mommy now."

Lynn craved sensations, as if they somehow made up for the sounds she never knew. Together with Bruce she piled up leaves in the front yard, enormous mounds pulled from the sidewalk and lawn. Lynn loved to jump in the pile, falling headlong into the soft bed of brown and gold and red, rolling over and over to feel the dry textures against her skin. She picked up double handfuls, held them to her face, felt their brittle surfaces and smelled the deep, clean odors of fall.

Halloween came at the peak of Indian summer that year. The sudden appearance of jack-o'-lanterns, witches and masks seemed to offer Lynn a kind of visual ecstasy. Looking back, we realize her world revolved around the faces of people. Without sound, with only limited gestures, her most important link to us came from watching our eyes, our mouths, our wrinkled foreheads, our expressions that talked and never stopped. With Halloween, *everything* started talking. Faces appeared in profusion, as if someone had turned up the volume.

One afternoon she climbed up on a chair and watched Louise sketch out smiles and frowns on several pumpkins. Then we carved these expressions into deep-set eyes, mouths with wicked-looking teeth, frowns, smiles. Lynn squealed with anticipation, watching in amazement as we created faces that spoke to her. She pushed her fingers into the eyes, reached through to feel the stringy, damp interior of these mysterious creatures. Later that night, in the darkness of the living room, when we lit the candles Lynn was transfixed by the shafts of light that came from the jack-o'-lantern faces.

I took Bruce out to trick-or-treat. Lynn spent the evening eagerly waiting inside the door for each group of masked children to appear. Proudly she helped pass out the candy. She never heard their shouts of "Trick or treat!" but she might just as well have. She read the message of their masks. She understood the meaning of outstretched hands, bags of candy, outlandish costumes, happy painted faces. Perhaps it was as close to music as she had ever known.

It is difficult to recall what we told others about Lynn's deafness that fall. Mostly we told them nothing. With friends we downplayed the seriousness of her impediment. "She can hear some," we said. "Her hearing will probably improve with a hearing aid." We didn't want them to feel sorry, to pity us, to view Lynn like a handicapped child. We had read that if we treated her like a deaf child, she might take on the characteristics of those isolated individuals we thought of as deaf-and-dumb.

We didn't tell the students who lived upstairs, and even though many of them saw Lynn day after day, they didn't suspect she couldn't hear. One crisp Saturday afternoon in November I heard shouts of laughter from upstairs.

"Mr. Spradley! Come and see Lynn!"

At the top of the stairs was a small room they used as a television lounge. There were pillows on the floor, a few chairs, and four or five students sprawled here and there watching a football game. Mike, a tall senior who majored in biology, stood at the TV set with Lynn.

"Watch this, Mr. Spradley," he said as I stepped into the room, a curious expression on my face.

He leaned down and turned on the now-dark television set. In a few seconds a bright picture of a college band marching across the football field appeared. Lynn had missed nothing. As soon as the set came on she reached over, and with an air of authority, she clicked the switch off.

"All gone!" she said, mouthing the words silently. At the same time she looked at the students sprawled around the room.

The comical expression on her face seemed to say, "I'm sorry, but I'm not going to let you see the rest of the game!" I laughed with the students. To all the world it looked like an intentional pantomime, as if she was keeping silent for some special effect. Their laughter told Lynn she had their attention. It told me that no one suspected the real reason behind her voiceless words.

With one couple, our friends and neighbors Bob and Mary Hughes, we did not hesitate to talk about Lynn. One day shortly after we first moved into the Ferris House, we had noticed something strange about Bob.

"Look at our neighbor! Don't you think it would be dangerous for him to drive?" I called to Louise from the living room. We watched as a slender man with dark hair who looked about thirty-five struggled to make his way down the walk to the street. His body lurched first one way, then the other; his hands moved through the air in uncontrolled gestures; his head bobbed back and forth. It took several minutes for him to open the door of a station wagon and settle himself in the driver's seat. How would he manage to control the car when he had such difficulty controlling his own body?

Later Bruce had begun to play with Jane and Alex Hughes. ·

Once Bruce climbed a tree in their backyard and Jane had to call me to help him down.

"Their mommy and daddy can't talk very well," Bruce said matter-of-factly. "And they walk funny, too."

"It's probably cerebral palsy," Louise said. We both felt uneasy, hesitant to take the first step in making our acquaintance with these neighbors who appeared so different. Bob worked at Wheaton College; I saw him going into Blanchard Hall and entering one of the business offices downstairs. I wondered what kind of work he could do.

I remember during my first year at Wheaton when I happened to catch up with Bob on my way up the long walk to Blanchard Hall. It was a cool day in late fall; most of the leaves had already fallen; the wind blew them in swirls across the lawn, scattering them in odd patterns. I could see Bob up ahead, struggling to put one foot down after the other. I strode quickly up the walk; he worked his way along as if on some invisible obstacle course. A vague sense of uneasiness came over me as I approached. Would he be embarrassed if I joined him in taking five minutes to cover the short distance that remained?

"Good morning," I said. I stepped out on the grass, looked quickly in his direction and nodded. I slowed my pace for an instant; Bob spoke but I couldn't understand him. In half a minute my long strides had taken me to the entrance of Blanchard Hall; as I opened the large door I was conscious that Bob Hughes was still struggling slowly up the walk only a few feet from where I had passed him.

We felt sympathy for Bob and Mary Hughes—and uncomfortable in the presence of their handicap. Then we discovered Lynn's deafness. Overnight we saw Bob and Mary in a wholly different way. Their struggle to talk, their effort to surmount enormous obstacles, their courage, they themselves suddenly became more significant. Louise talked to Mary about her first suspicions that Lynn might be deaf. "Well, if she is deaf, she can adjust to it," Mary assured Louise. "And you can get special help.'' Louise listened while Mary recalled her own school experiences. Slowly we learned about cerebral palsy, the stigma of being different, the special schools Bob and Mary had attended, and their painstaking effort to learn to talk.

"There are a lot more CPs than people realize,'' Bob told us. "And most can get along fine.'' As our friendship grew, so did our understanding of their world. One day after a windy storm, Bob called to ask if I could come over and light the pilot light on their furnace which had gone out.

"Could you drop over for a few minutes tonight, Tom?'' he asked as I started out the door. "We're having a party for a group of our CP friends. Three of them can't walk and I'm not much good at helping them. Could you give them some assistance?'' That evening as I wheeled each one into Bob and Mary's living room, I felt as if I was looking in upon another society. I had never seen so many strange movements and heard so many strange sounds all at once. But I also sensed the closeness that came from sharing the same handicap. In a society that stigmatized, overlooked, avoided or stood with gawking eyes, Bob and Mary were not alone. Later that night I returned to wheel the same three individuals back to their cars.

"CPs have good driving records, better than the average person,'' Bob said as we stood by the curb in the darkness and he and Mary waved good-bye to their friends. "But because we have cerebral palsy, it's been difficult to get insurance.''

When we returned from the John Tracy Clinic that fall and moved to Emerald Street, we still visited Bob and Mary. Louise went right over to tell Mary what we had learned about Lynn's deafness. We felt lucky to have them as friends. Had we chosen someone to teach us how to encourage Lynn's independence in the face of deafness, we couldn't have found more patient, courageous teachers.

Neither of us will ever forget one winter morning during the last year we lived next door to Bob and Mary. A freezing drizzle had crept into Chicago in the night; it had left a thick sheet of ice on the roofs, streets, lawns, sidewalks and cars. Even the power lines and branches glistened in the morning sun as I walked carefully to school; each twig was encased in ice. I smiled as I saw several students who had replaced their shoes with ice skates and now glided over the campus walks on their way to class.

Louise and Bruce watched out the front window as Bob Hughes made his way across Seminary Avenue. The sparkling world of ice that slowed most people down had created for Bob a treacherous, if not impossible, task. One step at a time, struggling to find footing, working to maintain his balance, Bob inched his way along. Suddenly Louise and Bruce were horrified. Halfway up the walk to Blanchard Hall, Bob slipped and fell. He struggled to get up, but each time he managed to place one foot under his body, the slippery ice made it impossible for him to rise. He lay sprawled on the walk, helplessly trapped. Louise ran for her coat, then noticed that two students had come to his assistance, lifted him to his feet and were helping Bob the rest of the way to his office.

We woke one morning in early December to find that a four-inch blanket of snow had transformed our world. It clung to the branches of the pine tree in our front yard, bending them under its weight, and outlined each branch and twig of the leafless elms that lined our street. Lynn, blinking her sleepy eyes, looked out our front window, awe-struck.

"Snow. That's snow. Snow," Louise said, looking at Lynn's questioning face.

Still in her pajamas, she ran to her room and returned in a few seconds holding her coat and boots.

Bruce was already outside. "Snow!" he called to her, throwing a snowball.

Lynn seemed to find a particular joy in the symphony of sparkling, dancing whiteness that covered everything, the rays of early-morning sun that cascaded off the roof. She threw great gobs of the powdery stuff into the air. She ran across the smooth sweep of our yard, pointing back at her deep footprints. After Bruce and I had gone to our schools, Louise and Lynn built a carrot-nosed snowman with a friendly expression that spoke to Lynn until it melted a few days after Christmas.

Bruce had begun to talk of Santa Claus, and Lynn had pointed to the decorations along Main Street in Wheaton. We tried to explain to her with pictures about Christmas. We showed her photographs from the year before, the tree all decorated in lights, presents stacked under it. "Christmas tree." "Lynn." "Bruce." Louise pointed to each picture. She pointed out pictures of Santa Claus and reindeer in magazines. Although eager and excited, Lynn looked at us in question marks.

"In a few days Christmas will come," we said to her in the same way we spoke to Bruce. But the mystery and silence didn't stop her from enjoying the preparations.

I had noticed a large branch that seemed out of place on a pine tree in the lot behind our house. The more I thought about a Christmas tree, the more out of proportion that branch became. One afternoon Louise and I went out to inspect it more closely. That evening a Christmas tree stood in one corner of our living room, looking for all the world like a huge bear about to lunge. Louise brought out the decorations and we all went to work hanging the lights, silvery balls of red, yellow and blue, candy canes, tinsel and homemade decorations. Even Lynn joined in, hanging tiny strands of tinsel on the lower branches.

We turned off the living-room lamps and admired the soft glow of lights reflected in the other decorations. Lynn was captivated, entranced; she ran to the tree and touched a red light; she rushed back, poked Bruce and pointed; she tugged on Louise's dress and pointed. And then, in all the days that followed, her expressions told of the intense joy she felt at seeing her silent world painted with the music of those lights and decorations. She would wake early, come into our bedroom and tug at the covers, the expression on her face begging to let her see the lights on before daylight filled the house and dimmed their glow. Every evening she showed us she wanted to stay up until the tree lights sent their brightness into the early-evening darkness.

I cannot describe how Lynn's face told us what she wanted.

It was as if she had taken our expressions, practiced them, improved on them and then spoke silent sentences that told us what she wanted and how she felt. Without any instruction from us she had learned to communicate. In contrast to Bruce, Lynn grinned, smiled, raised her eyebrows, nodded, threw her head from side to side, shrugged her shoulders and gestured to a much greater degree. "She's so eager and responsive," people would say. "She seems so bright and expressive."

At the same time, Lynn drew from us the kind of expressiveness she could understand. When we merely spoke, our faces lacked the communicative quality that came with laughter or anger. Lynn came to depend on seeing our faces filled with these stronger emotions. It was as if watching our mouths alone was not loud enough; smiles, angry looks, a head thrown back in hearty laughter, these reached across the gap that her deafness had created. She loved to make us laugh and in the process became a tiny comedienne.

One evening Louise turned the water on in the tub for Lynn's bath. Lynn, stripped down to her diaper, grabbed the red plastic bucket she played with in the tub, put it on her head and dashed into the living room, where I sat reading. She pulled a red-and-white candy cane from the Christmas tree, and just as Louise came looking for her, Lynn began to dance. I reached for my camera to record this special performance; Lynn stopped, assumed a sultry pose, held it until the burst of light from my flash faded, then continued her dance as we laughed and exclaimed.

Christmas Eve she sensed the excitement. The next morning she unwrapped her presents in silence, as captivated by the bright paper and ribbon as by the contents inside. She said no words. She heard nothing that Christmas. But she understood and did not lack for imagination. She opened one package and discovered a tiny tea set; immediately she took several sips from an empty cup, poured another full one for Louise and daintily offered it to her.

Another present came from Lynn that Christmas. We had expected it, wondering when it would arrive. One Saturday morning a few days before Christmas the doorbell rang, Louise answered it and the postman handed her a package; the return address said "Chicago Hearing Society."

"The auditory trainer is here!" she called excitedly.

We took it into the kitchen and eagerly began tearing the wrapping paper from the package. Amid the packing paper inside, I located a set of headphones, a microphone and a black control unit with a dial. I set them carefully on the kitchen table, looked in the bottom of the box and found the instructions. Lynn came into the kitchen and climbed up on the chair beside Louise.

Filled with anticipation, I began reading the instructions to Louise. The auditory trainer was battery-operated; the headphones and mike each plugged into the control unit. It worked simply; we were to speak into the microphone and Lynn would hear our amplified voices through the headphones. The volume control dial went from 1 to 10; we should begin with a medium volume and work up as necessary.

"I'm really glad this came before Christmas," Louise said, her words filled with relief and excitement at the same time. "If she can just hear us a little bit, even if our voices are faint, it should make a big difference."

"And it should make it a lot easier for her to learn to read our lips," I added as I made sure the batteries were in place. I picked up the headphones and plugged the jack into the control box.

"Maybe you should listen first, Tom, to see how it sounds."

I put the earphones on my head, adjusted them, plugged in the mike and turned the dial to 3. I spoke into the mike.

"Hello. This is Daddy. Hi, Lynn." My voice, uncomfortably loud, vibrated inside the headphones, as if I were shouting directly into my own ears. I turned the dial all the way up and then spoke softly into the mike: "Hi, Lynn . . .!"

I stopped instantly and pulled the headphones from my ears. My voice had come with deafening loudness. I could feel pinpoints of pain against my eardrums. I rubbed my ears. "She should be able to hear that!" I said to Louise.

Lynn had watched every move, and now, standing in the chair, she reached for the headphones.

"Let's get one of her books," I said and jumped up at the same time. Louise adjusted the headphones for Lynn while I quickly found her favorite book. I felt my heart pounding as I came back into the kitchen. The auditory trainer had made my voice sound louder than anything I had heard at the John Tracy Clinic or at Children's Memorial Hospital. Lynn's tiny head looked dwarfed between the cushiony black headphones; she smiled proudly up at me. I placed the book in front of Lynn and opened it to the first page, which showed a pair of brown shoes. I turned the volume control to 3, pointed to the shoes and spoke directly into the microphone: "Shoe."

Lynn looked at me, then back at the page. She pointed at the shoe in imitation of my movements, as if she was trying to grasp the rules of this new game. I turned the dial up to 6 and when she looked at me, I spoke again: "Shoe. Shoe."

I could detect no response. She looked back at the page, then tried to turn the volume dial back and forth. Perplexed, I turned the dial all the way up to 10. I couldn't understand why she hadn't heard. Perhaps there was a great difference between 6 and 10. Would the full volume hurt her ears? I spoke more softly this time: "Shoe. Shoe. Shoe."

Lynn didn't look up, but tried instead to turn the page to the next picture. I could see a look of keen disappointment spreading across Louise's face. I fought back the doubts and pointed to the picture on the next page. I spoke loudly into the mike, recalling the reverberations that volume had caused inside my ears only a few minutes before: "Wagon. Wagon."

No response. She didn't reach for the headphones. She seemed completely ignorant of my voice. I pointed to the wagon and spoke again. She pointed, looked at my face, then fiddled with the dial on the control box.

"Do you think she heard me?" I asked Louise, trying to sound unconcerned.

"No," she said slowly. "I didn't see any response."

For the next five minutes we tried other words, other pictures. We said things she knew how to lip-read, things we knew she had seen on our faces before. We said them while she looked away, we spoke them when her attention was on other things. We pointed and repeated.

No response.

It was as if the black box, the shiny microphone, the headphones were all like the other games we played together in silence. Finally she grew impatient and tried to take off the headphones. I set them on the table as she crawled down from her chair and ran into the living room.

Louise looked at me. I stared at the electronic equipment before us. Extreme disappointment swept over us. Was this what we had waited for with such anticipation? Why had she not responded? Surely it was loud enough. Was she only pretending not to hear? Had she ignored us?

"Well," I finally said to Louise. "Lynn has lived for so long without hearing us that she probably couldn't make sense out of the sounds she heard. She probably just needs time to *learn* how to listen, to use her residual hearing. Maybe that's why they call it an auditory trainer —it isn't for talking, the way her hearing aid will be, it's for training her to use her hearing. We'll just have to use it, to practice with her until she begins to recognize the sound of our voices."

Seven

Christmas vacation ended. Students returned to a campus caught in subzero temperatures and a wind-chill factor of more than 50 below. Each day at school I met my calculus class and two sections of algebra. At home Louise struggled to teach a far more demanding subject to Lynn: *language without sound*.

Talk. Talk. Talk. The informal instruction continued from the moment Lynn awoke until she fell asleep at night.

"It's morning."

"Bruce is eating breakfast."

"Cheerios."

"Bowl."

"Milk."

"Daddy. Mommy. Bruce. Lynn."

"I'm doing the dishes. Washing the dishes."

"Chair. Lynn is standing on the chair."

"Broom. The broom is for sweeping."

"Telephone. Talk to Grandma on the telephone."

"Pajamas. Lynn's pajamas."

"Pants. Shirt. Shoes."

"Making cookies."

"Flour. This is the flour."

"Sugar. Egg. The egg can break."

"Cookie for Lynn."

"Shopping. Drive in the car."

"Door. Steering wheel. Mirror. Keys."

"We're going to the store to shop."

Like a magnet, Louise's moving lips seemed to draw Lynn's attention. We didn't know how much Lynn understood, but she often responded as if she knew exactly what we said. Louise had a deep reservoir of patience and a capacity to teach Lynn informally which I lacked. She could capitalize on the most routine experiences, transforming them into quiet lessons in lip reading.

One Thursday morning Louise drove to the Jewel Food Market, talking as usual to Lynn perched in the car seat next to her. Inside the store she lifted Lynn into the basket seat and started down the first aisle, shelves crowded with bread, cereal and coffee.

"Let's get some Cheerios," she said to Lynn, offering her the box to hold before it went into the basket. "Cheerios. Cheerios." Lynn's eyes lit up in recognition.

They turned down the next aisle and passed a woman with a boy about Lynn's age. Lynn pointed eagerly, smiling and waving.

"Hi! Hi! Hi! Hi! Hi!" the little boy called loudly from his seat in the shopping cart. Lynn watched and waved until he disappeared at the end of the aisle.

"Cookies. Cookies. These are cookies." Louise spoke as she placed a package of Oreos into the basket. Lynn looked back and forth from the package to Louise's face.

"Milk. We better get some milk for you and Bruce."

"Eggs. Eggs. Here's some eggs."

And so the lesson proceeded. Down one aisle and up the next. A few other shoppers smiled at Lynn or looked at them as they passed. Louise kept talking of butter and coffee and napkins and waxpaper and oranges and potatoes. As she started filling a bag with apples an elderly man smiled at Lynn. "Hi there, little girl!" he said. Louise smiled, weighed the apples, and went on to the carrots and celery. Ten minutes later she pushed the load of groceries to the checkstand, went to the front of the basket and started unloading it onto the moving belt. Lynn sat alone at the other end of the basket, looking out at the store and passing shoppers. Louise stopped to wait so the checker could catch up; about half the basket was unloaded.

"Hi there! Are you helping Mommy today?" The friendly man from the vegetable department was back again, this time standing in line behind Lynn. Unafraid, she communicated as best she knew how with sparkling eyes, bright smile and an eager expression.

"Did you get to go for a ride in the shopping cart? I wish someone would push me around like that!" Lynn laughed out loud as the friendly stranger poked her gently. He smiled at Louise and went on talking to Lynn. "I've got a little granddaughter who isn't as big as you. I'll bet you'd like to play together."

Feeling a little uneasy now, Louise unloaded the remaining items quickly. She glanced at the man as she searched in her purse for the checkbook.

"What's your name, little girl?"

Lynn smiled a silent answer to his question.

"I'll bet it's Johnny. Is that right? Come on, tell me your name. What's wrong? Cat got your tongue? I'll bet you just can't talk today!"

A woman had joined the line and was also smiling at Lynn. It was too late to say anything. An explanation now would only embarrass this kindly gentleman. Louise quickly finished writing out the check, pulled the basket forward, smiled at the stranger, who was still admiring Lynn, and lifted Lynn out of the shopping cart. As they followed the young man with their cart full of loaded bags, Lynn flashed a smile at her friend and waved "bye bye."

After that we often tried to head off this kind of social trap. A brief comment like "She can't hear you, she's deaf" or "She can't talk yet because she has a hearing problem" usually sufficed.

Every day that winter Louise set up the auditory trainer. Somewhere we have a snapshot which I took during that time. It captures the hours they spent together at the auditory trainer. Lynn, obviously aware of the camera, large black earphones protruding from her head, a cheerful smile on her face, is sitting at a small table in the living room. Louise, on the opposite side of the table, is holding a shoe in her hand. Beside the black control box and microphone are Lynn's red ball, a large kitchen spoon and one of her favorite books.

"Shoe. Shoe. Shoe. Shoe. Shoe." With each word, Louise showed Lynn the shoe, watching for some indication that her voice had penetrated the barrier of silence. Then she put the microphone to Lynn's mouth, hoping she would imitate.

"Ball. Ball. Ball. Ball." As Louise spoke Lynn watched each word; the lines of concentration on her tiny face seemed to say she was trying hard to hear, to figure out what was expected of her.

Sometimes when Louise pushed the microphone to her Lynn would move her mouth in a silent mimic that seemed to mean "ball" or "shoe." Day after day in January and February we practiced and waited. Did she ever hear us? We couldn't be sure. By the end of February she made sounds like "aaaaaahhhhhh" and "uuuuuuhhhhhhhh" more often when she wore the earphones.

We knew it would be futile to force this kind of learning. So Louise would spend ten to fifteen minutes on it during the day; when I came home I would set up the equipment and go through the same procedure again. We rarely could hold Lynn's interest beyond fifteen minutes. Yet we knew that any practice would eventually bring results. Someday she would begin to recognize sounds. Someday she would see their connection to the words she saw on our lips. Someday she would talk to us.

On a dark, overcast evening in the middle of January, we drove to Chicago. John, a senior who lived upstairs, came down to baby-sit. Bruce and Lynn greeted him with delight. "We should be home by eleven," Louise said as we went out the door.

The side streets and secondary roads, covered with rutted, slippery snow, meant slow going, but once on the expressway, we made good time. The Chicago Hearing Society had announced a series of meetings for parents of deaf children. We hoped to attend them all, even though we would have to drive nearly an hour in each direction through wintry weather. In the distance, the lights in empty offices of Chicago's skyscrapers lit up the cold night.

We found the building and entered a high-ceilinged room. About forty folding chairs had been set up; less than half remained empty. We found two seats on the end of a row. After several minutes a tall, friendly woman in a green business suit stood up at the front.

"Welcome to this first meeting for parents of deaf children," she began. She talked about the Chicago Hearing Society and then introduced a film on the human ear and the causes of deafness.

The lights went out. We settled back to watch. Black and white numbers flickered in rapid succession on the screen; scratchy music came over the speaker.

"Look at the people around you," the narrator began as the camera focused on a blind woman slowly making her way along a crowded street. "You can see the blind, the wheelchair of the paraplegic. You notice the palsied and the amputee. But you probably will not recognize the deaf and the hard-of-hearing. They are usually invisible. Yet nearly fourteen million Americans have impairments of hearing. Of this number, about seven million have a significant loss of hearing in both ears. Approximately one million eight hundred thousand can be called deaf; that is, their hearing is nonfunctional for the purposes of everyday life."

The film then shifted to the ear, showing the intricate mechanisms inside that enable us to hear. The narrator gave a long explanation of the way each part of the ear works, how sounds reach the brain, and the difference between a conductive hearing loss and a sensory-neural loss. The film ended forty-five minutes later with a discussion of residual hearing and the way deaf children learn language.

The lights came on, the woman stood up at the front of the room. Several people asked questions about deafness and residual hearing.

"Will a hearing aid help my little boy who is profoundly deaf?" one man asked.

"That is something an audiologist will have to tell you," the leader answered. "Sometimes, on the basis of a test, a child will appear profoundly deaf; then, a year later, that same child will respond to more sound than anyone thought possible. It may be that, in the meantime, the parents have worked daily to stimulate the child's residual hearing. Most audiologists will recommend a hearing aid even if they aren't completely sure if it will help. And often the results are surprising."

I wanted to ask whether a hearing aid would amplify sound more effectively than an auditory trainer, but the subject changed, so I decided to wait. We slipped out just as the discussion was ending; it would be after eleven before we reached home.

A week later we sat in the same room. A special-education teacher was introduced and began her talk.

"I know that the first wish of every parent who has a deaf child is to hear Johnny or Susie talk. Just to hear your child's voice say 'I love you' will be worth all the work and sacrifice it takes to teach speech to the hearing-impaired child." All the whispering and shuffling had stopped; I could see a late couple tiptoeing across the back of the room to two empty seats.

The speaker then emphasized that speech was the birthright of every child. But that was only one reason we must begin teaching hearing-impaired children as early as possible. In our desire for immediate communication with our deaf child, we must never forget that all of us live in a hearing world. A deaf child encounters that hearing world from the first day he sets foot outdoors to play with normal children. From that time on, he will have to compete with hearing people for the rest of his life. Without the skill of lip reading or the ability to talk, how could a deaf child make it in a hearing world?

The deaf child who learns to communicate orally can succeed. And later an employer will be more inclined to hire a hearing-impaired person who has learned to use oral skills. People are more reluctant to employ a deaf person, someone they will have to give instructions to by gestures or by scribbling notes.

"With an oral education," she said, "you can share the joys of raising a family as if you had a normal hearing child. You can see your child go on to a successful life. I know hearing-impaired children who have finished high school with hearing kids, who have gone on to graduate from college and who are now successful in their careers.''

I shifted in my seat. Louise smiled at me for a moment, slipped out of her coat and put it around her shoulders. I looked around the room. In front of us sat a man in construction boots and overalls; his wife looked tired and overweight. A black couple had taken seats to our left. Two rows ahead I could see a young man and woman who hardly looked old enough to have finished high school. An older man, perhaps forty, in a business suit—who might easily have been a lawyer or an accountant—sat next to them. Next to him I could see an Oriental couple. There must have been forty or fifty parents there that night, all brought together by deafness.

The speaker pulled my thoughts back to the front of the room. ''Let's start at the beginning. Let's say you have detected that your child of two years is deaf. Although this may be a review for some of you with older children, it never hurts to go over the important principles again.''

I could see several people writing things down. The teacher spoke easily, emphasizing her words with a tone of authority.

''Treat your son or daughter like a normal hearing child.

''Work consistently to stimulate your child's residual hearing.

''No matter how great your child's hearing loss, auditory training can improve his ability to hear.

''If a deaf child does not have constant auditory stimulation, he will lose the ability to use whatever hearing he has.

''The most important thing is to take every opportunity to talk to your child. Face your child as you speak. Remember, if you have a deaf daughter, for instance, and you treat her like a deaf girl, she will begin to act like a deaf girl. She can be 'very deaf' if you let her.''

Toward the end of her talk she stressed the necessity for specially trained teachers as a child grows older. We were encouraged to enroll our children as early as possible in schools that provided such teachers. Some children could start as early as three years of age.

Then, just before the speaker finished, almost as if she had forgotten to stress it enough; she gave two warnings.

"I want to caution you first about discouragement. You may meet people who will try to discourage you. They will tell you that lip reading is extremely difficult, that too many sounds can't be seen on the lips. They will say that only a few gifted hearing impaired children ever learn to speak clearly.

"Don't believe them!" Her voice rang with authority as she repeated herself. "Don't believe them! I have worked with hundreds of deaf children. It's true, some do not learn to talk clearly or very well, but why not? It is because their parents did not start early, did not have the patience, did not work with determination to provide a pure oral environment for their child. If you have ever seen a group of deaf teen-agers or adults talking away for all they're worth, you will have had all the proof you need to know that your Janet or your Billy can grow up to communicate effectively in a hearing world.

"The second thing I want to warn you about is shortcuts to communication." She paused for a long moment as if to let the importance of this danger sink in. "Don't get sidetracked. Some misinformed people say you should use gestures as well as lip reading. If you gesture, it can prevent your child from ever learning to speak. If you gesture, your child will start thinking in gestures."

That idea caught my attention. Thinking and language were certainly tied together. How could anyone think at all without language? It would have to be in pictures or gestures or something. More than ever I could see how important it would be for Lynn to learn to talk and lip-read.

"I've seen deaf children in their teens who can hardly say a word, gesturing to one another, trying to communicate, completely cut off from the hearing world. And gestures can cause your child to develop a deaf personality, until he eventually will act deaf. His facial expressions will begin to seem unnatural. The noises he makes will sound unpleasant. The deaf person who relies on gestures will end up living almost entirely in the deaf ghetto."

The lecture brought a great many questions. The first hand went up near the front of the room; I tried to see who it was. The speaker pointed in the direction of the hand and nodded. An elderly black woman stood up.

"I'm a grandmother," she began hesitantly, looking around to include the whole group. "I have an eight-year-old granddaughter, Sally, who's stone deaf. Her mama couldn't come tonight. Now, Sally, she's been goin' to school for five years, ever since she was three. And her mama and papa, they talk to her all the time just like the teachers say they should. And I talk to her and all my daughter's other kids talk to her. Sally seems to understand quite a bit by readin' our lips."

The room had become intensely quiet, all eyes fixed on this gray-haired woman; I tried to catch each word.

"It just worried me and her mama," she continued, "'cause Sally still don't talk. Can't say no more than four or five words that anybody can understand. No conversation at all. We just can't make any real sense out of the noises she makes.

"I have another granddaughter," she went on, speaking louder now, more emphatically. "She is only four years old, but she talks all the time. Sally can't tell us how she feels. Sally can't tell us what she wants. Sally can't tell us what she's thinkin'. Sally can't even say her own name! When do you think we can expect Sally to begin talkin'?"

The hush that had fallen over the group continued after she sat down. Someone finally coughed, breaking the tension that seemed to fill the room. We waited for the teacher to speak.

"We must all remember," she said, looking around the room to include everyone, "that there are always individual differences. Some children take longer than others to start talking. That's true for a hearing child, but individual differences stand out even more for deaf children. Some deaf children will start talking when they are only four years old, but others not until they are six or eight.

"You keep talking to Sally," she said, looking back at this grandmother, "and you'll be surprised when one of these days she starts talking back. I've seen some kids who didn't speak much, who had learned to lip-read fairly well, and then one day, almost spontaneously, they began to talk. It just takes patience."

Then someone asked about the John Tracy correspondence course. Should they send for it? Would it help in teaching their severely deaf son?

"I'm glad you brought that up," she said, and went on to recommend it as one of the best ways to assist deaf children. It was especially good for the first few years before the children started regular school. She had hardly finished when a barrel-chested man at the back raised his hand and got to his feet at the same time. His wool shirt looked worn; wisps of sandy hair stood up on the back of his head.

"I don't like that John Tracy course," he blurted out in a booming voice. I could see startled heads all over the room suddenly turn to look.

"Our boy, he's deaf. When he was three we started that course. We wanted to help him all we could. At first it went okay, then it started to get more difficult to go through a lesson with him. Now he doesn't want to sit still for more than two minutes at a time."

His voice grew louder. I could see his white knuckles on the back of the chair.

"The more we tried to teach him"—he paused—"the more we fought with him. For a couple years we all managed to put up with it. I think we helped him a lot. But now he's six and a big kid for his age. He's really upsetting the whole family routine."

He stopped as if to catch his breath, to slow the unexpected rush of words.

"We can't understand more than two or three words he says. And he don't understand us. If we're all talking around the table, he gets angry and frustrated. It's getting so we don't like to take him out in public. He'll throw a tantrum in a restaurant or a store and it's embarrassing to the rest of us.''

As he spoke I could see the woman next to him—it must have been his wife—nodding her head in agreement, worried lines of despair written on her face. People now began to shift uncomfortably in their chairs. But this father hadn't finished.

''What I want to know,'' he went on, looking directly at the teacher in the front of the room, ''is why can't the city of Chicago have a residential school for deaf kids?'' He slowed for an instant and I could hear several muffled gasps. ''Why can't they have a place where all these deaf kids could be together all week?'' Now both his hands pounded the air in great downward jabs as he spoke. ''My boy could be with hundreds of other kids like himself. They would all be much happier. We could take him home on weekends, but all week long is just too hard on the rest of us.''

He ended abruptly and sagged heavily to his seat, as if it had taken all his strength to say what he felt so intensely.

Heads turned slowly back to the front of the room. Whispered exclamations broke out nearby and I could see the lowered heads that made these comments. I gave Louise a knowing look; she seemed perplexed. I sat up straighter in the metal folding chair wondering what the teacher would say to this man. I found myself feeling sorry for her. She waited for a long moment in complete silence, her face flushed. Then she spoke in carefully measured words.

''Have you ever thought that maybe *you* are unwilling to face *your* responsibility to *your* deaf son?'' Her question brought a sudden relief to the tension in the room, as if someone had thrown open a window on a stifling hot day. I wanted to nod vigorously in agreement, but I knew the man could see me from where I sat.

''You are the parents,'' she continued. ''It is *your* son who is deaf. No one said that life with a deaf child would be easy. It sounds as if you want to turn the problems over to someone else.

Sure, it is difficult to communicate with your son at six years of age, but pushing the difficulties off on other people will not solve them. That's not the way your child is going to learn how to talk. It takes time and it takes patience."

She stopped, almost in midsentence, and looked around the room for other questions. No one asked anything after that, and the meeting ended. All the way home we talked about this man and his problems. I could still see the pained look on his face; the anger and despair in his voice rang in my ears. His comments had raised new doubts for Louise. Would we have the same kinds of problems with Lynn?

"I don't think we need to worry," I said, as much to calm my own doubts as those Louise expressed. "Lynn is only twenty-one months old. Lynn can already lip-read a number of words. Lynn has already started to mouth some words. Lynn enjoys the lessons with the auditory trainer."

Later that week I had to make another trip to Chicago and all the way driving in and back, that one father's questions kept coming back to me. It made me more determined than ever to work patiently with Lynn. I vowed I would never give up as this man seemed to have done.

In the weeks that followed we planned again and again to drive in to the Chicago Hearing Society's meetings, only to be prevented by some new winter storm or teaching responsibilities. One afternoon when I walked home from school it began to snow. Enormous eggshells of white were slowly drifting down. By the next morning nearly two feet of snow had fallen, and before it ended, a record-breaking four feet of snow lay on the ground.

We were disappointed not to be able to attend the remaining lectures at the Chicago Hearing Society. But the gap created in our education about deaf children was soon filled when a large brown envelope arrived one day. I could see the return address read "John Tracy Clinic." Inside we found the first installment of the "Correspondence Course for Parents of Little Deaf Children."

I opened the envelope eagerly. I leafed through the pages, excited to have finally received the first lesson. At last we had something specific to work on, lessons worked out by experts. I immediately set about reading the introductory materials. Ahead of us stretched months and months of lessons that would come from the clinic as we completed each unit of work with Lynn.

Eight

I stopped reading from the first installment of the John Tracy correspondence course and looked up at Louise, who was listening from across the living room. Lynn, dressed in pajamas, snuggled down on Louise's lap, and slowly turned the pages of a storybook.

"Now, there's a case of someone profoundly deaf from birth," Louise began but did not finish her thought as Lynn wriggled off her lap to get another book. I knew what she was thinking.

I had read to her the story of a young woman in Alabama, a college graduate, who worked as a laboratory technician in a large hospital. Profoundly deaf all her life, this woman could talk to her fellow workers and understand what they said. She had adapted to a hearing world.

The John Tracy correspondence course offered more than we had hoped for: ideas, lessons for Lynn, scientific information on deafness. Most of all, it gave us something to do. It showed us how to plan a lesson, explained what to include, and then showed us step by step how to teach that lesson. Lynn settled into bed a few minutes later, and we spent most of the evening reading and discussing the course.

On Saturday morning, a few days later, I sat at the kitchen table with Lynn. Rays of bright sunlight streamed in the window and filled the room. Louise had collected blue, red, orange, green and yellow ribbons left over from Christmas wrappings. I cut each ribbon in two strips about four inches long. Lynn, kneeling on a chair, elbows on the table, chin in her hands, watched me with curiosity.

"We're going to match these colors," I said. She had no way

of knowing this would be the first of hundreds of lessons from the John Tracy course. She looked at my lips without understanding. Louise listened from the sink behind us as she dried the breakfast dishes.

I carefully placed the ribbons in two rows in front of Lynn, making sure that the various colors were mixed in a random arrangement. I picked up a blue ribbon from the first row and held it up to Lynn, whose bright, eager eyes followed my every movement. At the same time, with my other hand, I pointed to the red ribbon in front of her on the table.

"No!" I shook my head emphatically as I spoke. I pointed to the green ribbon. "No!" I shook my head again, still holding the blue ribbon in my hand. I moved it closer to Lynn, pointed to the matching blue ribbon on the table, picked it up, held it beside the one in my other hand, and nodded enthusiastically. I did my best to convey that I'd suddenly discovered a most important connection between these two pieces of ribbon.

"Yes! This is the right one. It matches. This one is blue too. See, I have *two* blue ribbons!"

Lynn looked back and forth from the ribbons to my face. A blank expression had replaced the interest. She turned to the ribbons in front of her, started to pick up the green one, let it fall back to the table, and then looked around at Louise, who was watching us.

"Now you can match colors," I said to Lynn, rearranging the ribbons in a new pattern. I picked up the red ribbon and held it out to Lynn, who took it. She looked at me quizzically and dropped it to the table; then, with a quick, sweeping motion she pushed all the ribbons into a pile at the side of the table. Several fell on the floor.

I looked at Louise, who was smiling at my valiant efforts. Patiently I retrieved the ribbons and again made two rows. For ten minutes I talked, sorted, rearranged, matched, shook my head, nodded, pointed. I matched all the different Christmas ribbons as if it were a game of solitaire. Lynn wouldn't play. Or couldn't. With the clear, decisive movements that told us her mind was made up, she pushed back her chair, slid to the floor and ran off to play. I gathered up the ribbons.

"Lynn's only twenty-two months," I said slowly. "The Tracy course says that some kids don't want to match colors until they're a little older. I think we should try the object matching sometime later today. Whatever we do, the instructions said we shouldn't try to force her. In time she'll catch on."

When Lynn woke up from her afternoon nap, Louise had collected a pair of shoes, two spoons, two cups, two forks, two balls and two blocks. This time I watched. Lynn and Louise sat on the floor with the matching pairs scattered in disarray between them.

"This is a shoe," Louise began, picking up the nearest one. "Can you find the other one?" Lynn appeared puzzled by the words on Louise's lips. After a moment Louise picked up the other shoe and held them together for an instant.

"See, they match." She returned one to the pile on the floor. The puzzled frown disappeared from Lynn's face. She picked up the shoe from the floor and held it high in the air as if she had made a great discovery.

"Good girl! You found the other shoe! You're so smart!" Lynn reached out for the shoe Louise held, then hugged both of them to her body as if she would never give them up. Back they went to the pile.

"This is a spoon." Louise held up the shiny metal utensil. "This is the spoon for eating our lunch. Can you find the other spoon?"

Lynn sized up the silent expectations written on Louise's lips and face without knowing that a fraction of her lip and tongue movement had formed a word. She reached out for the other spoon and held it up.

By now I couldn't sit on the sidelines any longer; I slid to the floor just in time to add my congratulations. From then on, every time Louise showed one object, Lynn quickly retrieved its mate from the pile. After five more minutes of matching, she grew restless. We tried the spoon again and then the block, but when

Lynn threw the matching block across the room we knew it was time to end the game. I gathered up the objects, put them in a paper bag and left it on the floor at the end of the couch.

That evening before dinner I sat reading the paper when Lynn found the bag, dragged it over to my chair and begged to play, one hand tugging on my pants leg, the other holding the bag. For six or seven minutes we matched shoes, spoons, blocks, forks, balls and cups two or three times. Lynn never hesitated as we went from one pair to the next. Her quickness made me sure she could learn anything.

Right from the beginning, the John Tracy course worked. But it also raised questions. How did matching colored ribbons, spoons and shoes prepare Lynn to speak? To lip-read? We had talked to her for months and she could already lip-read some things and even mouth a few words. Why couldn't we simply hold up a blue ribbon and say "blue"? Wouldn't she see the connection? The John Tracy course even told us *not* to expect Lynn to lip-read the names for colors and objects. We were only to work on matching.

I went back to the first two installments of the course and read them more carefully. What did the psychologists and audiologists at the John Tracy Clinic have in mind when they designed this course? A footnote in the first chapter indicated it had been developed from another course, used at the Wright Oral School for the Deaf in New York City. It was not haphazard. The references to scholarly works on the growth and development of children increased our confidence in the lessons.

I was impressed with a special section written by Dr. Arnold Gessel, who had been director of the Clinic for Child Development at Yale University. He emphasized that with patient help from parents, a deaf child *could* learn to speak to a gratifying degree.

Searching for the underlying rationale of the course, I came across one statement that seemed to answer many of our questions:

Every single thing a deaf child learns during the first years of life, every word he learns to lip-read or to speak, every action he learns to perform at command, *is consciously taught by somebody*.

I read that sentence again. I read it aloud to Louise. How different it had been with Bruce, who seemed to have learned everything spontaneously. Except for toilet training and a few "no no's," we couldn't recall having *consciously* taught him very much. He listened and picked things up. He watched and remembered. His first word came effortlessly. We never planned lessons. We never matched objects. He learned his colors without special teaching. Deep inside there must have been some principle of growth and learning that worked spontaneously.

Deafness. How powerful this invisible handicap had become. It sealed Lynn away from our words, from our thoughts, from everything we knew.

We would have to teach everything consciously. *Training*. That word kept recurring throughout the John Tracy course. Auditory *training*. Memory *training*. Concentration *training*. Imitation-*training*. Observation *training*. Sensory *training*. Association *training*.

The matching games were designed to train Lynn in the art of association. Putting things together. As her ability to match colors and objects developed, she could more easily take the next step: *connecting them to our lip movements*. But that would require more training. It was easy to see that two blue ribbons went together or two old shoes, but the leap from these associations to matching a ribbon with tiny lip movements for the word "blue" would be much more difficult.

In time she would have to match words like "falling," "running," "jumping" and "eating" with the actions. That meant more training. And someday she would go further and match lip movements with unseen ideas contained in words like "justice," "love" and "fear." Finally she would have to learn another association, one all normal children take for granted: *that lip movements go together with the sounds of the human voice.* And then she would learn to make those sounds even though she couldn't hear them.

Slowly Louise and I began to realize the enormity of our task. What started as merely *talk, talk, talk* must now be transformed into *train, train, train.* We began to see why the John Tracy course emphasized a solid foundation in sensory training and association training. Merely talking all the time would not lead to lip reading. Each tiny step had to be specifically taught. And we were Lynn's first teachers.

Late one evening, after Lynn and Bruce had fallen asleep, we discussed the things that Lynn would have to learn. We tried to imagine what it would be like. I asked Louise to say something to me without using her voice to see if I could understand it.

"Tomorrow . . . Lynn . . . Bruce . . . school." Her lips moved so quickly I could only guess at the words.

"Tomorrow I'm going to take Lynn shopping while Bruce is in school." I filled in the missing words that I could not decipher from Louise's lips. I'd seen her say those exact words dozens of times. I tried to lip-read other sentences, and then Louise read my lips. Sometimes we could understand entire phrases, even complete sentences. Even when the words were hidden inside our mouths we could get the sense of what the other person said. It never dawned on us that we were saying common, oft-repeated phrases. We didn't grasp the fact that we already *knew* the words. Lynn did not. We only had to recognize them. Lynn had to start from scratch. We had already mastered the grammar of our native language. Lynn only knew a few isolated words. For us it was like picking out a familiar face in the crowd. For Lynn it meant looking for someone she had never seen, about whom she knew nothing.

"Let's turn on the late news and see if we can understand without sound," I said, looking at my watch. It was a few minutes after ten o'clock. The local news had already begun when the picture came on. We both concentrated very hard on the rapidly moving lips of the newscaster. The minutes crept by.

". . . city . . . Daley . . . Vietnam . . . station . . . President Johnson . . . Chicago . . . winter storm . . ."

I was stunned—most of the words were undecipherable! The newscaster disappeared and silent pictures came on that were difficult to interpret. Then back came the moving lips and more words, disconnected, without meaning. I strained to understand but could do no more than recognize a phrase here, a word there. Isolated words that seemed familiar but didn't communicate. I looked at Louise in dismay.

"That's really hard to understand!" she said, shaking her head. "Can you make out what they're saying?"

"Not very well."

"And Lynn doesn't even know the words to watch for," she went on. "It must be like watching someone speak Chinese on TV with the sound turned off! How could you ever understand what they said just from watching their lips? Wouldn't you have to learn Chinese first? Even then it would be a superhuman task to lip-read a whole language. I wonder if Lynn can really learn something that difficult."

"Maybe being deaf actually makes it easier for her," I answered, half trying to convince myself. "We've never tried to lip-read because we've never had to. Lynn practices it all the time and has from the time she was a small baby. That's all she's ever known. And later, with a trained teacher, I think she'll be able to do it."

I was surprised and excited one day early in March to learn of a graduate student at Wheaton College whose wife had been trained in Australia to teach deaf children. She was unemployed and interested in part-time work.

Jill Corey arrived on a warm March afternoon; the last patches of snow had disappeared, neighborhood bicycles had taken over the sidewalks, and I could see the first buds on the tall elm in our front yard. Louise was out and Lynn cried vociferously when Jill came up to her. I put Lynn on the floor and we sat down to discuss her deafness and what Jill might be able to do.

Jill Corey was young and vivacious, enthusiastic about teaching the deaf. She agreed to come every week until the end of the semester. I wanted to watch Jill as she worked with Lynn; perhaps I could learn some of her skills by observation. From the little I knew, I half expected she would take Lynn on her lap, place Lynn's hand on her throat as she talked and begin to teach Lynn to speak the words she could already mouth silently. I had seen pictures of teachers working with deaf children in this way.

"Lynn is really too young for me to do much with now," Jill said in a matter-of-fact tone. "I can help both of you and give you some ideas about how you can help her."

I tried to hide the sudden surge of disappointment I felt. "Is she really too young to start talking?" I asked. "She is already mouthing words; we hoped it might be possible for her to start adding her voice. We just don't know how to get her to do it."

"She's not too young. But it is best to emphasize lip-reading skills at this age. You want to build a solid foundation for later speech."

Lynn slowly lost her fear, crawled over and pulled herself up in a chair next to Jill Corey.

"I'd suggest that we start with one word and teach her that until she can lip-read it in any situation, until she has mastered that one word. Does Lynn have a ball?"

I retrieved the red ball we had used for matching games, then settled back to watch. Jill began the first lesson. Kneeling beside Lynn, she rolled the ball across the floor to catch her attention.

"Look at your *ball* go." She looked at Lynn as she spoke, rolling the ball in her direction. "This is a fast *ball*. Do you like the *ball*? Can you roll the *ball* to me?"

Lynn watched in silence. Jill picked up the ball and hid it behind the pillow on the couch. "Where did the *ball* go? Can Lynn find the *ball*? "

Lynn could not be passive any longer; she pulled herself up to the couch and found the ball. I repressed the urge to tell Jill that we had played these games before, dozens of times. I waited to see what she had in mind. She hid the ball behind a pillow on the chair, rolled it across the floor, held it high in the air, then began bouncing it across the living-room floor. Between bounces she cradled it in her arms like a baby or rolled it toward Lynn. The way she handled the ball, the way she looked at it and talked about it, all suggested a reverence for this ordinary rubber toy. Lynn followed her movements as if transfixed.

"Bounce the *ball*. Bounce the *ball*. Can Lynn see the *ball* bounce? A bouncing *ball*. Bounce the *ball*. Bounce the *ball*."

After a few minutes Lynn began to lose interest and started for the dining room. Jill followed. Her enthusiasm for the ball picked up. She bounced it around the dining-room table and on into the kitchen, pretending to hide it in the sink. I followed, feeling strangely like a bystander. For nearly thirty minutes Jill, Lynn and the red ball took over the house. Finally Jill worked her way back into the living room and sat down.

"Well!" she said, catching her breath. "Lynn is a bright little girl and catches on fast. You must have been working with her because she watched my lips most of the time." I nodded, waiting for her to go on, to explain what would come next, what we could do.

"This week, before I come back for Lynn's next lesson, I want you to think up twenty games you can play with the ball. Different ones from what you saw me do today. Both you and your wife should play these games with Lynn several times a day. Always talk about the ball and make sure Lynn can see your lips."

Before Jill returned the following week, Lynn had seen the word "ball" at least a thousand times on our lips. She slept with the ball, bathed with it, ate with it, and all of us played with it at every opportunity. Before breakfast I'd bounce it around the house with Lynn still in her pajamas. Bruce entered into the games enthusiastically, as if we had created them partly for his benefit. I would play one or another hide-the-ball game before going off to school. The ball went shopping with Lynn and Louise; it sat on the table while Lynn watched her make bread; it went into the crib at nap time. Had someone been able to observe us that week and the ones that followed, they would surely have concluded that we all believed that little ball was a living, breathing creature, something sacred, almost supernatural.

I decided to test Lynn's lip-reading ability just before Jill came back for the second lesson. I sat down on the floor with Lynn and put the ball, a shoe, a book and a spoon between us.

"Give me the *ball*," I said. Her hand went out to the nearest object and she held up the shoe.

I tried again. "Which one is the *ball? Ball.* Can you give me the *ball*?"

This time she gave me the spoon. Each time I rearranged the items she would watch my lips closely, then reach out for the nearest one and hold it up triumphantly. A feeling of helplessness swept over me. I remembered a student who had stayed after class earlier that week to ask about an algebra problem from the previous night's homework assignment. I had discussed it in class and everyone had understood except Sandy. I couldn't understand her questions. I went through the problem on the board, but she shook her head and looked blankly at the symbols I had written. After class I went through it again, explaining each part of the process, moving slowly so she couldn't miss the steps involved. At last she shook her head slowly, gathered her things together, and with tears in her eyes, she said, "I just don't get it!"

I sat on the floor long after Lynn had grown tired of the game and left the room. I looked down at the ball and the shoe in front of me. We knew Lynn had already learned to lip-read some of our words. Now I began to doubt that she had lip-read them at all. She had merely read the situations in which we had spoken. We must have given off a hundred other clues that helped her understand what we had said.

"Shoe," Louise had said only that morning while dressing Lynn. She immediately raced across the room, picked up her shoes and brought them back to Louise. But "shoe" had become part of a daily habit—it was morning, it was time to get dressed, it was part of a sequence of getting dressed that followed the socks. Lynn could read the pattern, but she could not read our lips alone. "Spoon" went with breakfast, lunch and dinner. "All gone" went with the disappearance of food and television pictures. "Bye bye" accompanied all the subtle preparations for leaving—picking up a purse or briefcase, finding a coat, last-minute kisses.

I said the word "ball" silently to myself several times. Then "spoon." And "shoe." Even without a mirror I could tell there wasn't much difference between the small clues on my lips for each word. I felt very tired, almost overwhelmed by the task that lay ahead for Lynn.

Jill Corey bounced Lynn's ball all over the house again for the second lesson. Near the end of her visit she put the ball aside, and when she had Lynn's full attention, she suddenly fell on the floor. Lynn was taken by surprise and laughed out loud.

"*Fall down*," Jill said, sitting up quickly and looking directly at Lynn. Then she collapsed again, repeating the words as she fell. Within minutes Lynn happily imitated this new action game.

"Continue to work on 'ball,' " Jill said as she prepared to leave. "But if Lynn becomes bored, you can go on to fall down."

Long after midnight Louise and I were still awake, talking about Lynn and Jill Corey and the John Tracy course and the auditory trainer and everything we had started teaching Lynn. The informal, constant talking had continued, but we now began to feel that the formal lessons were more important.

In the back of our minds we worried about Lynn's going to school. At four, Bruce had started preschool classes; now he went off to kindergarten at Holm School. Watching and listening to Bruce only underscored the necessity to work hard *now* to help Lynn learn to lip-read and speak.

"We started reading groups today," Bruce had announced one day when he came home from school. "Mrs. Owens had to go over the letters in the alphabet because some kids don't even know it yet." Every day Bruce told us about school, special projects or field trips planned by Mrs. Owens, what he had learned, who had misbehaved and which friends he had played with. He called his friends on the phone, he visited their houses, he brought them home for lunch, they stayed for an an afternoon of play.

We began to realize that in addition to making school difficult, Lynn's deafness could also isolate her from other children.

We redoubled our efforts to teach Lynn the lessons set forth in the John Tracy course. In a strange way, the lessons helped us as much as they helped Lynn. We worried less because we had something to do. We felt more acceptant of Lynn's handicap and our responsibility to prepare her for a hearing world. We kept reassuring each other that eventually Lynn would speak. We recalled examples of successful deaf people reported in the John Tracy course. We talked to Jill Corey, who was impressed with Lynn's brightness. "She'll learn to talk and *eventually* go to school," she assured us. We slowly came to accept the fact that "every word a deaf child learns has to be taught consciously by someone."

Spring vacation arrived the third week in March and we packed our camping gear and headed through Indiana for the Great Smoky National Park in Tennessee. One important fact I could not leave behind: we had no time to lose in teaching Lynn to lip-read and speak. "Let's bring some ribbons and things from the kitchen for matching," I had suggested to Louise.

After only two hours on the road I had prodded Louise at least three times: "Why don't you work on matching ribbons with Lynn?"

"I just want to relax for once and watch the scenery," Louise said, a note of irritation in her voice. "Can't you ever forget that you're a teacher, just for a few days? Bruce and Lynn need to be able to act normal some of the time."

'But don't you understand that Lynn's only chance at being normal depends on us helping her at every chance?"

Louise sat quietly for a long minute looking out the window. "Tom," she finally said with a sigh, "all this matching and talk-talk-talk at every chance is stealing from us the times we used to relax, share things or just encourage each other. I think we need a vacation sometime."

In the back seat Bruce and Lynn were laughing. Lynn pointed

excitedly at a small herd of cows grazing near an old barn. The smell of newly turned Indiana soil, waiting to be seeded with corn, filled the air. For an hour we drove on in silence.

We stopped briefly in Selvin, a tiny town in southern Indiana. The main street looked deserted but we found an old country store still open. Bruce and I climbed the wooden steps to a porch which badly needed a coat of paint; Lynn and Louise waited in the car. The place was dimly lit, pleasant smells of rope and chicken feed and smoke filled the air. On my left, behind a rough counter, I could see shelves piled high with coffee, sugar and canned vegetables. The store was long and narrow; the walls that ran to the back were covered with shelves and hooks. I could see stacks of work pants and work gloves; hammers, shovels and other farm tools hung in straight rows. Near the back I could make out several men sitting around a large woodburning stove. Curious eyes turned silently in our direction as we approached.

"Just passing through," I said hesitantly and came up to the edge of their circle. I looked nervously around in the moment of stillness that followed my comment. Bruce had spied a cardboard box with baby ducks and was trying to pick one up.

"Ancestors came from this area," I went on. "Would any of you know if there are any Spradleys living around here?" My eyes moved from one man to the next as I spoke. I could see two of them turn slightly to look at an older man, a white-haired farmer in faded overalls. His face was leathery from the sun; friendly lines appeared at the corner of his eyes as he said, "Spradley, eh?" He spoke slowly without removing the darkly stained pipe held precariously in the corner of his mouth. I waited. He stared at the floor in front of him for maybe half a minute. "No, not now there ain't. None I know of. But there's plenty of them up on the hill." He gestured toward the front of the store and a hint of a smile came to the other corner of his mouth.

"Which hill?" I asked.

"Go two blocks, turn right. Follow the dirt road. It'll take you up to the hill. Probably ten or fifteen of 'em up there. Must have had means, too. Some of the biggest markers. But you'd better hurry. You won't have any light in twenty more minutes."

"Thanks," I said, hurriedly found Bruce's hand and headed for the door.

A narrow, rutted road took us to the edge of the cemetery. Trees and stone markers covered an area of about one acre. Weeds had grown up around many of the graves.

"Cemetery," I said to Lynn as I lifted her out from the back seat. "We're going to look for some graves." We started hunting.

"See these names," I said to Bruce, pointing to the first marker. It said "Abigail Johnson" and gave the dates of her birth and death. "Look for markers like this that have Spradley." We fanned out in a row, working our way around the outside, then moving toward the center, Louise and Bruce going in one direction, Lynn and I in another. It would soon be dusk.

"Tom, I've found *you*!" Louise called excitedly from near the middle of the cemetery where it turned out most of the oldest graves were located. "I've found *you*!" she said again with a grin when I came up to the flat stone marker, worn from years of wind and rain and snow.

THOMAS S. SPRADLEY
1842-1887

A feeling of insignificance swept over me as I stared down at the name and dates. My thoughts rushed back several generations. I imagined the family and friends standing beside his freshly dug grave. How had he died? What kind of person had he been? What kind of lives had these people lived? Part of me longed to go back, to live in that simpler time. I felt a part of the rich black Indiana soil.

"Here's another one!" Bruce called excitedly from farther up, near the crest of the hill. As we started in his direction I could see the western sky behind him, dark purple, tinged with a rosy glow. The sun had disappeared nearly an hour earlier and now I could hear the first crickets beginning to chirp in the grass. A cool wind was blowing the trees and I pulled Lynn's sweater more closely around her.

With dusk turning slowly to darkness, we came to a large headstone. I could make out the name "Spradley" from some yards away. We moved closer, straining to see in the dim light. The name became clear.

ANDREW BYRUM SPRADLEY
1809-1874

I shivered and felt cold as the wind rustled the tall weeds beside the gravestone.

"That's where your great-great-great-grandfather is buried," I said to Bruce, recognizing the name that had been handed down from generation to generation and now belonged to one of my brothers.

For almost a minute we stood in silence, outlined against the sky. Somewhere near the edge of the cemetery I could hear the clear whistle of a meadowlark. I was holding Lynn; Bruce clung to Louise's hand. The darkness thickened and settled over the graves around us as it had done for centuries. I looked back at Andrew Byrum Spradley's gravestone. Then I wondered how the deaf had lived in his time. Had they gone to school? Had there been any deaf children in this little farm town? Was Lynn the first Spradley born without hearing? Probably not. Six or seven generations would include thousands of people and there was a good chance that one or more had been born deaf. I wondered what that had meant in those days. Deaf-and-dumb. Mute, unable to communicate except by crude gestures. Deafness had often been confused with mental retardation. Some deaf children had undergone surgical operations on their tongues in a futile effort to enable them to talk. In some societies the deaf were considered less than human, even put to death. An education for the deaf was, at one time, considered impossible. I looked at Lynn, then back at my ancestor's grave. Then we turned and walked through the darkness back to the car, glad to be living in the twentieth century.

We drove south to Kentucky, turned southeast into Tennessee and the Great Smoky National Park, where we camped for several days. Then we drove back to Wheaton, arriving by the end of the week to find a letter waiting from the University of Oklahoma, where I had applied for graduate work. It offered me a full-tuition scholarship and a teaching assistant position in the math department. We could hardly believe it. I reread the letter at least six times that night after I mailed a reply accepting their offer. Louise wrote to the Brandts telling them we would be joining them at the university. We were overjoyed. I tried to explain what it meant to Bruce and Lynn. I could begin courses in summer school, so we began immediately to make plans to leave for Norman, Oklahoma, in June. Our four years at Wheaton would soon come to an end.

Nine

Jill Corey came for Lynn's third lesson the next week. It became more difficult for her to hold Lynn's attention; she worked hard on "ball" and "fall down" but quit after only twenty minutes. We saw no change in Lynn.

"She's still young," Jill reminded us as she prepared to leave. She knew the questions that lay unspoken at the back of our minds.

That evening, after dinner, I sat in the living room grading a set of algebra quizzes. At the same time I listened to Louise, who sat on the floor with Lynn. A fork, cup, spoon, ball and shoe lay scattered on the floor between them, and as each of us had done many times before, Louise was testing Lynn.

"Where is the spoon?" Louise asked. Lynn watched her mouth, then reached for the cup. Louise shook her head and tried again. "Can you give me the fork?"

This time Lynn picked up the shoe.

"Where is the ball?" Louise asked. Out of the corner of my eye I could see Lynn reach across the pile. She picked up the ball! I froze. An accident, I thought to myself, and waited for Louise to try again. She rearranged the objects on the floor and made sure the ball was the farthest away from Lynn.

"Can you find the ball?" she asked again. Instantly Lynn leaned forward and picked up the ball.

"Tom!" Louise called softly, trying to keep the excitement out of her voice. "Lynn just read my lips! Watch, I'll do it again." I stayed on the couch, not wanting to distract Lynn by moving.

"Where's the cup?" Louise asked, testing to see if Lynn would reach for the ball again. A puzzled look crossed her face and she picked up the spoon. But the next time Louise asked for the ball, Lynn broke into a smile of recognition and picked up the ball. Louise praised Lynn and gave her a big hug.

"Let me try," I said and slid to the floor, my heart pounding with excitement. For the next five minutes Lynn picked up the ball six times. No matter what other words I said, if ball appeared on my lips, she went for the ball. "Fork, spoon, ball." "Give me the ball." "Find the ball." "Hide the ball." "Throw the ball." Lynn would make a wild guess if I said "cup," "fork" or "spoon," but missed each time.

"She's got it!" I shouted after I was certain we had ruled out chance.

For days we walked on clouds—a breakthrough! Lynn had read the first word from our lips unassisted by any gesture. A tiny step, but it foreshadowed thousands more. We could hardly wait to tell Jill Corey. Each day after that when I came home from school, if I said, "Go get the ball," Lynn would dash off and return with it. Within a week she was mouthing "ball" in her silent fashion. It seemed too good to be true. We redoubled our efforts. The weeks and weeks of repetition, despite our doubts, had overcome what seemed to us like the biggest hurdle of all on the path to speech.

We soon discovered this was only the first of a long series of hurdles. Louise sent a progress report to the John Tracy Clinic for the first installment of the correspondence course. She wrote out several questions: "How can we get Lynn to use her voice more?" "Should we use such phrases as 'eat your food' only in natural situations or at other times with pictures or just pretending?"

But one occurrence puzzled us most of all. Louise had explained: "Lynn confuses the phrases 'throw the ball' and 'fall down.' Sometimes we will ask her to fall down and she runs and gets her little red ball to play with."

Mrs. Thompson, director of the correspondence department at the clinic, answered our letter:

You asked how you could help Lynn not to confuse the two different phrases such as "throw the ball" and "fall down." Evidently about all Lynn is seeing is the sound of "all" which occurs in both phrases. In using any noun we usually suggest varying a phrase. Talk about bouncing a ball, rolling a ball, throwing a ball, hitting a ball, picking up a ball, and occasionally say, "here's a ball, I have a ball" and so on. In that way Lynn may gradually get to know that ball is the name of the object and she won't have to identify the complete phrase.

Louise had also reported that although Lynn would gesture "come here," she made no attempt to use her voice to say the words.

When Lynn wiggles her finger to say "come here" [the letter from Mrs. Thompson went on] she is probably communicating as best she can. If you always say "come here" when you want her she will gradually begin to understand the word and then if you give her an encouraging look, someday she may spontaneously say it.

That was the day we both dreamed about, hoped for and knew would come if we continued to work. One thing could speed up the process: a prescription hearing aid.

Shortly before Lynn was two, after learning that the audiologist at Children's Hospital had moved to Canada, we went to St. Luke's Hospital in Chicago for another hearing test. After the test was performed, the audiologist brought out a hearing aid with straps and cords attached. A small gray box about half the size of a package of cigarettes, the aid came with a harness that made it look like a miniature backpack. Louise placed the harness over Lynn's shoulders and the audiologist helped Lynn put the ear-molds in place. Interest and anticipation filled Lynn's hazel eyes as she watched the audiologist click the switch to "on" and turn the volume control to 6.

"Bub, bub, bub, bub, bub, bub." The audiologist spoke in a

normal voice, as if she had no doubt that the hearing aid would enable Lynn to hear. We watched for the slightest response.

"Bub, bub, bub, bub, bub." Suddenly Lynn raised her eyebrows slightly, looked at Louise for an instant, then smiled at the audiologist.

"I think she heard something," the audiologist said evenly. "Why don't you say something to her?" I glanced at Louise. It almost seemed too good to be true.

"Hi, Lynn!" I hesitated, watching her face for the slightest clue. "Bub, bub, bub, bub. Can you hear me?"

She gave me a quick grin, then looked at Louise and the audiologist in quick succession. It seemed to us that she had recognized my voice.

The audiologist wrote out a prescription and we went to have Lynn fitted. The Bishop Hearing Aid dealer did business from a two-room shop on Madison Street not far from the Loop. The dealer, a middle-aged man with a shiny bald head, gave us a friendly smile and invited us to sit down and talk about hearing aids. "Zenith makes one of the best aids," he began.

I looked around the small consultation room. It must have been the only room in the store besides the front reception area. A bronze plaque hung on the wall to my left; pamphlets on hearing loss and modern hearing aids were strewn on a small table behind the chair where the dealer sat. He wore a white laboratory coat.

"I've worked with deaf children for five years now," he went on. "I really enjoy it and I've helped a lot of them." He pointed to the plaque on the wall. "I received this award for service to hearing-impaired children. You'll notice a real difference after your daughter starts wearing her hearing aid. For some youngsters, when they put on their first hearing aid, they are able to hear Mom or Dad for the first time."

After a few minutes, at his suggestion, I took Lynn in my lap. He brought out a small lump of plastic material and pressed it firmly into each of Lynn's ears. She squirmed but didn't resist.

"This will harden in just a minute or two," he explained.

"From these impressions we can make earmolds that will fit her ears perfectly. You're lucky your daughter is being fitted while she's still young. I've had kids who don't come in until they are three or four years old.

"You can pay a hundred dollars' down payment," he went on. "The rest will be due when you pick up the hearing aid next month. The total cost will be three hundred dollars plus tax."

Driving home, we both felt elated. Finally Lynn would have her own prescription hearing aid. It seemed to us that we had waited too long already. Instead of being tied to brief periods with the auditory trainer, Lynn could wear this unit in the car, walking in the woods, at meals, when she played. All the time. And it was designed more for hearing than for auditory training.

A few days after Lynn had been fitted for her hearing aid, we received the first issue of the *Volta Review*. The John Tracy Clinic had advised us to subscribe to this journal, published by the Alexander Graham Bell Association for the Deaf in Washington, D.C. Bell had considered teaching deaf people to speak his most important work. One of his first pupils, a girl who had lost her hearing at age five, later became his wife. When Bell invented the telephone, the French government awarded him the prestigious Volta Prize and with the money he received, he founded the Volta Bureau in 1887. This world-wide information center on deafness was later renamed after him.

On the cover of that first issue was a four-year-old girl wearing a hearing aid with cords running to each ear. She almost looked like Lynn. With outstretched hands she was presenting the 1967 Alexander Graham Bell Award to President Lyndon Johnson.

Thumbing through the first pages of the journal, I eagerly read the advertisements about special schools for deaf children, about Gallaudet University, which is the national college for the deaf in Washington, D.C., notices about recently published books on deafness, and advertisements for hearing aids.

Even before I had read a single article, a strange feeling swept over me. We weren't alone! I felt in contact with a whole world of people scattered across the country, people with problems like ours, teachers concerned with deaf children, professional researchers investigating deafness. The *Volta Review* seemed to end our isolation.

One full-page advertisement showed an old New England school. Gracious lawns spread out under beautiful evergreens; a huge ivy-covered building dominated the picture. Across the top it said: "The Clarke School for the Deaf, Northampton, Massachusetts." I read and reread the description of their program.

> Clarke School has employed the oral method exclusively since its establishment in 1867. Residual hearing is worked with continuously from admission to graduation. Pupils are admitted at four and one-half years of age and progress through the lower, middle, and upper schools. The course of instruction is planned to fit pupils for high school work with hearing children.

But it was the hearing-aid advertisements in the *Volta Review* that held our interest. In less than two weeks Lynn's aid would be ready. The J. L. Warren Company in Chicago had a full-page advertisement about their compression auditory training units, which could be worn like hearing aids. "Even a whisper is heard distinctly by the aurally handicapped child using the new Warren Wearable Walkaway Units," it said. The descriptions of hearing aids emphasized that most children had some measurable hearing, no matter how deaf they appeared. Hearing aids could build on the tiniest fraction of hearing. The powerful amplifiers did things we didn't understand. They "cushioned sound" and "minimized distortion." An advertisement for the Zenith Corporation stated that deaf students could hear the teacher at any volume. "Trust Zenith to remove clamor, clutter, and too often confusion from classrooms for deaf youngsters."

When we went back to pick up Lynn's aid, the dealer inserted the first earmold in Lynn's right ear with a swift twisting motion.

"Aahieeiou!" she cried out and without hesitating pulled out the earmold; the discomfort showed on her face. The dealer tried the other one in Lynn's left ear; she instantly removed that one, too, while looking defiantly at this stranger.

"They'll be tight for a few days," he said. "She shouldn't wear them until you get home. Leave them in for short periods, then you can lengthen the time as she becomes accustomed to them."

I thought we might test the hearing aid in the shop, but I was almost glad for his suggestion. In the privacy of our own home we could sit and talk to Lynn without someone watching us; we could take our time and observe more carefully whether she heard us. If Lynn wanted to speak, she wouldn't be inhibited by the new surroundings or this stranger who had pushed these uncomfortable things into her ears.

"This volume control goes from one to seven. I'd suggest that you set it at about six." Then he pointed to the switch beside it which had three settings marked by tiny etched letters in the plastic top. I could see an M, T and R.

"This switch allows you to put the hearing aid on MIKE, TELEPHONE or BOTH. When your daughter gets older she can set the switch to T and place the earpiece of the telephone next to the aid and listen to people on the phone."

How great! I thought to myself. I glanced at Louise, nodding my head slightly. Bruce loved to use the telephone, calling his friends up and down the street to see if they could play, running to answer it first when he heard it ring. We had taken for granted that when Lynn grew older her friends would call. We hadn't thought much about the fact that it might be impossible. She might not even hear the telephone ring—much less the voices of her friends. Now this problem could be solved with her hearing aid.

We paid the dealer and drove home. I thought about the hearing aid, which Lynn held in her lap. I hoped it would amplify sound better than the auditory trainer she had used. It seemed important that these earmolds, which carried the amplified sound, went *inside* Lynn's ears. That would bring our voices even closer than the headphones had done.

A brilliant sun speckled the front lawn with shadows from the new leaves covering the highest branches of the elm. We went to the backyard and sat on the grass. Louise slipped the harness with the hearing aid in it over Lynn's head. She fastened it in front.

The single cord from the amplification unit had a Y connection where it forked into two cords that ran to the earmolds. Lynn quickly appraised the situation, and when Louise began inserting one of the earmolds, Lynn struggled and cried out, trying to protect her ears. She wanted no part of those painful things! I took her in my lap and held her arms gently while Louise tried again. She pulled Lynn's earlobe down to open the canal slightly, moistened the earmold, then pushed it into place with a quick twisting motion. The second one followed.

Lynn calmed down once each earmold was in place. Louise turned the volume control to 6 and we looked at each other, wondering who would speak first.

"Hi, Lynn! How are you? Can you hear me?" Louise knelt on the grass, leaning slightly forward, her face not more than fifteen inches from Lynn. We both watched for the slightest indication she might have heard; in the brief moment of silence Lynn watched Louise's face as if she was waiting for her to continue.

"Hi, Lynn! Bub, bub, bub, bub, bub." Still no response. Lynn spied a blue jay, pointed and looked up at me to see if I had seen it. I moved her to the grass between us, then when her eyes were on Louise, I spoke from behind. "Bub, bub, bub, bub, bub, bub. Hi, Lynn!"

Nothing. She did not look around or make any movement that suggested she heard anything. She was unaware I was trying so hard to communicate. I could see the disappointment on Louise's face. Hundreds of other tests flashed before my eyes—the fire engines, popping paper bags, standing behind Lynn in her high-chair, calling to her crib as she stared at the ceiling.

I looked back at Lynn, who was tugging at the right earmold. "Lynn. Can you hear me?" My voice came louder now. She was looking at Louise and pointing across the yard. I was filled with consternation. Why didn't she respond?

"Well," I said slowly, trying hard to sound confident, "Lynn is tired and irritable. That was a long drive to Chicago. This whole experience is new for her. She may have heard us but just doesn't know what sound is. She *has to learn to use* her hearing aid."

"You're probably right, but I thought she would show *some* response," Louise said. "She seemed to hear the audiologist through a hearing aid."

"Wait a minute!" I said to Louise, jumping up. "I've got an idea." I ran into the house and found Lynn's red ball. She could lip-read "ball" in dozens of different sentences. She mouthed "ball" whenever we played the games we had invented. If she was going to say anything at all today, it might just be "ball."

When I came back outside, Lynn was sitting near Louise, who easily distracted her whenever she reached for the earmolds. Lynn saw me coming, pointed at the ball and immediately began mouthing "ball," "ball," "ball." I sat down in front of her and held the ball between us, bouncing it lightly.

"Ball! Ball! Ball!" I directed my words toward the hearing aid, strapped to Lynn's chest. We both waited, almost holding our breath.

"Ball." Lynn's lips moved in a clear, silent enunciation. She had responded to what I said. But why the silence? Why didn't she make some sound? Even a hoarse whisper. I could see the same questions written all over Louise's face.

"Ball! Ball! Ball!" I repeated, bouncing the ball more vigorously. Then, before we could stop her, Lynn pulled out both of the plastic earmolds and began tugging at the harness.

Louise held our dashed hopes in her hands—the tangled cords, the harness, the earmolds. Dejected, we carried Lynn inside and put her down for a nap. Neither of us spoke. I put the hearing aid neatly back into the box. We went into the living room and sat down.

"It doesn't mean the hearing aid didn't help her hear," I said finally, fighting to regain some perspective.

"You're probably right." I could sense Louise's trying to cheer me up. "It's just *so* hard to wait. But as you said, she'll have to learn to use it."

Painfully we faced the truth. Hearing aid or no hearing aid, Lynn could not speak. Even with amplified sound, she still had to learn where the sounds came from, how they were made, what they meant. She still had to learn the sound of her own voice, to discover that changes in her vocal cords changed those sounds. It would take time for her to recognize the faint sounds that came through the earmolds. Like listening to some distant bird amid the city noises. Like hearing a cricket chirp at night on a busy boulevard.

It might take months or years to fully develop her residual hearing. As with the auditory trainer, it required repetition, association training and auditory training. We had to hope that her residual hearing would develop. No one is completely deaf. Every time we read that statement in the *Volta Review* or in some new book on deafness, our hope revived.

The last week in April, Lynn wore the hearing aid for brief periods each day, never more than ten minutes. Never without protest. Then her tiny ears became red and sore inside. When we tried to insert the earmolds she cried out in pain. We waited. Slowly the irritated passages healed. A week or two later she began putting the earmolds in by herself and leaving them for five minutes. The tightness had disappeared. Louise discovered it was better to put the harness on backward; Lynn could still pull out the earmolds but could not change the volume control or the selector switch.

All during May we tested Lynn over and over again while she wore the hearing aid. Louise came up behind her and spoke distinctly while I watched for any response. Lynn never turned around. Not once did she react to our voices or show she heard us.

Day after day we struggled with our feelings about the hearing aid. We became discouraged at the struggles to keep her wearing the uncomfortable earmolds for more than ten minutes at a time. We wondered if the aid was worth the money. It was difficult to understand why she easily mouthed ''all gone'' and ''ball'' but never made the sounds to transform them into words. The questions crept back into our thoughts again and again, as if spawned by our deeper fear that she would never learn to talk. A fear we could not express out loud.

About this time we discovered something about deafness that helped us understand what Lynn was up against. It came from a children's science demonstration, part of a monthly series that Bruce received in the mail. This particular demonstration focused on different kinds of deafness and the physiology of the ear. It included a recording that simulated what a deaf person actually heard.

A clear voice read the first few lines from the Declaration of Independence as it sounds for a person with a conductive loss of 40 decibels. It sounded distant, but we easily understood it. The same sentences were repeated, this time simulating a loss of 60 decibels. We could barely hear the words.

The demonstration continued, this time for a sensory-neural loss. We noticed a marked difference at both 40 and 60 decibels. With a conductive loss, the voice sounded weaker, as if the volume had been turned almost all the way down. With a sensory-neural loss, not only did the volume decrease but the words became distorted and muffled. Finally, the recording repeated the same sentences, showing what a person with a 60-decibel loss would hear when the sounds were amplified with a hearing aid. For a conductive loss, the amplification made the sounds loud and clear. For a sensory-neural loss, the louder sounds became even more distorted.

''I can't understand any of the words!'' Louise said as we replayed the recording. ''They're all garbled and run together; it's like someone talking underwater!'' We could hardly have recognized it was human speech except that we had been told exactly what the narrator would say and knew the words by heart.

"And Lynn's loss is somewhere around 100 decibels for most of the speech range," I said, trying to fight back the doubts that she could ever hear our words clearly. We played the recording over again, listening carefully to the last part, which amplified the words for both kinds of hearing loss. The amplification for a conductive loss was like using a powerful magnifying glass that clearly enlarged a line of extremely small print. With the sensory-neural loss it was as if the magnifying glass revealed that the tiny print consisted only of broken and missing letters, so that not a single word could be deciphered.

Painfully the realization sank in. Lynn would never hear the way we heard, the way Bruce heard. With a profound sensory-neural loss, her hearing aid could make her aware of our voices; it could not make our voices clear enough for Lynn to understand what we said. But with lip reading, with whatever amplification she did receive from her aid, and with increased ability to use her residual hearing, we believed she could learn to speak.

We secretly clung to hope. And each issue of the *Volta Review* nourished our hopes for Lynn. It was Linda McArthur, a young lady we had never met, who helped most that spring. We had read about Linda in one of the first issues of the *Volta Review*. Linda McArthur was deaf. But Linda was also a freshman at California State Polytechnic College in San Luis Obispo.

I can still remember sitting in our backyard under the trees looking through the *Volta Review* which had arrived in the mail that morning. The tulips had begun to bloom; bright-yellow crocuses lined the back fence. "Learning to Be Self-Sufficient" was the title of Linda's story. I started reading it to Louise. The similarities to Lynn struck us both immediately.

Linda had been deaf since birth. Profoundly deaf. She had a 90-decibel loss. We both found it difficult to believe she had written the article herself.

My parents should receive much of the credit for my achievements to date. Their secret was continuity. In fact, my mother recalls one incident after she spent a month-long vacation away from me in my early pre-school years. She says, "All I could get out of you was a squeak." And it took her three months to get my voice back.

Linda attended special classes for the deaf in an elementary school, but when she was eleven she lip-read and spoke so well that she changed to the regular school near her home. We had dreamed about Lynn going to school with hearing children. It had seemed impossible, given her deafness, that Linda had gone on to high school and even participated in competitive athletics. Now, in her first year at college, she was majoring in physical education. She made friends easily and seemed to live a normal life. Was she typical of deaf adults? We didn't know, but one thing was certain: Linda McArthur, profoundly deaf, had adjusted to the world of hearing people.

Soon we began to discover others through a national association of deaf people called O.D.A.S.—the Oral Deaf Adult Section of the Alexander Graham Bell Association. These deaf adults had become part of the hearing world by mastering the oral approach—learning to lip-read and speak. Each month the *Volta Review* devoted several pages to O.D.A.S. We learned about its national meetings, about the common problems of oral deaf adults, but mostly we read the personal stories of individuals. We knew nothing about those other deaf adults, the ones who used manual gestures, who could not communicate with normal people. With hard work, we believed that Lynn could follow in the steps of the oral deaf adults we read about.

Wheaton College, the town, our neighbors—they all held four years of rich memories for Louise and me and Bruce. Lynn had lived all her life in Wheaton. We knew hundreds of students. Some would return in the fall; others had scattered throughout the world. As we prepared to leave for graduate school in Oklahoma, it seemed unlikely that we would ever return except for nostalgic visits.

All the events of those four years seemed to pale, however, alongside that Fourth of July two years earlier. How much those screaming sirens and booming fireworks had changed the course of our lives!

As we said good-bye to students and friends during final-exam week, it felt good to know that our friends Dave and Melva Brandt would be waiting to greet us when we arrived in Norman, Oklahoma.

Before we left we asked Dave's mother to visit us. A wise and sprightly woman, Mrs. Brandt had come to Wheaton to live near her son when her husband died. She stayed in Wheaton when Dave and Melva moved to Oklahoma. For Lynn and Bruce, Mrs. Brandt had become a substitute grandmother. Her eyes sparkled with warmth and tenderness for children. She treated Lynn and Bruce with the same love she gave unreservedly to her own grandchildren.

Lynn loved Mrs. Brandt. Whenever we visited, Lynn would dash off to find her. They seemed to enjoy a special kind of silent communication; Mrs. Brandt played with Lynn, observed her from the vantage point of long experience with children, and most of all she *understood* Lynn. Lynn's deafness called forth a unique love from this magnificent woman. And she had a great deal of faith in Lynn, a faith that buoyed us many times.

"Lynn will make it," she used to say with a twinkle in her eye, "even though she's deaf. I can tell she's a smart baby. She catches on fast."

It was a warm evening in late May when Mrs. Brandt came for a barbecue in our backyard. We had finished eating. Lynn and Bruce ran off to play. As we relaxed and talked about Wheaton and Oklahoma, our conversation turned to deafness.

"I think Lynn's hearing aid is helping some," Louise said. "Just in the last few days I've noticed she makes more sounds when she wears it."

Then Mrs. Brandt recalled an experience from her childhood

in Canada. "When I was sixteen, there was a deaf girl living in our neighborhood. Beth was her name. On warm summer nights my friends would come to our house, and Beth too. We talked by the hour. We went for walks. And Beth would join in the fun. She couldn't speak a word, but she watched us with an intenseness that made us all feel she understood what was going on. She would watch our lips and follow along whatever we did. She would make gestures or act things out and we understood her most of the time.

"But I can remember times when we would all be talking and laughing and I would turn and look at Beth. Maybe I would catch a glimpse of her out of the corner of my eye. Her face had the saddest look I think I've ever seen in my life. Her deep brown eyes would fill with a forlorn, lonely expression. She wanted so much to join in with us, to understand our laughter and talk, to tell us about her own feelings. But there was no way she could follow our train of thought, no way she could tell us what thoughts lay behind those lonely eyes.

"Beth felt the isolation terribly. She was smart and could have learned, too, if only people had known then. But it will be so different with Lynn. She'll be able to communicate; her deafness won't be such a barrier. I think about Beth every time I see Lynn. I wonder whatever happened to her."

There was a long silence after she spoke. Louise shifted in her chair next to me and pulled her sweater over her shoulders. I watched Lynn run across the yard. I thought about Beth. A sense of sadness filled the cool evening air around us, sadness mixed with hope. Someday she would speak. She would not be alone.

Ten

Louise stood in the middle of our front lawn and motioned me back with her hands. Cautiously I backed the orange-and-black U-Haul truck over the curb, across our front lawn, and stopped a few feet from the front porch. Bruce and Lynn watched from the safety of the porch railing, then Bruce climbed into the truck when I opened the back. He shouted to catch the immediate echo of his voice; Lynn, hands outstretched, begged in her silent way for me to lift her into the back of the truck. I slid out the loading ramp until it met the porch and together we started loading the truck.

For days Lynn had been excited about finding boxes, emptying shelves, unloading cupboards and labeling packing containers; it all seemed like a great new matching game designed especially for her. And each box or cupboard became the source of things for Louise to name and talk about as the casual lessons in lip reading went on and on.

"We're going to Oklahoma. We're moving," Louise repeated endlessly to Lynn. "We have to pack all these things so we can move to Oklahoma where Daddy's going to school." Without words, without tenses to indicate time, communication about the future was hazy at best. So many times we wished that, like Bruce at her age, she could understand "tomorrow," "in a few days" or "next week." But Lynn didn't seem perturbed by her own ignorance.

At sunup the next morning we left Wheaton. Bruce, in the truck with me, talked of his friends and commented about familiar landmarks. I could see Lynn in the car seat beside Louise as they led our little caravan. Lynn, uninterested in the passing scenery, kept peering out the back window to make sure the black-and-orange truck with her father, brother and toys stayed close behind.

"What's Lynn pointing at?" Bruce asked in the middle of the morning. Louise was nodding her head to Lynn.

"It's another U-Haul truck!" Bruce shouted. Then I saw the orange-and-black vehicle, going in the opposite direction. As it passed Lynn waved and pointed, looking back to make sure we saw it too. A truck! Boxes and furniture and toys! Another family moving! An idea that Lynn had experienced in that fleeting moment, like matching objects for which she had no word.

About noon the next day we drove into Norman. We located our apartment in the housing for graduate-student families several blocks from the university. Driving up, we could see the row of apartments stretched out for a mile along a forested preserve. The wide strip of grass that separated the buildings from the woods gave a country-club appearance to the otherwise drab stucco buildings that had served as U.S. Army officers' quarters during World War II. Each two-story building had eight living units.

"Hi! Can we give you a hand?" Before I had even opened the back of the truck, Bill Connley, an English student, and Craig Atherton, who I discovered was working on a Ph.D. in mathematics, came out to help. Within minutes we felt at home. Louise talked to their wives about markets, schools and places to visit on a graduate-student budget. Swarms of children came from every direction and soon Bruce was talking with several boys his age; he learned their names. They told him about the creek and most of the animals that lived there; they explained that the creek led into a pond several blocks away. They gave him directions to the local store that sold candy. Just around the corner from our building sat a large sandbox partly overgrown with weeds, and nearby stood a permanent swing set. It looked as if we had moved into the middle of a park filled with children. All sense of isolation in a new city at a big university disappeared.

Then I noticed Lynn. She stood around with Bruce, his new friends and other children her own age. Smiling, pointing, trying to be friendly, she drew confused looks from the others when she did not respond to their questions. She did not learn about the creek or the turtles that lived there. She heard no names to associate with the faces of these new playmates. In spite of her isolation she showed no hint of loneliness.

A day or two later we went to the Brandts' for a picnic supper on the grass behind their apartment, several buildings away from ours. Afterward, in the cool of early evening, we explored the woods. We crossed the parking lot in back, and beyond it the wide grassy area which the university kept mowed.

"Hurry up!" Davy called to Bruce, eager to show him the stream, and they raced toward the woods on the other side of the field. I could see large spreading elms crowded among ash, oak, Southern pine and others I didn't recognize. Tangled undergrowth and smaller trees gave the entire area a semi-wilderness atmosphere. Twenty feet into the woods the ground dropped away to a small meandering stream six feet below us. Fallen logs were scattered here and there; mushrooms poked their way through the damp cover of dead leaves from the previous fall. The woods were alive with birds—English sparrows, robins, mockingbirds and bright-red cardinals with a pointed crest and a bib of black beneath their beaks.

We followed Bruce and Davy upstream to a large oak; it stood on the high bank of the stream, its root system partially exposed by erosion. Someone had fastened a two-inch-thick rope with a large knot at the end to a branch that jutted out over the water. Bruce, his legs firmly wrapped around the rope, was already swinging back and forth in a wide arc over the narrow stream.

"Rope swing," I said, looking at Lynn; she pointed and begged for a turn, then closed her eyes tightly as I pushed her into the air above the water.

Bruce wanted to visit the duck pond, so we went back to the house for bread and started down the street. We went parallel to the woods and stream for about three blocks, crossed a busy street and then walked toward the woods again. The stream ran under the street and into the duck pond before winding its way on through that part of the city. A small park area surrounded the pond, and more than a dozen white ducks paddled among the reeds close to shore. Bruce and Lynn began throwing pieces of bread crust to them and before long the ducks were eating out of their hands.

"Ducks. Ducks," Louise was saying each time Lynn looked in her direction. Lynn danced up and down and squealed with excitement; then she struggled and cried when we finally had to pick her up to start back.

During most of the two years of her life in Wheaton, Lynn had been a cooperative, eager-to-please child. Seldom did we have to do more than shake our heads "No! No!" or remove her from a forbidden area. Perhaps we had trained ourselves as much as Lynn; since we could never shout "Come back!" or "Don't touch that!," we often intervened. But the stirrings of independence and eagerness to explore the wider world grew noticeable almost at once after we arrived in Oklahoma.

I came home one afternoon during the first week of school. It was warm and humid. Even the short ride home on my bicycle had left me drenched with perspiration.

"Hi! I'm home!" I called as I came in and set my books on a kitchen chair.

"How was school?" Louise asked routinely.

"Good. How was your day?"

"Busy. I went shopping and then worked with Lynn. She matched all her colors today except one." Louise turned around and headed for the bedroom. "I wonder where Lynn is?" Her voice carried a tone of worry.

She came back into the kitchen. No Lynn. Now an anxious expression had appeared on her face. We headed out the back door together. The water in Lynn's blue wading pool shimmered in the sun; two children played at the edge of the grass near the parking area. Lynn was nowhere in sight. We walked quickly around the corner to check the sandbox and swings. No Lynn.

"Where *could* she have gone?" Louise asked anxiously. "She was here only five minutes ago!"

"Bruce!" I called. The sound of urgency in my voice brought

him running. "Have you seen Lynn? He shook his head. "Come on! We've got to find her!" I looked at Louise and we both thought of the same thing at the same instant. The woods! We all began running. I crossed the parking area and picked up speed on the seventy-five yards of grass.

"Lynn! Lynn!" I called at the top of my lungs. If only she could hear us! Perhaps she was with someone who would call back. I dashed to the stream and looked up and down. No Lynn! I ran through the trees, the thick underbrush tearing at my pants. The rope swing swayed gently in the warm breeze. I was scanning up and down the streambed when Louise and Bruce came up. No Lynn!

"Tom!" Louise was out of breath and her voice sounded on the edge of panic. "The duck pond!"

I could feel the blood drain from my face. "Let's go!" I started running at top speed, Bruce and Louise followed. I came out of the woods, cut diagonally across the field and dashed between two apartment buildings. The busy street. The pond. I fought back the vision of Lynn floating face down in the muddy water. I reached the boulevard, quickly appraised the traffic and flew across against the light, down the long slope toward the water.

There was Lynn, alone, squatting at the very edge of the pond.

"Lynn! Lynn!" I screamed. Oblivious to my voice, she didn't move. Then I saw she was not alone; four ducks were approaching her outstretched hand. My heart was pounding. A great sense of relief swept over me. Then Lynn looked up and saw me. She pointed happily at the ducks. I came up and knelt down beside her, shaking my head "No! No!"

In a few seconds Louise and Bruce arrived all out of breath. Louise, her eyes moist, picked Lynn up and held her close for a long minute. Then we tried to explain.

"No! No! The duck pond is no, no!" Louise shook her head vigorously and tried to look angry.

"You cannot come to the duck pond without Mommy or Daddy," I added, shaking my head sternly.

We started back together, holding Lynn's hands tightly; my

legs suddenly felt weak and shaky. For days after that we constantly kept watch whenever Lynn went out in the yard. For Louise it meant an unrelenting vigilance.

Since the day Lynn had learned to walk, watching over her had grown into a full-time job. We hesitated to discipline her when we weren't sure she understood our commands. When she was less than a year, even before the audiologists had confirmed her deafness, the loud "No! No!" had not worked. In our immediate presence her actions presented little difficulty; outside our presence, even if she was only in the next room, it was another matter. Once, when she was about eleven months, Lynn had crawled into Bruce's room to explore. The books on a lower shelf caught her eye and she scattered them all over the floor. Amid head shakings and "no no's" Louise took Lynn back into the living room. Later that same day, down came all Bruce's books again and he exploded angrily. "I wish someone would put her in the garbage can!" He slammed his door shut and began to replace his books again.

"I think she needs a good spanking," Louise said.

"I don't think she understands, and what good will it do to spank her?" I asked, then reluctantly slapped her hands, hoping she knew what we wanted.

Then a few days later Bruce struck on an idea. He recalled Lynn's fear of dogs. Louise had taken her out for a walk in the stroller when a little black dog came dashing up, put two feet on the stroller tray, wagged his tail and licked Lynn's face. Terrified, she burst into tears. After that, even an approaching dog sent her into near-panic. Bruce replaced all his books for the sixth or seventh time, then placed a floppy-eared stuffed dog on guard in the doorway to his room.

He called us to watch. In a few minutes Lynn crawled down the hallway while we followed at an inconspicuous distance. She could see that the door stood open and headed straight for another game with the books. Then she saw the toy dog! In a flash she whirled around and almost ran on hands and knees back down the hallway. After that whenever that silent sentry stood guard to Bruce's room, Lynn withdrew to a safe distance.

One afternoon in early July a few days after Lynn's excursion to the duck pond, Bruce came running in. "Mom! Quick! Lynn hurt herself! Come quick!"

She had fallen out of the swing and cut a gash in the back of her head. Lying on the ground, blood all over her head, Lynn was screaming at the top of her lungs. Louise got a diaper and held it to the wide gash on Lynn's head. I carried her to the car and we drove to a nearby hospital.

"It's all right. It's all right," Louise kept saying between Lynn's cries. "You'll be all right. We'll have the doctor fix it." We wanted to tell her where we were going, to prepare her for the stitches, but all we could do was hope our moving lips gave some comfort.

In the emergency room we told the doctor Lynn couldn't hear. He looked at the matted and bloody hair, inspected the gash, gave her a shot and then began sewing up her head. It required twelve stitches.

The next day Lynn was sitting in her highchair and pushed against the table. Her chair rocked back and over it went, hitting her head again. The stitches held, but after that Lynn began waking up in the middle of the night screaming and crying. We would pick her up in the darkness, hold her for a few minutes, then put her back into the crib. An hour later she would be crying again.

We began to realize how frequently we had used our voices to keep in touch with Bruce through the blackness of night. She missed the calming influence of our voices and although we left a small light on, she couldn't read our lips. If only we could reach out across the darkness and reassure her. In time the wound healed and Lynn slept peacefully once again.

Lynn's new independence extended to her hearing aid as well. She started asking for us to put in the earmolds and fasten the harness. She would walk into the kitchen, tug at Louise's dress, then point to her ear with repeated jabbing motions: "I want my hearing aid." She would only tolerate it for twenty or thirty minutes, but with her aid she still made more noises—babbling, humming and vowel sounds.

One morning Lynn came in and pointed to her ears. Louise fastened the harness and inserted the earmolds; Lynn waved good-bye and headed out the back door and around the corner of the building. Louise walked her to the sandbox, then went back inside, returning every few minutes. On this particular day it seemed the other children were more intrigued by the strange things in Lynn's ears than building sand castles or fighting over the tricycles. The third time Louise came out to check, Lynn was sitting in the sand, still in her small harness with the aid in its pouch, but the Y-cord with both earmolds had disappeared! On several previous occasions we had seen children come up to Lynn and pull them out of her ears, but we had quickly retrieved them. Now Louise began the search.

"Have you seen Lynn's earmolds?" she asked a small boy nearby, pointing to Lynn's ears.

"No," he said, shaking his head. Neither had any of the other children until she came to one three-year-old who wouldn't speak but shook his head "No." He then reached in his mouth and produced one soft plastic earmold.

Louise sifted through the sand and five minutes later discovered the other earmold. But the Y-cord had vanished. That afternoon when I came home we sifted all the sand again and searched the entire area around the sandbox before giving up. The next day it turned up, hidden in the grass, nearly a hundred feet from the sandbox.

One thing made it easier to keep tabs on Lynn—the closeness of our neighbors in the graduate-student housing complex. Within days after our arrival everyone knew Lynn was deaf. I can still remember Bruce introducing Lynn to some of the other children at the sandbox one afternoon during our first week in Norman.

"This is my sister, Lynn," Bruce said. "She's deaf. She can't hear."

Wide-eyed with amazement at this childhood anomaly, a six-year-old boy with red hair and freckles moved a bit closer. "Hi, Lynn. Can you hear me?" Lynn gave him a big smile but answered nothing.

"Can she really not hear?" he asked Bruce, who nodded proudly.

"Lynn! Are you deaf?" another boy shouted as loud as he could. Everyone looked at him—everyone except Lynn. Unaware of the tests presented by these backyard audiologists, Lynn had failed with flying colors.

Word passed quickly from one child to the next and back to their parents. We talked easily with all our neighbors about Louise's bout with rubella, Lynn's deafness and the problems we faced in teaching her to lip-read and speak. They listened and offered the best resource we could have asked for—understanding. As the summer wore on, we began to feel safe when Lynn went outside—just knowing that other mothers and fathers and older children knew she couldn't hear.

In her world of silence Lynn craved color and movement and reactions from others that spoke louder than the minuscule mouth movements which she did not understand. She teased us all to evoke the responses she could read. I recall one morning when I sat at my desk typing a letter to my parents in Los Angeles. Our bedroom door opened and there stood Lynn in her pink pajamas. A wide grape-juice mustache highlighted the grin that said, "I want to play!"

She came over to the desk and I picked her up, held her and talked to her for a moment, then put her back down. "I'm writing a letter to Grandma and Grandpa. You run along and play." I went back to my typing, trying to ignore her silent insistence.

Then came a tug at my sleeve. "Up," she mouthed and pointed to the corner of my desk where she often sat to watch me work.

"No!" I shook my head and continued typing. Another tug and more pointing. I took her by the hand, led her out of the bedroom and closed the door. In less than thirty seconds the door opened and there she stood, mouthing "Up, up."

I finally gave in. She sat on the narrow perch and I returned to my letter writing. Half a minute passed. She reached over and tried to catch the typewriter levers as they flicked up and down. I removed her hand. Again she reached out for the dancing arms that made letters across the page.

"No!" I shook my head angrily. I was fast losing patience and Lynn loved it. She laughed and grinned as if to say, "Now I know how you feel!"

Next she turned to the mirror over my desk and tried to get my attention by making faces at herself. She scowled, stuck her tongue out, pointed and laughed. I nodded and smiled, trying to remember what I was typing. Suddenly she reached over and pulled the paper from the typewriter.

"No! Bad girl!" I shouted. I picked her up with one swoop and rescued the wrinkled page.

As we headed for the living room, peals of delighted laughter came from Lynn. Finally Louise came to my rescue and distracted Lynn for a few minutes of play and color matching.

Bruce had also teased us, demanded attention and pushed us to the limits of our patience. But Lynn was different. For one thing, at her age Bruce could understand much of what we said. He had an expressive vocabulary of more than four hundred words. He could speak in two- and three-word sentences. I could type a letter and keep up a running conversation with Bruce that satisfied him. With Bruce we could explain, postpone, delay— all things that required words.

With Lynn, the months and months of repeating words often seemed like a steady rain that falls on the hot desert sand; our words disappeared as quickly as we spoke them. But somehow they had reached the roots of understanding deep within Lynn's mind and now her consistent successes held promise of someday communicating through language.

I remember one oppressively hot afternoon in late July when a violent thunderstorm swept through Norman.

"Could you call Bruce and Lynn?" Louise asked. As I ran around to the side of our building the sky opened with a deluge and the temperature must have dropped fifteen or twenty degrees.

I found the children, arms outspread toward the darkened sky, faces upturned, dancing in the rain as if the shower had been provided especially for them. Bruce heard me instantly, turned to tap Lynn on the shoulder and point in my direction. They both came in, streams of water running down their faces, hair matted wet, but cool and refreshed.

"Rain. Do you like the rain? Thunder. Lightning. The thunder will come again." Lynn watched my lips as I spoke. At the next sharp explosion Lynn looked up at me, then pointed to her ears and to the kitchen ceiling. It was hard to know whether she had heard the sound or merely felt the vibration.

"Dad! Watch what Lynn has learned to do!" Bruce took Lynn by the hand as soon as Louise had finished drying her off, led her into the living room and got her bag of matching objects. He sat her on the floor and took his place opposite her. She knew exactly what he had in mind and waited for his instructions. I stood in the doorway and watched in silence. Bruce reached into the bag and pulled out only *one* of each object—the ball, a toy car, an old shoe, Lynn's hat, a plastic bird and a cow. He set them in front of Lynn in a row. Lynn watched patiently.

"Where's the ball?" Bruce looked directly at Lynn as he spoke; her hand shot out and picked up the ball. Back it went into the row.

"Cow." Again she picked up the correct object.

"That's really good," I said to Bruce. Lynn had learned "ball" and "cow," but I didn't think she had learned to recognize the others consistently.

"Car!" Bruce said. I half expected Lynn to reach out for the cow again, since it looked so similar on the lips. But now, with a steady hand, she reached out, picked up the car and showed it to Bruce. The bird, hat and shoe followed. Then Bruce went through all of them again in random order. Lynn read his lips perfectly without one mistake!

I went over and knelt down on the floor, praising them both for their success. "You're a better teacher than Mom or I," I said to Bruce. "You've taught Lynn to lip-read four more words!"

By the end of July we could count eight words that Lynn lip-read in test situations. In addition to the six objects she also knew "up" and "hot." Informally she responded consistently to "eat your food," "wipe your face," "take a bath," "put your hat on," "fall down" and "go bye bye."

An event that gave Lynn dozens of new words to lip-read was our Saturday-morning jaunts into the beautiful Oklahoma countryside. I remember one Saturday we left right after an early breakfast.

"Barn. See the barn with the silo." Louise pointed off in the distance and at the same time looked around at Lynn.

"Look, Dad! A turtle!" Bruce shouted and pointed. We stopped to look. Its bright-painted shell must have been ten inches across. "Turtle. See the turtle."

Lynn squatted down and reached out gingerly to touch its hard back. In the car a few miles later we came upon her favorite animal —Jersey cows. Lynn pointed and tugged at Louise's shoulder. We pulled over and talked about cows for five minutes. As we started away, Louise looked directly at Lynn and said, "Cow. Cow." Unexpectedly, without hesitating, Lynn mouthed a silent "cow." Louise and I looked at each other, surprised and excited. That tiny lip gesture had made our morning! If she could mouth new words, we felt sure she would soon learn to speak them.

By early August, when summer school drew to a close, Lynn lip-read so many objects from the bag that we had moved on to pictures. The John Tracy correspondence course suggested a file with matching pictures. Louise spent hours going through discarded magazines and newspapers collecting matching elephants, airplanes, houses, dogs, trucks and dozens of other pictures. She also found people doing things which allowed us to teach Lynn verbs. On almost any day, late in the summer, I might come home from school and find Louise and Lynn sitting in front of pictures spread out on the floor.

"Running. Where's the boy running? Running." Lynn would look over pictures of a boy running, a girl jumping, a baby sleeping, an old man laughing, a woman cooking, then pick up the one that matched the picture of a running boy in Louise's hand.

"That's right! You found the boy who is running!" Louise handed Lynn the matching picture and she put them together back on the floor. Then it was on to the girl jumping and the woman cooking until all had been matched. Every magazine and newspaper became a source for that picture file. And slowly Lynn moved on from merely matching the pictures to selecting the right picture by matching it with the word on our lips.

It would not be accurate to say that we spent most of our time giving Lynn *formal* lessons in lip reading. They did involve considerable amounts of time but increasingly we emphasized casual instruction in everyday situations. Now that she could lip-read a handful of words, we felt sure she had finally acquired the *idea* of a word. And so we tried to capitalize on every situation by speaking new words that referred to things she could see.

At times we wondered how important it was to stick to our schedule of planned lessons. Near the end of that summer Louise sent in the third lesson from the John Tracy course and asked for advice.

"Most of our activities with Lynn have been very informal, and unstructured," she wrote. "We have tended to shy away from some of the more organized activities suggested in the course. Do you feel it's advisable to do some of the more formal color matching games, etc., as long as we are doing them informally? Will lip reading in informal situations throughout the day meet the same objectives?"

The reply from the clinic encouraged us to use our own judgment, keeping up the informal but also the formal lessons as Lynn's attention span increased.

One thing could not come from the casual talking with Lynn and that was the *certain* knowledge that she was reading our lips and not some situational clue. When we tested Lynn with objects we could be sure she read our lips. At first we had used two bags. We would reach into one bag and pull out a block or fork or shoe, show it to Lynn, then wait while she reached into her bag, felt around the various objects, then proudly presented the matching one.

Over the summer Lynn had moved slowly from matching what she saw to retrieving what she read on our lips. One evening as I studied for my final exams, I listened to Louise say the names and wait for Lynn to find the right object.

"Shoe." Lynn's hand went in, searched for a few seconds, out came an object.

"Good girl. You found the shoe."

"Spoon." Again a pause while Lynn retrieved the spoon. I was conscious that Louise must have gone through nearly twenty objects without a single mistake on Lynn's part. I looked up from the problem I had been working on and watched as they proceeded.

"Cup," Louise said and waited. Lynn searched with her sensitive fingers, trying first one shape, then another inside the bag. I thought back to that day in the spring when I had tried so hard to see if she could match "ball" on my lips with the ball in front of her.

"Ball," Louise said and I could tell she had saved the easiest word until the last.

"Tom! She did all twenty-five of them without a mistake!" I felt a shiver go up my spine. To think she had progressed so quickly! She *could* learn. I felt proud of Lynn, proud of Louise, proud of Bruce, and proud of what we had all accomplished together. And I felt sure Lynn would start talking soon; perhaps by the time she was three or going on four at the latest.

Eleven

Janet lived in one of the upstairs apartments. Her father was writing his Ph.D. dissertation in English. Janet was nearly six months younger than Lynn. At the swings, Louise and I must have pushed Lynn and Janet together a hundred times that summer; we alternated between them to keep their swings going at the same tempo. They loved to look at each other at the highest moment, Janet squealing with excitement, Lynn beaming with a wide grin.

Janet loved to swing, and flying back and forth, she hummed and sang and laughed and screamed and talked. The sounds came so effortlessly. Moving her lips. Playing with sounds. Pushing air out past her vocal cords. She could say several hundred words and it was as if the excitement, the feeling of movement, the experience of falling were somehow incomplete without this verbal accompaniment. I didn't understand everything she said; the baby talk and word play were mixed freely with intelligible speech. But even when she was not clear, I grasped the meaning in her rhythm, her tone and her very expressiveness itself. How we wished Lynn could express herself as easily!

We didn't know it then, but we had come to the edge of another invisible barrier—the great chasm that existed for Lynn between the *expressive* and *receptive* sides of language.

For Janet, or any hearing child, for that matter, understanding words and saying those words were like two sides of the same coin. Both involved sound. For the vast majority of the human race, reception and expression are synchronized, part of the same process. I remember how quickly Bruce repeated the words he heard us say. ''No! No!'' we would admonish him. Soon he was toddling all over the house saying "No! No!" to us, "No! No!" to his toys, and even "No! No!" to himself.

Certainly hearing children listen and understand words long before they can say them. But after the age of two, the expressive and receptive sides of language are never far apart.

For a long time we had expected it would be the same for Lynn. She could lip-read a word like "up"; she could mouth "up"; soon she would say "up." We assumed from all we had read that lip reading and speech were invisibly connected. Like hearing and speech. One would inevitably follow the other as surely as the rise and fall of our backyard swing.

Slowly we discovered that for Lynn, for any deaf child, lip reading and speech were not synchronized. They were not part of an interconnected process. But that summer our understanding of the process hadn't gone beyond the basic rule that came in a letter from the director of the John Tracy Clinic correspondence department:

"Just keep pouring the words into her and sooner or later, they will all come back to you."

At two and a half, most children have a wealth of expressive language. They can coordinate more than a hundred different muscles to move the diaphragm, lungs, throat, vocal cords, mouth, jaw, tongue and lips in a delicately balanced sequence of rhythms. They can utter the sounds that make up nearly five hundred different words. They can combine these words into two- and three-word phrases. They can use prepositions, adjectives, adverbs, nouns, verbs and pronouns. They can carry on lengthy conversations.

Lynn could not speak one word.

And so, as her lip reading steadily improved, Louise and I turned our attention more and more to speech. We pored over the John Tracy lessons in search of ways to help Lynn prepare to speak. It soon became apparent that for Lynn to gain control of her long-unused muscles it would tax our patience to the limit. One of our first discoveries occurred at a birthday party.

Johnny, a lively two-year-old, lived in the next apartment. His black skin and frizzy hair fascinated Lynn. She joined six other children about the same age for his party. After games and presents, the noisy children sat around a small picnic table behind the apartment playing with balloons and waiting for the birthday cake. In addition to a large cake with two candles, each child received a cupcake and a single flaming candle in the middle of the dark chocolate frosting. Without hesitation, each one blew out his candle at the same time Johnny extinguished the two in front of him.

Everyone but Lynn.

Like the others, she had leaned forward to the burning candle and her mouth had formed a tiny circle, but the puff of air never passed her lips. A single bright flame flickered at the picnic table as the other children looked at Lynn. She tried again, leaning closer, straining to make her lips into a tighter circle. The air refused to come. A few seconds passed, then Janet leaned over and blew out the candle for her. An instant later everyone began to devour the cake and ice cream.

We couldn't remember teaching Bruce how to blow out a candle. But now we set about in earnest to help Lynn learn this simple act that most children acquire incidentally as they learn to talk. Louise began by lighting two candles at the kitchen table. Bruce blew out one of them; Lynn watched, then tried and tried to blow out the other without success.

"Maybe if she could feel the air rather than just see the candle go out," Louise said to me one afternoon a few days later. And so we started taking every opportunity to blow on Lynn's hand, on her arm, her tummy and her face. She loved this new game and would hold her own hand up to her mouth, purse her lips and try to blow, but still the air refused to come. She tried our hands without success.

Next Louise combined the sense of touch and sight by placing a feather in Lynn's hand. When we blew, Lynn felt the air and saw the feather fly off her hand. Week after week we blew out candles, blew on Lynn's hands and sent feathers fluttering to the floor. We wondered if something was wrong with her muscles or lungs that she couldn't grasp the simple idea of blowing, but what we read in the John Tracy course suggested this was a common problem for deaf children. We also discovered Lynn didn't know how to drink through a straw like other children.

Weeks turned into months and we continued to work with Lynn on blowing. I thought of all the sounds that required some expression of air from the lungs—words like "hi," "cat," "hat," "pat," "party," "tiger," "trip," "try," "bed," "ball," "ship," "shore" and hundreds of others. I said the alphabet out loud to myself with my hand held close to my lips to discover all the sounds that involved even the slightest puff of air. I began to realize Lynn had to gain the idea of blowing, then learn to control the amount of air required by these different sounds.

Months later, not long before Lynn's third birthday, the solution came unexpectedly. Louise bought some party whistles, the kind with a coiled tube of paper that unrolls when you blow the whistle. Bruce and Lynn were both in the kitchen helping her unload the groceries and fold the paper bags when she had emptied them out.

"Look what I bought for you," Louise said to both of them after the groceries had all been put away. She opened the cellophane bag that held the whistles and gave a silvery blue one to Bruce, a red one to Lynn. Bruce immediately blew on his, the paper tube rushed out to stop a few inches from Lynn's face. She was fascinated. Into her mouth went the whistle. She tried to blow, but the red paper tubing didn't budge. She took it out of her mouth to examine it more closely. She tried again but to no avail.

So Bruce took her red whistle and demonstrated that it also held the same kind of magic. For ten minutes Bruce demonstrated and Lynn valiantly struggled with the whistles. Then she tried blowing the four others that were left. All worked instantly for Bruce; none responded to Lynn. Mystified, she finally gave up.

Later in the day Bruce took the whistles into his bedroom and demonstrated each one again to Lynn. He must have worked with her for half an hour when he came charging out of the bedroom shouting, "Mom! She's got it! Lynn can blow the whistle!"

Sure enough, there came Lynn behind him, the red paper magically shooting out at least an inch and then retreating. When the tube had completely unrolled it emitted a shrill noise, but Lynn could not blow that hard yet. By the end of the day she filled the house with the screeching sounds and proudly watched the bright-red paper unroll to its full length.

"Let's try the candle," I said to Louise that night after dinner. "If she's learned to blow the whistle, she can probably do the candle now too!" So out came the candles and Lynn looked on with interest as I lit two of them, one for Bruce, one for her. Bruce quickly extinguished the flame on his, then Lynn leaned forward and tried to blow. But nothing happened. After a few minutes Bruce brought in her whistle. She blew it hard and the paper tube flashed out and the shrill whistle filled the kitchen. Louise took the whistle from her and pointed to the candle. Lynn rounded her mouth and strained forward, trying to blow. Nothing happened. Not even a flicker!

Why could she blow the whistle but not the candle? Perhaps having the whistle in her mouth made the difference, stimulating her to tighten the muscles of her diaphragm and expel the rush of air. But Lynn *had* learned to blow! We celebrated with a trip to Baskin-Robbins for ice cream cones.

In the weeks that followed, Louise practiced with the whistle and the candle together. First Louise blew the whistle, then quickly blew out the candle. She lit the candle again and then Lynn blew the whistle, rounded her mouth and made every movement as if she were going to blow out the candle. But the air did not come until one day, after a couple weeks, the flame flickered.

"Good girl! You almost blew it out!" Louise said as Lynn watched her lips. She tried again. It flickered again. And then, before the session ended, Lynn had blown out her first candle!

And none too soon, for the following week she proudly blew out three candles on her cake while the other children at her party watched.

The previous summer the John Tracy correspondence course had been suggesting other ways to prepare Lynn to use her voice. We learned that language was not simply words, but words spoken in the rhythm of sentences. Words spoken with punctuation and stress. And so we began to teach Lynn the *rhythm* of speech even without the *sound* of speech.

Nursery rhymes fascinated Lynn. She watched our lips and looked at the pictures of mice running up grandfather clocks, bakers and butchers floating in tubs, and children dancing in circles. After reading her a nursery rhyme, we now added rhythm with our hands and bodies. "Ring-around-the-rosy" was one of Lynn's favorites, and we were careful to move and fall in rhythm with our voices. "Pat-a-cake, pat-a-cake, Baker's man" gave us a chance to clap our hands in time with the silent words. And slowly, through movements she could see and experience, she began to acquire a sense of rhythm that would be important for fluent speech.

If Lynn was to use her voice, she had to know it existed. But how could we make her aware when she couldn't hear? Even when she cried, she could only feel her moving lips, the vibrations in her throat, and the tense muscles pushing air from her lungs. That first summer in Oklahoma we became aware that she didn't understand when other children cried. Because she couldn't *hear* or *see* herself when she cried, she had not connected the grimaces, the tears, the strange faces other children made when they cried with her own crying.

One afternoon early in the summer Bruce had come running down the hallway and burst into our apartment. Through his tears and screams we learned he had fallen off his bicycle and scraped his knee. The blood had already begun to ooze through his torn pants leg. Lynn seemed delighted at Bruce's antics and started laughing and pointing. I picked her up at the same time Louise started to help Bruce out of his pants to clean up the wound.

"Bruce is hurt!" I said to her, looking concerned and shaking my head in sympathy. I pointed to his knee. "That hurts. You shouldn't laugh." Louise carefully slid his jeans down and Bruce cried out in even greater pain. Lynn looked at me with a smile and pointed at Bruce; she began laughing again.

All our explanations failed, and for weeks Lynn laughed whenever she saw Bruce or some other child crying. Then one morning Lynn fell against her tricycle; she burst into tears and screams of pain. Louise had been weeding her flower garden next to the porch and ran to see how badly Lynn was hurt.

An idea struck her. She picked Lynn up from the walk and rushed inside to our apartment, Lynn still crying loudly. She took her directly to the large mirror in our bedroom. Ignoring Lynn's injured arm for the moment, she held her up to the mirror.

"Look at yourself! You're crying!" Louise moved her a few inches closer. "You're crying just like the other kids when they're hurt!" Tears streamed down both cheeks. Her lips quivered, the corners of her mouth turned down between each gasp of air. The painful grimaces came and went, creating a sequence of distorted expressions.

For the first time Lynn saw herself crying. For an instant she stopped, surprised by her own performance reflected in the mirror. She looked at Louise, then began crying again. She had made the connection, at least once. Though the crying of other children always caught her attention, she slowly came to understand that this accompaniment of pain and anger and disappointment was not intended to entertain her.

Lynn could easily *see* the facial expressions that went with crying. To *feel* the tiny vibrations in her throat was another matter altogether. Somehow she had to become aware of her own ability to produce vocal sounds. The John Tracy course told us to capitalize on informal situations where Lynn was "giving voice" without realizing it. And so we tried to watch for situations like the following, which, with minor variations, repeated itself many times each week.

Lynn was splashing happily outside our back porch in the

wading pool. It was time for her nap, so Louise went to the porch and waited until she caught Lynn's attention.

"Come in now. It's time to come in," she called loudly, motioning for Lynn to come in. Lynn looked blankly at Louise, then went back to washing her rubber doll and pretended not to understand. Finally Louise went out to the wading pool, picked up the towel from the ground nearby and pointed toward the house. "Time for your nap. You have to get out of the pool now!"

But Lynn wasn't ready to come in. She pointed to the water, kicked her legs defiantly and shook her head. Louise lifted Lynn from the pool and began wrapping her in the towel. Lynn kicked harder than ever and then in a burst of anger she tried to struggle free. "Aaahhh! Eeeeaaah!" she screamed.

Instantly Louise stood her up, let the towel fall to the ground and stooped to gain eye-level contact with Lynn. "You're talking! You're using your voice!" Louise quickly pointed to Lynn's throat and tried to get her to make the angry noise again. "Good girl! You used your voice."

But by now Lynn was struggling to go back to the wading pool. In a few seconds the lesson was over, but not lost. Patiently, in dozens of similar situations when she *gave voice* spontaneously, we turned her attention to the existence of her own voice. We knew this wasn't the whole answer, but it was one way among many to begin preparation for the day she would begin to talk.

By late summer Lynn graduated to a new kind of matching game. She had mastered the task of putting two identical objects together. She could find the corresponding picture for anything we presented. She also matched objects and pictures with the movements on our lips. Now we had to teach her the most difficult thing of all: *that the objects and our lip movements went together with the sound of our voices.*

"Yellow. Which one is yellow?" Now Louise grasped Lynn's left hand and held it firmly to the side of her own throat so that Lynn could feel the vibrations of her mother's vocal cords as the words were spoken.

"Yellow. Pick up the yellow one." With her free hand Lynn picked up the yellow paper, looking back and forth from Louise's face to the floor.

"Blue. Where's the blue one?" While Lynn's hand went out to pick up the blue paper I could hear her making a sort of humming sound as she felt the vibrations on Louise's throat. One time through all the colors and Lynn had come to the end of her patience. She tugged at her hearing-aid cords and the earmolds fell from her ears. She began to pull on the harness.

Auditory training had become a continuous thing whenever Lynn wore her hearing aid. For some time we had been working on *gross sounds*. The John Tracy course suggested ways to help her pay attention to gross sounds like an automobile horn, a drum or a police whistle.

We devoted many hours to one particular auditory-training game recommended by the clinic. Together we discussed it and figured out how we could teach it to Lynn. We reread the instructions several times. It would take a week or two for Lynn to grasp the nature of this game completely; each day on the kitchen floor was a step toward understanding it. We could not explain the game but we knew she would discover the rules, and playing the game enabled her to use her residual hearing.

The objective was simple. Louise was to sit behind Lynn on the floor with a metal wastebasket kept out of Lynn's sight. Five blocks would be stacked in front of Lynn. Louise would bang on the wastebasket bottom with a wooden spoon to create a gross sound that would echo throughout the kitchen. Each time Lynn heard it, she was to knock one block from the top of the stack. This way we could be sure she heard the sound.

But the game did not start that way. Lynn and Louise sat facing each other, the wastebasket and large wooden spoon to one side. Louise stacked the blocks into a tiny tower while Lynn watched. As soon as the blocks were in place, Lynn reached over and knocked them down, something she had done dozens of times before.

"No. Not all at once," Louise said as she restacked the blocks.

This time she restrained Lynn's hand. ''Now, you take this wooden spoon and hit the wastebasket,'' she said to Lynn, reaching over the pile of blocks to grip Lynn's hand in her own and hit the wastebasket with a resounding bang. Lynn looked up at me as if she had heard the sound.

''Hit the wastebasket again and then I'll knock down one block,'' Louise said as she helped Lynn hit the wastebasket and at the same time reached over and knocked the top block off the stack. Together they hit the wastebasket again and Louise pushed over another block. The fourth time Lynn was ready to hit the pan by herself and watch Louise knock the block from the pile. Round one was finished!

''Bang!'' Lynn struck the wastebasket.

''You can push the block over, too,'' Louise said to her and moved Lynn's other hand to knock one block from the top of the pile. Then she pointed to the wastebasket.

''Bang!'' Again she helped Lynn displace another block. Slowly they worked down the stack of blocks until all five lay scattered on the floor. It had taken nearly ten minutes and now Lynn grew restless. The game ended for the day.

The next time they played, Lynn quickly began to beat the wastebasket, holding it tightly between her outstretched legs. Now Louise had to restrain her from hitting it more than once before she had removed the next block. After two loud bangs on the waste basket, Lynn reached over and pushed two blocks from the stack.

''No, only one block at a time!'' Louise replaced one block and waited for Lynn to hit the wastebasket again. By the end of the lesson Lynn had gained a clear idea that it was her job to hit the wastebasket, and it was her job to knock the next block from the pile. She also was beginning to grasp the notion that displacing the block always followed hitting the wastebasket.

The next phase went more quickly. ''I'm going to hit the wastebasket, and whenever I do, you push the next block from the stack,'' Louise explained, hoping Lynn would understand her actions. For the rest of that week they worked on this pattern—Louise hitting the wastebasket, Lynn knocking over the blocks.

Several days later, after numerous reviews, Louise was ready for the next step. She moved the wastebasket around behind Lynn, who couldn't see it unless she turned around.

"Now, we'll pile the blocks in front here and every time I hit the pan, you push one block off the stack." We both spoke to Lynn *as if* she could hear; she couldn't, of course, so we depended on some example, a demonstration or a clue to get across our message. When Lynn was not looking, Louise struck the wastebasket. Lynn waited for about ten seconds and then looked around with a puzzled look on her face. The five blocks stood in a neat stack as if waiting for Lynn to hear.

"Okay, we'll have to let you see me for a while until you get the idea," Louise said. While Lynn watched she hit the wastebasket. Lynn smiled, looked back at the blocks and removed the top one from the stack. Back and forth they went, Lynn watched Louise hit the wastebasket, then turned around to displace the next block.

Sometimes I played this game with Lynn when I came home from school, at other times Bruce played and always Louise repeated it. Often we hit the basket when Lynn wasn't looking to test her; sometimes she seemed to hear and knocked a block from the stack, but we couldn't be sure because she was inconsistent.

Almost always Lynn played this game while wearing her hearing aid. One morning Louise sat down to play without taking the time to put on Lynn's hearing aid. Lynn was watching the blocks intently.

"Bang!" Louise whacked the bottom of the wastebasket as she had done hundreds of times before. Lynn dutifully pushed the top block off the pile. Louise was surprised and puzzled. She banged the wastebasket again. Without hesitating, Lynn removed the next block.

"Good girl! You heard it!" Louise was cautious but filled with excitement.

"Bang!" Off went another block. "Bang!" Another block. It seemed too good to be true, so she ran through another round of the game. When I came home, Lynn successfully responded to two rounds with me, this time with her hearing aid on. We didn't understand how she had heard without the aid, but it didn't seem important. Now she began to respond consistently whenever we hit the wastebasket—with or without her hearing aid.

One morning not long after this, Louise had set out the waste-basket and blocks. Before they could sit down, Lynn grabbed the wooden spoon and with an impish grin pointed for Louise to sit down. She placed the blocks in front of Louise and moved the wastebasket around behind her.

"Bang!" Lynn struck the wastebasket as hard as she could and then pointed over Louise's shoulder to the blocks, nodding her head. Louise smiled and dutifully knocked over the first block. Lynn laughed proudly. She struck the wastebasket again and waited expectantly for the second block to fall. Mommy obeyed. The game went on for three rounds of blocks. From that time on it grew increasingly difficult to play this game with Lynn. After two or three minutes she demanded to become the teacher, or she grew impatient and ran off to play.

When my mother and father arrived for a short visit, Lynn was especially excited because Grandma became such a responsive student. She lip-read Grandma as easily as she read the familiar words off our lips. But within hours after they arrived, Lynn pulled Grandma over to a place on the couch and dumped out the blocks and cars and hats and other objects from her matching-bags.

"Find the matching block, Grandma!" her nodding head and pointing finger seemed to say as she held up a block. Grandma caught on quickly. In her own silent way Lynn praised her for each success. Slowly they worked through the entire set of objects and colors. Then she moved on to the auditory-training game. They both sat down on the floor. Lynn set the wastebasket behind Grandma, the blocks in front of her. It took Lynn several attempts to demonstrate the rules, but soon Grandma was knocking over one block at a time as Lynn gleefully banged the wastebasket for all she was worth. If Grandma looked around, Lynn shook her head "No! No!"

With increasing frequency now, Lynn became angry and frustrated at our inability to understand her. She pulled on my arm, pointing to the back door; I followed her outside, thinking she wanted to be pushed on the swing. At the swing she shook her head, stamped her feet and pointed toward the woods. More than once I made a trip across the field and into the cool woods, only to find her as upset and unsatisfied there as at the swing. Back to the apartment we went, with me still unable to interpret her gestures and facial expressions. In the end she often gave up, having forgotten her original interest.

Sometimes Lynn's inability to communicate brought added strain to family relationships. When we struggled unsuccessfully to grasp the meaning behind her insistent gestures, we were all left feeling helpless and angry. When Bruce played with friends, he did not want to be bothered by Lynn's fruitless attempts to make herself understood. "Can't you make her stay away from us?" Bruce would complain. Sometimes Louise and I would blame each other for the frustration we saw building in Lynn, feeling that this recurring problem was due to one of us not working hard enough with her.

The John Tracy Clinic suggested a way that would allow Lynn to communicate with us without speech: an experience book. We still have those two loose-leaf notebooks, each crammed with hundreds of pictures pasted on 5" by 8" cards. The blue books are worn on the edges, fingermarked from Lynn's dirty hands. She would come running in from playing outside, grab one of the books, dash over to us while turning the pages in search of the picture that would say she had seen a blue jay or wanted to swing.

Lynn missed her grandparents when they left for home but with this new way to "talk" to Lynn about them, it seemed to ease the hurt that came with their sudden disappearance. I don't know what we would have done without those experience books.

Lip reading allowed us to talk to Lynn in only the most limited ways. She couldn't communicate with *us* at all. She couldn't ask questions. She couldn't tell us how she felt. She couldn't tell us what had happened outside when she came in crying. She couldn't tell us where she wanted to go, what she wanted to do.

We went through all our photographs and picked the ones we thought had meaning to Lynn. Daddy riding a bicycle along the sidewalk in front of our apartment. Lynn swinging on the rope across the creek in the woods. Bruce climbing a tree. Opening presents at a birthday party. Lynn sitting in the sandbox, heaping sand over her legs. Lynn sitting in her wading pool. Mommy driving the car. Lynn riding on Daddy's shoulders. Mommy putting on Lynn's hearing-aid harness. A cow standing beside the road. An armadillo in the middle of the road. Grandma and Grandpa standing beside their car. Grandma and Grandpa waving good-bye.

The list went on and on. We added to it with pictures from magazines. We started taking new snapshots of ordinary things— Lynn going to bed, Lynn asleep, Lynn taking a bath. Slowly the books began to fill up. Each evening we looked through them together and "talked" about experiences and people and things she knew. Wherever we went, the experience books went along, and they reduced communication problems dramatically. We would start for a drive in the country and Lynn would begin looking out the window. She couldn't say, "I'm looking for cows," but now she reached over, opened her experience book, pointed to the picture of a cow, then went back to looking out the window.

Before she pulled Louise or me to follow her outside, she searched through the experience book. If she didn't come to us with a picture, we handed her the book with a questioning look on our faces. She often turned to a favorite picture of herself, standing in tennis shoes and a red gingham dress at the edge of the duck pond. The white ducks bobbed up and down in the water at her feet; she held a small bag of breadcrusts. Instead of making futile trips to the swing or the woods, we immediately set off for the duck pond.

Lynn caught on quickly and in many situations communication by pictures was unnecessary. She simply understood. When we started loading sleeping bags and the tent into our car at the end of August for a two-week vacation in New Mexico, she seemed to know what lay ahead. On the second afternoon of our trip we pulled into a National Forest Service camp a few miles northeast of Santa Fe. We started unpacking and as I laid out the tent, Lynn began handing me stakes to pound into the ground. She had watched me do this before and needed no coaxing to lend her assistance.

Once the tent stood in the shade of a large pine tree, Lynn ran off to rummage through the two boxes of our camping gear, obviously searching for something. She pulled out a gallon plastic water jug she remembered seeing us use the previous summer. Without any instructions—no one pointed, no one said anything—she dashed off to a nearby faucet, filled the bucket, and within minutes struggled back into camp with water for cooking and drinking. After dinner Louise collected the trash and paper plates in a bag, without a word handed it to Lynn, who knowingly walked off to deposit it in the nearest trash can.

Our vacation ended all too quickly. We drove back through Santa Fe in the early afternoon. A late August sun reflected off the white hood of the car as we made our way slowly through the downtown business district.

On the outskirts of town Louise pointed to a sign as we neared an intersection. ''That's the school for the deaf,'' she said. A cluster of stucco buildings stood back on a sloping incline to the right. A driveway ran up to the school, which was surrounded by lawns and trees.

''It's the New Mexico Residential School,'' Louise added. We came to the sign and I pulled to the side of the street, the engine idling.

''Shall we go up and visit?'' I asked, almost thinking out loud. I wanted to go in, to see what the school looked like, to ask about their educational program. At the same time I felt a sense of uneasiness, foreboding. *The Residential School.* For months

145

we had heard those words. In California, in Illinois, in Oklahoma. Almost every state had a residential school for the deaf, a place where young children were separated from their mothers and fathers.

From what we had read, from all we had learned at the John Tracy Clinic, from what audiologists and speech teachers had told us, we were confident it would never be necessary to send Lynn to a residential school. Only the few deaf children who did not develop speech attended residential schools to learn a manual trade and to learn to communicate with one another by means of gestures. What could we find out here that would benefit Lynn?

I looked at Lynn, then back at the school. She had no way of knowing what it meant, no way of knowing that other children like herself lived there. But in a sense, the children there were not like Lynn. Out of such schools, we had heard, came the *manual* deaf adults, the ones who couldn't communicate with the rest of society.

I looked at Louise. ''What do you think?''

''Should we take the time?'' she asked, and the tone of her voice reflected my feelings.

I pulled away from the curb and headed out of town. Soon the residential school was far behind us. But each of us thought about it for hundreds of miles. At the same time we hoped and prayed that a good oral school would accept Lynn soon.

Twelve

A hint of fall filled the air one day in late September when Louise and I set out for Chickasha, Oklahoma, to register Lynn in the Jane Brooks School for the Deaf. It was about forty miles west of Norman

For more than a year we had felt that if Lynn was to learn to talk, it would require professionally trained teachers. The few lessons Jill Corey had given Lynn underscored everything we had read. *Start your child in school as early as possible.* The earlier, the better. Most hearing-impaired children, we learned, didn't begin school before the age of three or even four. Some waited until six or seven, with disastrous results.

During our first week back I had gone to a professor associated with the speech and hearing program at the University of Oklahoma, which had a special school for deaf children. To my surprise, I discovered that Lynn was *too* young to attend. We would have to wait until she reached three or three and a half before they would accept her.

"But we wanted to start her right away," I said to him, trying to hide my disappointment.

"There's an excellent private school in Chickasha," he suggested. "It's an oral school. It's on the campus of the Oklahoma College of Liberal Arts. They might take your daughter even though she's only two and a half."

A nationally recognized institution, the Jane Brooks School for the Deaf had been founded by Mrs. Margaret Brooks as an outgrowth of teaching her own daughter, Jane, who became deaf at an early age when stricken by meningitis. Our first letter from the school emphasized that it offered an *oral* education for deaf children. We were invited to make a visit. We had pored over the admission requirements and discovered that Lynn would not be accepted if she had multiple handicaps. The letter read: "We function as a school for the severely deaf, teaching oral communication skills, and we cannot accept a student if he knows or uses the manual language." Lynn's only handicap was her deafness. She still used her own gestures but certainly did not know the manual language, whatever that referred to. We had consistently avoided responding to her gestures except with spoken words.

The goals and expectations of the Jane Brooks School were impressive.

> When a deaf child starts to school at the age of three we expect to have him ready, by age seven to begin formal academic work in the first grade; reading, spelling, number concepts, phonics, speech-reading and speech . . . The Jane Brooks School provides rehabilitation for the congenitally deaf child and for the child with an acquired deafness so as to prepare them to enter high school in public school as does a hearing child.

The letter said that while most classes had waiting lists, there was an opening two days a week in a preschool class for Lynn.

We drove into Chickasha, a rural town of 15,000, and quickly located the Oklahoma College of Liberal Arts. We stopped to ask a student for directions to the Jane Brooks School; she pointed to an old brick building in the distance. We entered a small windowless door, climbed a short flight of stairs, and walked down a narrow hallway to the director's office.

Mr. Harold Taylor wore rimmed glasses and spoke in a pleasant Oklahoma drawl. "Please come in and sit down." His office seemed more like a large living room in an old house. We sat on a maroon overstuffed sofa that faced Mr. Taylor's desk.

"Have you had your daughter's hearing tested?"

"Yes," Louise said, "at the John Tracy Clinic when Lynn was seventeen months. Then at several places in Chicago since then. All the tests have shown that she is profoundly deaf."

"Well, we have many children come to the Jane Brooks School who are severely and profoundly hearing-impaired and we have had a fine record with them. Each child who has completed the ninth grade has gone on to a public high school in his hometown and graduated. Of course, there are a few who don't complete the ninth grade. We had a boy two years ago, he was fifteen, and we had to send him to the state residential school in Sulphur. They learn the manual language there and finish school.

"An oral education is the most important thing you can give your daughter," Mr. Taylor went on. "And no school can do that job alone. We expect parents to continue our work at home. And if the parents are faithful to the oral approach, in all probability their child is going to be successful."

We nodded in agreement. We certainly didn't want to turn the entire job over to the school. At the same time, we needed professionals who knew how to teach the deaf. The Jane Brooks School had a staff of nine full-time teachers and two part-time speech instructors. Classes were kept small. We talked about tuition, and although the $35 each month was a substantial chunk of the $222 we had to live on, it was worth it.

"I think it would be good if Lynn began two mornings a week, and she can come for the remainder of the school year." Louise nodded eagerly when Mr. Taylor asked us if we would like to visit some of the classes in session.

As we started down the hallway we met a young woman. Mr. Taylor stopped. "I'd like you to meet one of our best teachers," he said with a friendly smile. "Carolyn Graves, this is Mr. and Mrs. Spradley. Their two-and-a-half-year-old daughter, Lynn, is going to start in our preschool."

"That's wonderful! I'm sure she'll like it here. And you're lucky to be able to start her that young. That's so important!" I liked Carolyn Graves immediately. She had sparkling eyes and there was a calm warmth about her that I could sense included a love for children.

When she excused herself and moved down the hallway, Mr. Taylor turned to us. "We are very proud of that teacher. She was a student here and is profoundly deaf herself."

Louise and I looked at each other in amazement.

"*Profoundly* deaf?" I asked incredulously. Mr. Taylor nodded. I couldn't believe it. Suddenly I wanted to look around, to see what Carolyn Graves looked like, to find some clue that revealed her deafness.

"She was a student here?" I asked, trying to sound unsurprised. This was the first deaf adult we had ever met and I quickly realized we had not been able to visualize what life would be like for Lynn when she grew up. We had read about oral deaf adults, but actually meeting Carolyn Graves had an immense effect on both of us. Not the slightest clue that she was deaf! Her speech had been perfect! She had read our lips perfectly without our even realizing it! And profoundly deaf!

We were still thinking about Carolyn Graves as we entered the back of the first-grade classroom. Instantly we were met by a barrage of strange noises. Groans, howls, wails, screeches, brays, grunts and snorts came from a group of seven or eight children sitting in a semicircle around the teacher at the front of the room. It was unnerving. Lynn's sounds, though few, were not unnatural like these. I wanted to leave but could tell that Mr. Taylor, the teacher and a teacher's aide all acted as though these were routine noises.

We moved closer to watch. The teacher worked on reading and speaking individual words printed in large black letters on cards.

"Dog." The teacher enunciated clearly and held up a picture of a brown-and-white collie with the word printed below. The children had become quiet. I waited, eager to hear the class repeat the word. I could see Lynn sitting in a class like this in two or three years.

Again came the same sounds. High nasal rasping. Grunting, animal-like noises. Vowel sounds that came out like groans. I was startled! Not one child had said "dog." Whatever they did say, I could not understand a single word from any child. I could see that most were at least three years older than Lynn. My God, I thought to myself, There must be some reason why they can't talk!

"Horse." The teacher was holding up the next picture with the word printed below it. There followed another chorus of hissing, moaning sounds, unnatural and weird. It was anything but speech. Questions flooded my mind that I wanted to ask the director. How long had these children been in school? How much had their parents worked with them? Why couldn't they speak? Were any mentally retarded?

I could tell that Louise was stunned by what we were hearing. Before we had a chance to collect our thoughts, Mr. Taylor calmly motioned for us to follow. We walked down the hall to a second-grade room, where the same strange noises greeted us, sounds that seemed to come from another world. Trying to speak, these seven-year-olds struggled to control the muscles in their mouths and throats. It took enormous effort. I felt my heart pounding. I wanted to turn and run out of the room, to ask what had gone wrong, to find some explanation. We moved closer to the front and I strained to understand the words these children were saying. A phrase went through my mind that I had read somewhere but hadn't understood: *sounding like a deaf person*. Now I knew.

Louise and I had envisioned teachers sitting with young children Lynn's age, teaching them to speak the words they already knew how to lip-read. By the time these children reached the first grade, we assumed they would certainly be able to talk clearly and only need to improve their pronunciation.

Now we left the second-grade class filled with doubts. We walked across the hall to a fourth-grade classroom and slipped quietly into the back. Five or six eight-year-olds sat attentively in small chairs around their teacher. It was Carolyn Graves! She was working on speech pronunciation. Fascinated, we edged closer and watched. A small freckle-faced boy was trying to say a word printed on a card held by Carolyn Graves.

"Baaoonnn." He strained to say the word correctly. It came out heavily nasal. We could hardly hear the consonants, but knowing the word he was trying to say, we recognized it as "bacon."

"No, not quite. Try again. *Bacon.* " Carolyn Graves shook her head and emphasized the middle consonant as she repeated the word. Her movements seemed to suggest to the boy how to move his muscles to produce the right sound.

"Baaadonnn."

"That's better. You're getting closer." Carolyn Graves watched his lips, his tongue, his teeth, and from the movement she helped him correct the pronunciation of this single word.

"Bacon," she said again, then waited.

"Bagon." The strange hollow quality remained, the nasal tone that permeated the word from beginning to end, but even we could sense the improvement. Carolyn Graves praised him for this nearly perfect utterance and then went on to the next child.

Leaving the room, I felt bewildered. The very tediousness of the task must be overwhelming. I marveled at her patience. How could she correct their speech when she couldn't even hear mispronounced sounds herself? She must have known by watching their mouths and tongues. Was her class an average fourth-grade class? Did all deaf children have to go through this kind of learning process? Would it take Lynn this long? I found it hard to comprehend why it was so difficult for these children to learn to speak. I thought of our last letter from the John Tracy Clinic. "Just keep pouring the words into her and sooner or later, they will all come back to you." We had presumed this meant Lynn's words would come *pouring* out in a stream of speech, the same way she had heard them. Was it possible that learning to speak each new word would be an even slower, more exhausting task than learning to lip-read them?

In the sixth-grade classroom that we visited next, Mr. Taylor took us to the front of the room. "This is Mr. and Mrs. Spradley. Their hearing-impaired daughter is going to start in our preschool."

"Hello." A chorus of six or seven voices greeted us. The hollow, nasal sounds were less noticeable, but still present.

"Mr. Spradley goes to the University of Oklahoma. He and Mrs. Spradley are visiting today." The teacher spoke to the class, which sat in a semicircle around her. I could see the children watching her lips as she spoke.

"John, can you speak to Mr. and Mrs. Spradley?" Mr. Taylor had told us that John was the teacher's son. He wore a pair of hearing aids, but unlike Lynn's, which was strapped to her chest because of its bulky size, John's small and less powerful aids fit neatly behind each ear. At the time we didn't recognize that this was a clue to the fact that his hearing impairment was not profound. We saw all these children as *deaf*. Lynn was deaf and so were they.

"I like the football team at Oklahoma," John said slowly, with some effort. The words were understandable, but still distorted. I remember thinking that Bruce could speak more clearly, though only half this boy's age. The teacher then had each of the other children read a sentence from their books. Although none spoke as clearly as John, we understood most of the words. But their voices all had a hollowness, the sound of struggle with every breath.

We left those classrooms deeply shaken, the sounds of deafness ringing in our ears. Driving home, we talked and wondered out loud about the children we had seen.

Each day for the first month, Louise deposited Lynn with Mrs. Park, the teacher. "I'll be back when class is over," she said firmly to Lynn, who began to cry and fought to free herself from Mrs. Park's hand. When she returned at ten-thirty, there was Lynn lying on the floor, her head buried in a pillow wet with tears. Each day Lynn cried herself into exhaustion and refused to enter into any class activities.

Louise would arrive home equally exhausted. "If I could just tell her that I'll be back!'' she would say. ''If there was only some way to explain about school, some way for Mrs. Park to talk to her, to say her name, to remind her that I'll return! Or if she could talk to the other kids. I think she just feels terribly alone and isolated.''

Then one morning after about a month, Lynn decided to join the class. She took her seat in the row of chairs, waved good-bye to Louise and met her with a smile at ten-thirty.

The week before Thanksgiving I took Lynn to school for the first time. The fields of corn were dry and brown, most of the leaves had fallen from the tall elm and ash trees along the way, and the air felt crisp. Lynn pulled on my hand to hurry as we entered the brick building; she walked to the rear of the room and hung up her coat, ran up and gave Mrs. Park a hug, then went to a board that had name tags pinned up for each child. I took a seat. Lynn picked out her own name, pasted it on the front of her dress and sat down.

''Good morning, children. It's time for our prayer and flag salute.'' Mrs. Park smiled and looked from one child to the next as she spoke. She bowed her head and recited a brief prayer.

The row of five little heads bowed together, revealing five sets of hearing aids. One child had an aid like Lynn's, strapped to her chest with wires running up to plastic receivers that protruded from each ear. The other three wore smaller, over-the-ear aids. The prayer ended and all the children stood up, hands over their hearts, ready for a simplified flag salute. Mrs. Park had written out the words on a large newspaper tablet; I could hear a few soft noises coming from the children but no one actually said anything except Mrs. Park as she pointed to the written words.

''Now it's time for roll call.'' Mrs. Park held up a card. ''Johnny,'' she said in a normal voice, looking directly at a little girl at the end of the row. The girl went to the teacher, took the card, walked over to Johnny in the middle of the row and held the card in front of him while looking back at Mrs. Park.

''That's right.'' She spoke distinctly but did not seem to emphasize her lip movements in any exaggerated way. The girl returned Johnny's card to the teacher and went back to her seat.

"Lynn." Mrs. Park held up the next card and a red-headed boy who looked older than Lynn went up, took the card and held it up in front of Lynn. She looked around to make sure I had seen this act of personal identification. I had often thought about the name we had given Lynn. Our names—Bruce, Mommy, Daddy—these words stood out clearly on our lips. But *Lynn* was almost invisible. The only clue that we had said anything was a quick, tiny movement of the tongue hidden deep inside the mouth. The lips remained motionless. Even when we called her Linnie, it only added one more flick of the tongue.

"Maybe we should change her name," Louise had said to me on more than one occasion. "She can't even lip-read her own name and it's so hard to see I don't think she'll ever be able to." But I had felt that eventually Lynn would be able to lip-read her name, and now, seeing her read the letters printed on the card confirmed my feelings. Someday she would even be able to say it.

Fifteen minutes later the door opened and several students from the Oklahoma College of Liberal Arts came in. Lynn went with a tall girl who wore glasses; they sat at a table to work on copying letters. Each child sat at a different table with one of the college students; Johnny went with Mrs. Park to a table at the front for an individual speech-therapy lesson. After about ten minutes Lynn's turn came and I moved closer to watch.

Mrs. Park sat at a low table. She lifted Lynn to the edge of the table so that their faces were on the same level. Lynn smiled at me as she squiggled back on the table for a firmer seat. A large mirror hung on the wall behind Mrs. Park. She helped Lynn pull a pair of black headphones over her ears, then reached across the table to turn up the amplifier unit.

"Ball. Ball." Mrs. Park held a microphone in her right hand; with her left hand she pressed Lynn's fingers carefully on the side of her own throat as she spoke into the microphone.

"Ball. Ball." She said the word again, then quickly moved Lynn's hand to her own throat and held the microphone close to Lynn's lips. Everything about her facial expression, her movements, the way she held the microphone seemed to say, "Now it's your turn. Say 'ball' and you can feel the vibrations in your own throat."

"Aaaaah. Aaaaah." Lynn struggled to make some sound. It was working. I leaned forward, tense in my chair, straining to hear her voice. It didn't seem to matter that she hadn't said "ball"; she had said something!

"Airplane. Airplane." Smoothly Mrs. Park moved the microphone back to her own mouth, then back to Lynn's at the same time that Lynn's hand went from Mrs. Park's throat to her own.

"Aaaaahhhhn." Again Lynn said something and I could see by her eyes in the mirror that she also seemed to feel a vibration in her own throat. Lynn was learning to speak by using her sense of touch. She had grasped the connection between the vibrations in Mrs. Park's throat and the movement on her lips, and she had now made the transfer to herself. In the future she would have to gain more control of the muscles that coordinated the vocal cords so she could make the right sounds. But could she actually feel the *right* sound? Probably not, I thought to myself; all sound must feel like the same vibration. In order to shape the sounds more precisely, to make them into the English words we spoke, she would need someone else to listen for her. And somehow communicate how to change her voice. On and on the lesson went with familiar words that Lynn could already lip-read. Although Lynn seemed far from speech, I could see she clearly understood the *idea* of speaking.

Mrs. Park dropped Lynn's hand after several minutes of intense work and began showing her the shape of several sounds. She turned so Lynn could see her face in the mirror.

"P-p-p-p-p-" I watched Mrs. Park in the mirror; her lips came together repeatedly, each time followed by the brief puff of air. Lynn watched her every moment.

"P-p-p-p-p." As Mrs. Park made the sound for "p" again, her animation and the look in her eye urged Lynn to try it.

She finished the sound and turned to Lynn, nodding her head, looking at Lynn's lips, waiting patiently, expectantly. Since Lynn had not yet learned to blow out a candle, I wondered if she could even come close to making this sound.

"Bh-bh-bh-bh." Lynn smacked her lips together, sucking air in as she struggled to imitate Mrs. Park. She had come close and her teacher nodded encouragement, then went immediately to the next sound.

"B-b-b-b-b." I watched in the mirror; her lips moved in a pattern that seemed identical to the "p" sound she had just made. I was aware Lynn could not hear the difference, but I could.

"Mh-mh-mh-mh-mh.' Again Lynn smacked her lips, sucking in air through her mouth and nose at the same time. I was amazed at the way Mrs. Park could get Lynn to respond, to use her voice and to come so close to the right sounds. Only ten minutes had passed, but it seemed more like half an hour. Lynn began to grow restless; Mrs. Park removed the headphones and Lynn ran off to one of the tables while another girl took her place.

Recess followed the end of speech therapy; the children went outside to play on swings. I talked with Mrs. Park while we watched them work off their pent-up energy.

"Lynn's really a good lip reader," Mrs. Park told me during recess. "I'm amazed that at only two and a half she has such advanced lip-reading skills. She will do well." We chatted casually about Lynn and about teaching the deaf. My respect for Mrs. Park and her talent as a teacher had taken a sharp climb in the last hour.

After recess Mrs. Park went through reading-readiness exercises. She placed pictures of a cow, a ball, a tree, an airplane, a cat and a car in slots on a large manila board. Inch-high letters printed on cards below the pictures gave the names for each object.

"Steve, give me the car." Mrs. Park looked directly at Steve as she spoke. "Where is the car?" Steve jumped up, ran to the board and pulled the picture of the car from the appropriate slot and handed it to the teacher. "Good for you!" Steve was obviously pleased and looked around at the others. The teacher returned the picture to the proper slot.

"Lynn, bring me the picture of the tree." She looked at Lynn, who went quickly to the board, reached up for the picture of the tree and gave it to Mrs. Park. Slowly they worked through the pictures until each child had retrieved all of them at least once. Then Mrs. Park went to the board and removed all the pictures; only the printed words remained.

"Steve. *Cow.* Can you give me *cow*?" Steve moved with the same quick assurance, picked up the card that said cow and gave it to the teacher.

"*Airplane. Airplane.* Nancy, can you give me *airplane*?" A little blond two-and-a-half-year-old with hearing aids over her ears retrieved the correct word and returned to her seat. Each time a student handed Mrs. Park a card, she would praise them and then place it back in its slot. Lynn went next and correctly read the word "cat." I sat entranced. All the months of talking, talking, talking to Lynn were beginning to pay off. At least she was progressing in a special school, with a teacher of the deaf who really knew how to teach.

In January and February the weather turned so nasty that Louise was unable to drive to Chickasha for nearly six weeks in a row. We hated for Lynn to miss school, but reminded each other that we were now doing many of the same things at home. A mirror hung on the wall over the dining-room table, where Lynn watched herself move her lips, where Lynn and Louise practiced the shapes of sounds and where Lynn sat to feel the vibrations in my throat or Louise's throat as she read the words on our lips.

During those weeks without school the John Tracy course was a constant reminder and resource. We reviewed Lesson Four, which had come early in the fall, and worked on lessons Five, Six and Seven. Talking to Lynn on every occasion had become routine; we did it without thinking. We felt confident that we had provided her with an *oral* environment. It was gratifying to both of us when we came across the following list of principles in one of the lessons. They summarized the things we practiced all the time:

1. Speak to the deaf child exactly as you would to any other child.
2. Show the child what you are talking about.
3. Do not speak in single words. Use complete sentences.
4. Do not talk baby talk. Use good English.
5. Keep your hands still. He will not look at your mouth if your hands are moving.
6. Don't try to talk to him when you are smoking or eating or chewing gum.
7. Don't talk to him if he is sitting or standing on the floor and you are rocking in a rocking chair.
8. If you are out of doors and wearing dark glasses, take them off when you talk to your child. They cover up the expression in your eyes, always extremely important to a lip reader.
9. Never forget that light is important to a lip reader.

By late fall our report to the John Tracy Clinic had showed that Lynn could lip-read fifty words. By spring that number had doubled to more than a hundred words. We now had stacks and stacks of cards she could pick up from seeing the names on our lips. Lip reading has been called an art; Lynn was obviously a budding artist and she had not yet reached three. We could now ask her dozens of simple questions which she understood. "Do you want to ride your bike?" "Shall we go outside?" "Where's the moon?" The possibilities for direct statements like "Get the box," "Come in the house," "Shut the door," "Get your coat," "Look at the rabbit," had far surpassed what we had anticipated. She lip-read so well that by March, Louise wrote to the John Tracy Clinic: "With many of the things we do together it almost seems she is not deaf for she responds immediately to suggestions to help and get ready to do something together."

By the end of the school year, Lynn could lip-read more than two hundred words. We often recalled the day in Wheaton only one year earlier when she had finally mastered the word "ball." It seemed far in the past. As our time in Oklahoma drew to a close, Lynn passed another hurdle.

It happened one evening after dinner. Sitting around the table we had listed the names for all the dishes, silverware and the nearby furniture. Lynn had made a variety of sounds, trying to imitate me or Louise or Bruce. She seemed more vocal than usual that night. She looked in the mirror and constantly checked her own mouth, to see if it looked like our mouths. I had pointed to Bruce and said his name several times. There was a moment of silence.

"Bruuuu," Lynn said and pointed at her brother with a proud smile on her face.

"That's right!" I almost shouted. "You said it!" I looked at Louise, then at Bruce. "She just said her first word!"

"Bruuu," Lynn said again, watching herself in the mirror, smiling proudly at all of us. She knew she had said it and now came a whole series. "Bruu. Bruuu. Bruu. Bruuu." I looked at Louise, who was wiping her eyes and trying to fight back the tears. For days after that we listened proudly to Lynn go around the house saying "Bruu, Bruu, Bruu."

Thirteen

Lynn stood expectantly at the end of our driveway, a few feet from where it met the street. Every few seconds she looked up and down the street.

"She's been out there for fifteen minutes!" Louise said, shrugging her shoulders in resignation. "I tried to explain. No bus. No school. It's *Saturday*. She just didn't understand."

From the window of our kitchen I saw that another smoggy day had begun to spread over Los Angeles and all the surrounding towns. Before we left Oklahoma I had applied for college teaching jobs in California but had finally taken an interim position at Northview High School in Covina. A few weeks earlier we had rented this green ranch-style house only a mile from where my mother and father lived.

I watched Lynn at the curb. She stamped her feet impatiently. One white knee sock sagged down toward her sneaker. The white straps of her hearing-aid harness contrasted sharply with the red flowers on her summer dress. Her sandy hair, cut short to keep from becoming entangled in cords, barely reached down to the protruding receivers. A car went past and I could see the driver do a double take; Lynn looked more like a miniature paratrooper than a three-and-a-half-year-old child.

"Shall I go bring her in?"

"No," Louise answered. "Let's wait; she may have to learn this one by herself."

Shortly after seven o'clock that morning Lynn had crawled out of bed, dressed herself and then headed straight for the kitchen as she had done every day for the past week. She walked right past Bruce lounging on the living-room floor in his pajamas watching a rerun of *Leave It to Beaver*. After a bowl of cereal she came to Louise with her hearing-aid harness partly on and pointed to the aid for Louise to fasten it. She pushed the earmolds into place herself, then went blithely out the front door.

She waited for half an hour; then, as decisively as she had left, she turned around, came back into the house and curled up in the wicker chair to watch a Bugs Bunny cartoon.

"At least she *likes* school," Louise said to me with a smile when we slipped into the kitchen out of Lynn's sight.

The yellow eight-passenger GMC bus had arrived one afternoon the week before school began. "Covina Valley Unified School District" announced the large black letters on the side of the bus; red lights blinked brightly on top. Bruce went with Lynn on that trial run; she came back excited and pleased. When the bus arrived on that first Monday morning, she climbed aboard without a backward glance.

Sunday morning Lynn woke early and came into our bedroom. We could tell she wanted breakfast immediately.

"No school today. The bus won't come," I said sleepily, shaking my head. At her insistence I crawled out of bed, went to the kitchen and fixed a bowl of cereal while Louise slept a few more minutes. As the Cheerios and milk disappeared I reviewed for the hundredth time the weekly cycle of days.

"Sunday there is no school," I said, pointing to the date, September 22, 1968, on the calendar. "The bus will come tomorrow, but not today. This is Sunday. No school today."

She watched attentively. I pointed to the squares on the calendar and named the days of the week. She finished eating, insisted that I fasten the harness, and though I shook my head and told her again that the bus wouldn't come, she headed out the front door.

Lynn threw me a confident grin through the window as she marched out to the end of the driveway. I let her wait for five minutes. Still in my bare feet, I went out on the lawn, picked up the book-sized Sunday edition of the L.A. *Times* and joined Lynn at the end of the driveway. I pointed up and down the street, shaking my head.

"The bus won't come today. No school. It's Sunday." Lynn looked confused. I took her hand and started back into the house, but she pulled away defiantly and turned back to look up and down the street. I left her standing there. It took forty minutes, but finally she grew restless and came in looking disconsolate.

Monday morning she went out to wait again. This time the yellow bus arrived on schedule. When she saw it, she looked back at Louise, who was watching from the house, and waved triumphantly as if to say, "See, I knew it would come if I waited long enough!"

The driver came around and opened the door for Lynn, who smiled at the other children as she crawled into a seat at the back next to the right-hand window. The bus pulled away and she waved to Louise.

Saturday morning, one week later, Lynn dressed herself, then came in and woke us up. All week long Louise had showed her the calendar. "The bus will come today," she had said, nodding, and marking a large X through each date. Now Louise went with Lynn to the kitchen, took the calendar down from the wall and showed it to Lynn. Five red marks had been made for each day of the week.

"Today is Saturday and there is no school today. No bus." She shook her head and pointed to the calendar, and together they drew black diagonal lines through Saturday to show it was different from the other days.

"Tom, she's gone out to wait again!" Louise said as she came back into the bedroom. "How can we make her realize it's not a school day? They're all the same to her. She just doesn't understand some days are different."

Saturday and Sunday couldn't be seen or touched like cows and cars and shoes. When Bruce was three and a half, he had heard us say the days of the week hundreds of times. He had repeated them in nursery rhymes. He asked questions like "Is tomorrow Saturday?'' With almost two thousand words in his vocabulary, he could use their names in sentences new to all of us. Lynn couldn't even lip-read the name of a single day, much less say their names.

Half an hour went by and then we heard the front door open and close. She had given up for now.

We continued crossing out the days of the week—Monday, Tuesday, Wednesday, Thursday, Friday—and we spoke them to Lynn as we showed her the calendar. But week after week, on Saturday and Sunday mornings, she took up her post, unwilling to be dissuaded from her loyalty to the little yellow school bus.

Then, near the end of the fifth week, Lynn came into our bedroom, still in pajamas, mouthing ''Oooool? Ooooool?'' Her eyes and wrinkled forehead filled in the missing words: ''Is there any school today?''

''Yes''—Louise nodded excitedly—''today is Friday. There's school today and the bus will come.'' Lynn's face broke into a wide grin of understanding. The next morning Lynn woke early as usual. Louise produced a picture of the school bus, pointed to the marks which now filled the calendar and said, ''No school today. It's Saturday. The bus won't come today.''

''Ooool?'' Lynn's mouth silently formed the tight circle that we had come to take for ''school,'' her eyes adding the question mark. ''No!'' She shook her head vigorously in answer to her own question.

A few minutes later Lynn left the breakfast table, ignored her hearing aid, which sat in a heap on the counter, went into the living room and walked over to the window. For one long, wistful minute she looked out at the street, then stretched out on the floor beside Bruce to watch cartoons. Within a few minutes she began to search for something more interesting to do. Television held slight attraction for her. The flapping lips of cartoon characters, even the precise speech of trained actors, remained a complete mystery. She had no way of following the development of a story.

"I think she finally understands!" Louise said with a sigh as we both sat down at the kitchen table for another cup of coffee. I looked around the room, thinking how strange our house would appear to an outsider. White cards pasted everywhere with the names printed in large black letters. CUPBOARD. SINK. CHAIR. TABLE. STOVE. OVEN. WASTEBASKET. TOASTER. FLOOR. WINDOW. DOOR. DRAWER. Even the broom standing in the corner had a name tag attached to its handle. In the other rooms, additional tags identified every item of furniture in the house. Lynn could already read many of them and we had noticed that reading the printed words also helped her lipread them when we spoke.

Through the kitchen window I saw the top of Mount Baldy, a deep purple on this October morning. We hadn't even known you could see it when we moved into this house. One morning strong winds blew the smog out of the L.A. basin and Old Baldy loomed close enough to touch, reaching higher than any of the other San Bernadino mountains. That year we not only watched the mountain change with the seasons but frequently drove to its base, shouldered our packs and set out to explore the trails that snaked back and forth along the steep canyons that led to the top. Lynn and Bruce loved these wilderness hikes even more than we did.

Before we had finished our second cup of coffee, the doorbell rang; several of Bruce's second-grade friends wanted him to play baseball in the street. Louise invited them into the kitchen while Bruce finished eating.

"Ooooooo. Aaiieee. Brruuuuu. Uuuuhnnn. Aahhhh." Lynn smiled and went through her complete repertoire of sounds.

"What did she say?" asked a tall boy with a Dodgers baseball cap pulled down over his eyes.

"She's talking German," Bruce replied in a serious tone, then gobbled down the rest of his cereal. The boys looked at Lynn in disbelief.

"Really?" one of them asked.

Bruce smiled faintly. "No. She's deaf. She can't hear or talk." Before they could ask another question Bruce added, "Come on. Let's go play." Then he got up and headed for the front door.

"Watch out for cars," I reminded them as they filed across the lawn and into the street. Working in the yard later that morning, I heard one of the boys holler routinely, "Car!" I looked up. Bruce in center field, his back to the oncoming car, walked to the edge of the street and waited as a pickup truck delayed their game for a few seconds.

Reed Avenue, where we lived, did not have sidewalks; the fences and hedges between houses went right out to the street. Even to walk from one house to the next meant going out in the road. We restricted Lynn to riding her tricycle on our walk and driveway, but she watched others her age pedal along the side of the street and soon begged for the same kind of freedom.

At first one of us walked alongside; later we marked chalk lines about three or four feet out in the street from our house down five houses in each direction. Saying "No! No!" repeatedly, we pointed to the white marks. At the fifth-house boundaries we pointed again to the chalk line. "This is as far as you can go. You must turn around and ride back to our house." Louise allowed her to ride over that line, then shook her head and pulled the tricycle back to make sure she understood.

For nearly two weeks, every time Lynn went riding in the street Louise or I went along. Slowly she assimilated the idea; we watched from the yard as she pedaled by herself in each direction, turned her tricycle around and pedaled back.

She was riding when I came home from school that Friday. She stopped and made me understand that she wanted to tie a small wagon to her tricycle as she had seen others do. In the wagon sat a stuffed dog and a small doll. I tied the wagon securely, then watched as she pulled her little trailer to the street, turned left and pedaled down her usual course, well within the chalk lines. She passed the fourth house and turned to wave to Mrs. Anderson in the yard. At the fifth-house boundary, she stopped, got off and turned the tricycle and wagon around.

I froze! Careening around the corner, tires squealing, a battered old Ford came speeding directly at Lynn. It couldn't have been more than fifty feet from her. The driver hadn't seen her!

"Look out!" I rushed into the street. "Look out!" I screamed again. The car crossed over the middle of the street and the teenage driver was looking at the passenger next to him. Lynn, intent on getting into motion didn't even look up. She edged into the car's path. She heard nothing!

Suddenly the driver saw her. He swerved back toward the center of the street, tires screeching loudly. He had missed her by no more than two feet. I ran into the street, pointing wildly at Lynn, shaking my fist, shouting angrily at the car. I dashed down the street.

I wanted to explain. To warn her. To tell her what had happened. Overwhelmed by the futility of words, I said nothing. My legs felt shaky as I walked back. Lynn pedaled happily along beside me, looking back now and then to check her passengers.

Bruce and Lynn now enjoyed the special attention that only grandparents can give. Both Louise's and my parents lived nearby and every few days Lynn brought her experience book, turned to a picture of either my parents or Louise's parents and pointed with a questioning look that said, "Can we go visit Grandma and Grandpa?"

I often wondered who she thought they were. These special people who came to our house, who smothered her with silent hugs and kisses, whose homes we entered without knocking. Did she understand even the most basic ideas about kinship?

"My mama, my daddy," I repeated each time we saw them, pointing first to my parents, then to myself. Did she understand this relationship? Did she grasp the idea that I had once been their little boy? We couldn't tell.

Early one morning that fall our phone rang, waking us both from a deep sleep.

"Dad's in the intensive care unit," my mom said. "He's had a severe heart attack."

"Grandpa's very sick," we said to Bruce and Lynn at breakfast. "He's in the hospital. He had a heart attack last night." Lynn looked at us mystified, watching impatiently as Bruce plied us with questions. Louise brought out the experience book and showed Grandpa's picture to Lynn.

"Sick. He's very sick." She made a pained face and tried to make Lynn understand.

Louise and I went together to the hospital. We talked to Dad for a brief moment, then picked up Bruce and Lynn and went to see my mom. A few minutes after we arrived Lynn pointed at Grandma and looked around. "Where's Grandpa?" she seemed to ask.

"Grandpa's sick. He's in the hospital." We drove past the Covina Intercommunity Hospital on the way home; we pointed and explained. Lynn looked at us blankly. Dad survived the crisis and several weeks later he came home to recuperate; only then did Lynn seem to grasp that something momentous had happened.

Lynn attended a regular elementary school that fall, one with two preschool classes for deaf children. Each teacher worked with six or seven children on lip reading, auditory training, speech therapy, reading readiness and a whole new set of matching games. Mrs. Monroe, a dark-haired woman in her late twenties, taught Lynn's class. Louise visited once a week to observe carefully, and we repeated some lessons at home.

School that fall presented a new problem, however. We both were surprised at how the children treated one another. Louise became apprehensive. "You're overanxious," I told her. "Her problems aren't that serious."

But when Louise described how the children behaved in school, I found myself wondering about it. I had never seen Lynn act the way Louise reported when she played with one or two hearing children at home.

"They all sat around the table coloring these pictures," Louise told me after one visit. "I saw Lynn reach over and make a big mark on Vanessa's paper. She didn't appear the least bit concerned when Vanessa cried, pointed at Lynn, then at the mark. It was as if Lynn had just turned to Vanessa and said 'Hi.' I think a lot of the problems come because those kids have no way to communicate with each other.

"I'm really discouraged. The teacher said that last week Lynn started bothering other children, as if she is the only one causing all the trouble in class." Later that same day, several children had lined up for a drink and Lynn seemed to bump intentionally one of the boys, who went crying to the teacher.

But Lynn wasn't alone. Except for Ruben, who could talk much better than the others, most seemed to have problems. Linda cried constantly. Mrs. Monroe and her aide struggled unsuccessfully to elicit even the briefest periods of cooperation from her. Later we talked to Linda's parents. When they suspected her deafness at about six months, they had gone to a new clinic in Los Angeles which advocated intensive hearing-aid therapy. Linda was given a hearing aid that amplified sound to enormous levels. The theory was to stimulate the auditory nerve and thus increase the residual hearing.

"They assured us that Linda would function as a normal child by the time she was three or four," her mother said wistfully to Louise one day. "I wish she could lip-read as well as your Lynn. Linda hardly understands anything we say."

Another girl constantly sucked on her middle finger; the sore between her first and second knuckle never healed. Lynn developed a habit of picking at any scrape or sore; each time the scab formed she picked around the edges. It took weeks to heal the smallest scratch.

The two classes of deaf children went out on the playground at recess. Lynn and another child filled a small wheelbarrow with sand; then they began pushing and fighting over who should dump the sand. Shoving, screaming, pointing at the wheelbarrow, each one struggled to gain possession. Lynn wanted to lead, to teach, to dominate; she pointed to a spot on the ground and nodded her head in a way that said to her playmate, "You stand there and wait!" Like the others, Lynn appeared bossy and aggressive. No matter how many times the teacher intervened, explained or showed by example, cooperation seemed beyond the children's ability. Whereas hearing children this age talked, argued, laughed and often achieved cooperation when someone assumed the leadership by shouting out a simple instruction to the others, the deaf children appeared to intentionally create chaos and hurt one another.

They all loved to ride tricycles on a course marked like a set of miniature streets and alleys. Some days each child had a tricycle, at other times they shared them with hearing children from a kindergarten class.

"Line up now and take turns," the teacher would say to the hearing children. They quickly lined up, talking and laughing. They took turns. When differences of opinion emerged, language proved to be the great arbitrator. "You're next. Wait your turn. Time to get off." The children waiting in line talked about the ones riding through the miniature city, bragged about their own skill, created fantasy worlds with real cars and grown-up business to accomplish.

"Line up, children. You must take turns," Mrs. Monroe said to the twelve or thirteen deaf children, trying to look at all of them so they could see her lips. In one rush, they descended on the two red-and-white tricycles. They screamed, pushed, pulled and hit out at one another. Lynn held the handlebar and straddled the front wheel of one tricycle. She shoved Vanessa, who also had a grip on the handlebar. A boy pulled on the seat.

"Line up! No! No! Children! Line up! You must take turns!" Without realizing it, Mrs. Monroe and her aide both were shouting as they pulled the deaf children apart and stood them against the wall, physically cutting off their path back to the tricycles. As the aide blocked and talked, Mrs. Monroe ushered Russell and Vanessa to the tricycles. But once through the course, neither wanted to give up their prize. Lynn broke from the makeshift line along the wall and the aide forcefully brought her back, then removed Russell and Vanessa, one at a time so that the next ones could take their turns.

Tricycles and wheelbarrows had one overwhelming advantage

for Lynn. It was easy for her to tug on shiny handlebars, to scream, to push others away. Everyone knew what she wanted. But how do you tell Mommy that you don't like your cereal with that much milk on it? How do you ask Daddy to swing you upside down when all he seems to understand is that you want to be held? How do you tell them that you want to go to other people's houses like Bruce? How do you make them understand you want the same kind of Kool-Aid that you had two weeks ago at your cousin's house and just now remembered? How do you say, "I forgot what I wanted"? Faced with such impossibilities, Lynn increasingly expressed her frustration.

Communication tantrums. They started about the middle of October. By Christmas they came several times each week. Sometimes we found what Lynn wanted; most of the time a tantrum ended with the mystery unsolved.

I can still see her marching up the front walk, a determined expression on her face. The door opened and shut with a decisive bang; she headed directly for the kitchen, where Louise had started an apple pie.

"Listen to me!" She pulled on Louise's skirt, harder than usual. Then she pointed to a small cupboard over the refrigerator, *her* cupboard. It held paper and pencils for drawing pictures, a couple of clothespins, a Baskin-Robbins ice cream cup. Louise held up each item; Lynn shook her head and pointed more insistently at the cupboard.

"Ooooooeeeeo!" Lynn began to cry out, pointing, demanding in her silent fashion. "Aaaahhhhheeee!" She pointed again, jabbing her hand into the air in the direction of the cupboard, shaking her head until everything that had found its way to the shelves had been presented.

"No! No! No!" Her hair flew as she shook her head in rage.

"Show me what you want!" Louise presented Lynn with a pencil and paper.

"Aaaaahhhheee!" An angry swat sent them flying across the floor. Now she pointed at other cupboards, more insistent, anger showing in her eyes. "Aaaaaaahhhhhheeeeee!" she screamed louder. Out came pans, dishes, a few plastic containers. Lynn refused them all.

Now she stopped, as if an idea had pushed its way past her anger. With her hands she drew a large half-circle in the air, pointing with each index finger as the picture was completed. "That's what I want! Can't you understand?!" The expression on her face punctuated the dramatic, baffling gesture.

"Tom! Can you come and see if you can figure out what she wants?" Louise called me from my books.

"What do you want?" I asked Lynn who had calmed down for the moment. Again the sweeping semicircles, the pleading expression for me to understand. Suddenly, in response to my puzzlement, Lynn began jabbing her fingers into the air.

"AAAAAAAAAHHHHHHHHEEEEEEEOOOOOOO!!!" she screamed. Tears of anger streamed down her face. I took her by the hand and we went to her room. I pointed at each of her toys.

"Is that what you want? Is that what you want?" Through her tears she screamed and shook her head, pulling on my hand back into the kitchen. I brought out her experience book. She hit it out of my hand and kicked out at me. I began pointing to the cupboards, the refrigerator, the stove.

"What *does* she want?" I looked at Louise, bewildered and angry myself.

Head shaking, screaming, Lynn now threw herself on the kitchen floor, kicking out in every direction. Louise knelt beside her. Overwhelmed with human helplessness, we waited. Slowly the torrent of anger and frustration subsided. Then Lynn got up, completely ignoring us, walked out the front door and climbed up on her tricycle.

"Tom, I don't think Lynn is ever going to talk." Louise looked at me dejectedly, fighting back the tears. "I don't know what's wrong with her, but I just don't think she's going to talk!"

Lynn's communication tantrums forced Louise and me to resort to limited gestures—pointing, imitating, pantomiming.

I recall one night when we had nearly finished dinner. Lynn sat at one corner of the table dawdling over her food. Both Louise and I had prompted her during the first part of the meal. "Eat your peas. Drink your milk. Look, Bruce is almost done." But still she picked at her food, rearranged the peas in a long row on her plate and took only the smallest sips from her milk.

"Eat your dinner," Louise said, exasperated. At the same time she unconsciously lifted an imaginary fork to her lips, imitating the action she wanted from Lynn. Instantly Lynn lifted her empty spoon, copying the gesture perfectly.

"Don't do that!" I said to Louise in an irritated tone of voice. "Can't you see how quickly she understands your gestures and copies you? She'll never learn to lip-read and speak the words if you always gesture!"

One Tuesday evening, the week following Thanksgiving, we had attended a meeting for the parents of children in Lynn's class. Mrs. Monroe wanted to discuss the curriculum and answer our questions. She introduced herself, then described how she conducted the speech-therapy sessions.

"Are there any questions about what goes on in class or anything else?" Mrs. Monroe had concluded her fifteen-minute orientation. Louise and I had taken the last two chairs; directly in front of us sat Russell's parents. To the left, dwarfing their small chairs, sat Vanessa's mother and Ruben's mother and father. Three more couples sat in the front. A sandy-haired man at the front raised his hand. He wore glasses and a pin-striped business suit. Mrs. Monroe nodded in his direction.

"Are deaf people able to obtain good jobs?" he asked. "You know, can I expect that my son will someday be self-supporting?" He looked uncomfortable on the small chair; with one finger he pushed his glasses higher on the bridge of his nose.

It seemed like a strange question. Can he really be serious? I wondered. I thought of Linda McArthur, majoring in physical education at Cal Poly in San Luis Obispo. And Carolyn Graves in Chickasha, Oklahoma.

"There are some things that deaf people can't do," Mrs. Monroe began slowly. Then she hesitated, almost groping for words. For the first time I sensed her feeling ill at ease. "But some do get good jobs and we just have to keep trying and hope they do all right.'' She stopped and looked around for other questions. I looked at Louise, surprised and wondering. Why hadn't she given this man more assurance? She had been working with deaf kids for seven years and I couldn't believe she didn't know. Mrs. Monroe pointed to Vanessa's mother, who had raised her hand.

"I'm worried about Vanessa,'' she blurted out. ''She lip-reads very well and we've worked on speech for a long time. But she doesn't say much. We can understand three words, but no one else can make them out. When can I expect that Vanessa will begin to talk?''

''That is difficult to answer,'' Mrs. Monroe began. ''Some children talk sooner than others, just as with hearing children. The important thing is to work on auditory training and speech therapy. The more you do at home, the better. I think we have to be patient. Sooner or later, if you maintain a good oral environment, Vanessa will talk. We have to keep trying and keep hoping.''

And now I felt more than uneasy. Was that all Mrs. Monroe could say? Vanessa's mother needed to know. Louise and I needed to know. When would we find someone who could tell us, ''Lynn will talk when she starts first grade,'' or ''Lynn will talk when she is about five and a half.'' When would all those words come pouring out? Why were professionals always so evasive?

Yet, at the same time I realized that there were enormous difficulties in teaching Lynn or any other deaf child to speak; you had to admire people like Mrs. Monroe for their persistence and courage. It had taken all fall just to teach Lynn how to say one word—''blue.'' Sometimes it came out ''bruu''; other times she said ''boo.'' The ''l'' sound came from deep within our mouths, and since Lynn couldn't see anything, she couldn't easily learn to make it.

Other questions followed which I can't recall. As we drove home that night I kept thinking over and over to myself, We just have to keep trying and hoping. Someday Lynn will talk.

Fourteen

"When you read, face your child and hold the book down low like this. That way your child can see your lips but won't see the pictures in the book." Dr. Barrington turned sideways as if to face an imaginary child and held a picture book up to demonstrate her point. I listened half-heartedly; Louise and I had read books to Lynn this way for nearly two years.

"With a picture book you can make up short sentences that identify things in the story; you may want to do that even when the author has written a story to go along with the pictures if it has too many unfamiliar words in it. Now, after you have talked about one page, show your child the picture and check to verify what has been understood on your lips. 'Where is the bird?' 'Point to the barn.' 'Where is the wagon?' "

Dr. Barrington shifted her position as she spoke and held the book to illustrate how her imaginary deaf child could look at the pictures and also see her lips.

I was tired. The announcement about this evening had arrived right after New Year's Day; Dr. Barrington, a psychologist, would speak on "How to Tell Your Deaf Child a Story." The baby-sitter had canceled out at the last minute; I decided to come alone and Louise stayed with Bruce and Lynn.

The cold rain spattered against the windshield as I drove along the Pomona Freeway. I had left home feeling at an all-time low about Lynn's progress, or what seemed more like total *lack* of progress. Even after Dr. Barrington began her lecture I couldn't shake the gnawing sense of depression. Day after day Lynn's anger had built up inside, burning more intensely whenever she needed to communicate, then exploding in an outburst of rage and exasperation.

I looked around the room at the fifty or sixty parents who listened so attentively. I wondered if those with young toddlers were filled with the same high hopes we had felt when Lynn started lip reading. It's good you don't get hit with *all* the problems at once, I thought to myself.

I recalled the scene before dinner, one that had been repeated over and over since we moved to Covina.

"Can Lynn play?" Lizzie, a five-year-old neighbor stood at the door.

"Sure," I said. "She'd love to. I think she's in her room, why don't you go see?"

Louise followed Lizzie down the hall and helped the two girls get started on a puzzle, then went back into the kitchen. I wondered how long it would last. Sustained play with others presented Lynn with enormous hurdles; she didn't even know the rules to the simplest games.

"Can Lynn come over to my house?" Five minutes had passed and now Lizzie and Lynn had their jackets on, ready to go out. I got up to check the bedroom.

The puzzle pieces lay scattered across the floor mixed with blocks, dolls, books and other toys. The drawers to Lynn's toy chest stood open; everything was emptied out.

"Who made this mess?" I asked.

"Lynn did it," Lizzie replied.

I tried to get Lynn to help pick things up. She resisted and I knew that without physically taking her hand in mine to force cooperation, it would be impossible. Lizzie and I finished the job and the two of them left.

Ten minutes later Lizzie and Lynn came up our walk, hand in hand.

"Lynn won't do what we ask her," Lizzie said, frowning. "I can't get her to come to my room. She won't take turns. She doesn't understand what I say."

Similar scenes took place when Lynn occasionally went to the homes of other neighborhood children. The phone would ring in ten or fifteen minutes. "Could you come and get Lynn?" somebody's mother would ask. "She can't seem to play with the other children. I can't leave my baby to bring her home."

Dr. Barrington ended her talk. She piled her notes and the children's books to one side, took a drink of water, and as people whispered to each other and shifted in their seats, she asked, "Does anyone have any questions?"

Instantly, hands went up all over the large room. But none of the questions that followed concerned reading stories to deaf children.

"When can I expect my son to talk? He's already five and a half."

"Why is my daughter so stubborn? I can't get her into the bathtub; once she's in, I can't get her out. Her older sister never fought us like Janet does."

"What can I do when my six-year-old wants something and we can't find out what he wants?"

"Billy is seven and hardly talks at all. He throws temper tantrums so often we don't like to take him out anymore. What can we do?"

"How do you get a deaf child to talk more? Our Sheryl is five and we've been working on the same six or seven words for almost two years. She doesn't seem to lip-read new words like she used to."

I didn't hear the questions or Dr. Barrington's answers that night so much as I heard the anguish, the disappointment, the fear, the sense of helplessness that pervaded the voices of those mothers and fathers. Suddenly I thought about that meeting of the Chicago Hearing Society two years earlier. I could see the kindly face of that black grandmother, I could feel the cry for help in her voice: "I have an eight-year-old granddaughter, Sally, who's stone deaf. It just worries me and her mama 'cause Sally still don't talk. Can't say no more than four or five words that anybody can understand. No conversation at all. We just can't make any real sense out of the noises she makes."

177

"Lynn won't turn out like that," we had reassured ourselves as we drove from Chicago back to Wheaton. "Look how early we have started on lip reading and auditory training."

Of all the questions that spilled out that night, none seemed so urgent as the ones about sleeping.

"My Bobby, he's four years old, he just don't want to go to sleep." A young mother near the front had stood up. She clutched a large leather purse with both hands as she spoke. She went on to describe her son's tantrums and I could see her husband nodding his head. He wore a checkered wool shirt and work pants.

"You might try reading him a story and make sure that he has a relaxing time before going to bed. Sometimes children are so keyed up that they can't go to sleep." Dr. Barrington's suggestions sounded like the ones we had read in Spock and Gesell, suggestions that had worked with Bruce several years earlier.

"We've tried that!" The words were blurted out from near the back. I looked around at a tall thin man about my own age. "Our daughter still won't go to sleep!" he shouted, his voice trembling. "She comes into our room and wakes us up. We've given up! We leave the light on now and let her stay up all night. We're beginning to think she's got the day and the night mixed up!" He sat down and other hands went up. Dr. Barrington listened patiently, reminded us that children go through stages, urged us to be patient and admitted it was more difficult with deaf children.

My chance finally came, and when she nodded in my direction I stood up. "We've had the same problem with our daughter. Lynn is nearly four years old and for the last six months she's had trouble sleeping. At first we took her back to her room. But every few mintues there she was, crawling into *our* bed, tugging at my shoulder, waking us up." I shifted nervously on my feet and looked around.

"We tried just about everything—talking to her, spanking her, making sure she played hard and was tired, quiet evenings—nothing worked. I started closing our door and thought at least she might stay in her room; she would stand outside our door knocking and knocking and knocking until my wife or I got up and let her in. Sometimes we just let her stay in bed with us all night.

"Well, we finally decided it wasn't worth the trouble. Now, when she wakes up in the night, she comes to our room, unrolls a sleeping bag we leave on the chair, climbs in, and goes to sleep."

The meeting ended, I drove home and talked about it with Louise for more than an hour. Strangely, we both felt encouraged. Lynn's problems were not unique. And in many ways Lynn had progressed further than other children who had reached six or seven and could only speak five or six words; Lynn came close to that already. She might not break into fluent speech immediately, the words she lip-read might not pour out tomorrow, but in time she *would* talk. We decided to start special speech therapy sessions immediately as an extra precaution.

Speech therapy made up part of each day at school, but it never seemed enough. Furthermore, Lynn's teachers had less training than a fully qualified, professional speech therapist. We helped Lynn at home, but we knew that a really good speech therapist might make all the difference in the world.

We found such a person in Pomona, a young woman who had graduated from UCLA and had also had special training at the John Tracy Clinic. Louise began taking Lynn each week for intensive therapy. Lynn wore special earphones and sat on a high seat so that she could easily touch the therapist's throat. Louise watched through a two-way mirror to learn each new technique. Much of that spring involved teaching Lynn the difference between short and long sounds.

"Ooo." The therapist paused for a second or two. "Oooooooooooo." As she spoke into the microphone, she pressed Lynn's fingers against her throat so Lynn could feel the difference.

"Aaa." A brief pause. "Aaaaaaaa."

"Nnn." Pause. "Nnnnnnnn."

Occasionally, while she listened and watched the therapist, Lynn moved her own mouth and made some soft vowel sounds. Once she had gone through a series of sounds, the therapist began again, this time adding another visual cue to help Lynn understand the length of the sounds.

"Ooo." The therapist held up a bright-red ribbon about two inches long which immediately caught Lynn's attention. "Oooooooooooo." The two-inch ribbon fell into the therapist's lap and in its place she produced one six or seven inches long. All the while she deftly made sure that Lynn's fingers were on her throat.

"Aaa." A short green ribbon. "Aaaaaaaaa." A long green ribbon.

"Eee." A short yellow ribbon. "Eeeeeeeeeee." A long yellow ribbon.

At home, Louise not only repeated the techniques she had observed through the two-way mirror, the therapist had also given her additional assignments. Louise cut up colored construction paper into short and long pieces.

"Ooo." Louise held Lynn's hand against her throat with one hand and picked up a short piece of paper with the other, then dropped it into a shoe box with a small slot in the top.

"Oooooooo." Now a longer piece of the same colored paper went into the box. Soon Lynn dropped the correct length of paper into the shoebox to match the sounds.

All that spring the speech therapist and Louise worked on long and short vowels and the consonants "p," "n" and "m."

The "m" sound came first. During February and March Lynn could close her lips in a silent "m" while she attempted to make the sound. I tried to feel the vibrations for "m" on my own throat and nose; only after many repetitions could I pick up the barest sensation with the tips of my fingers.

Early in April, a few weeks before Lynn's fourth birthday, a rusty, unused voice joined her lips in a soft smacking sound. "Smmmmmmk. Smmmmmmmmk." We were overjoyed! The speech therapist looked encouraged.

"Mmm. Mmm," Louise would say, Lynn's hand on her throat.

"Smmmmmk. Smmmmmk," Lynn repeated.

"Good girl! You're talking!" Any sound at all gave the speech therapist something to work with. And so the task shifted to helping Lynn improve it. By the beginning of May the "k," which came at the end of her lip-smacking "m," had disappeared. Later that month we heard her say "mmm" for the first time. It seemed like a monumental achievement.

That spring in Covina we finished the last lesson in the John Tracy correspondence course. That course had shaped our thinking for nearly two years and we still reviewed many of the games from early lessons. We had also progressed to newer exercises, designed to teach Lynn to "hear" the rhythm in words of more than one syllable.

We must have spent at least a hundred hours that spring helping Lynn "hear" the difference between "jump," "run" and "fall down."

"Run." I sat on the floor next to the dining-room window; the three cards sat on the window ledge. I pointed to the ledge and waited. Lynn picked up the right card.

"Good girl!" I exclaimed. "You got it right!" I gave her a big hug.

"Jump." Again, the right card.

"Fall down." Louise watched as Lynn correctly retrieved each of the cards.

A few days later I added the next step. "Jump." Lynn turned, picked up the card for "jump." "Right! Now let's jump!" Already on my feet, I grasped her hands and together we bounced up and down around the dining room. Lynn loved it!

"Run." Lynn read my lips, read the card and picked it up with an expectant look on her face. I turned and started jogging through the house, Lynn in hot pursuit.

"Fall down." Lynn reached for the printed card, I pulled her toward me and we both went crashing to the floor in a heap. She laughed and rolled over, and I could tell she was enjoying these lessons in semantics. We played this game for twenty or thirty minutes before she lost interest.

Now I began hesitating slightly after she picked up the right card to test whether she would run, jump or fall down. It took only a few sessions until she scored 100 percent every time. Then things grew more difficult.

I positioned myself in back of Lynn as she faced the three printed cards on the window ledge. Crouching down to her level I spoke over her shoulder so her hearing aid would pick up my voice.

"Fall down," I said with resounding force, emphasizing the rhythm of sounds. Lynn reached out and picked up the card printed "run."

"No." I shook my head and returned the card to the ledge.

"Fall down." Before she could pick up any of the cards, I turned her head slightly, so she could see me repeat "fall down"; then I allowed her to take the card. We both tumbled to the floor. We worked our way through each word several times with many mistakes.

Day after day we played, and slowly, ever so slowly, Lynn began "hearing" the right word. I'm still not sure how she did it. Perhaps she only sensed the rhythm or her residual hearing had improved or she had learned to use it more efficiently. Maybe she picked up vibrations, something from the way I crouched behind her. But it didn't matter. She was responding to my voice, not merely my lips.

I kept up the games for weeks and soon she recognized the right word 75 percent of the time. Then she made only an occasional error. Not long after her fourth birthday she achieved a perfect score. Run! Jump! Fall down! Only three words, but to us they seemed like three hundred.

Years later we would look back and wonder at how hard we had worked. I'm amazed at the patience with which Louise and I taught Lynn, at our persistence as we practiced and practiced those language games. Most of all I'm amazed at the strength of our hope. What bolstered our spirits? How did we manage to keep going? Why didn't we get more discouraged? What prevented us from giving up?

Progress. No matter how minute, every new sound Lynn made spurred us on. "Hearing" one new word meant progress. Slow, tedious, exhausting, but every step she took was living proof that our work was not in vain. Run. Fall down. Jump. She had "heard" them. She knew these words. And that was a step closer to speech. "Bruuu." "Blluuu." "Ooopbenn." It didn't matter that others couldn't understand these words. And every word Lynn spoke shouted a deeper message with ringing clarity: "Someday I'll talk!"

Equally important, our hope rested on this basic fact of life: the oral approach offered the only adequate solution. There was nothing else to do. We couldn't just give up. We couldn't consign Lynn to a world of silence, loneliness and dependence. Yes, it would take longer than we had anticipated. No, we couldn't count on sudden breakthroughs. But Lynn would learn to talk. Slowly we scaled down our hopes. She might begin to talk by five or six; fluent speech would probably come much later.

But during all those months and years of teaching Lynn to talk, nothing bolstered our spirits more than stories of deaf adults who had succeeded. We literally devoured the reports that came each month in the *Volta Review*. Sometimes we learned unexpectedly of someone whose example we talked about for days.

One morning I woke before the alarm went off. I looked at the clock; in a little more than an hour I would have to leave for Northview High School. Barefoot, I walked sleepily through the living room and out the front door to bring in the L.A. *Times*. The grass, thick with dew, had soaked the outside page of the paper. I broke the string, unfolded the paper and sat down in the wicker chair; all around me lay the scattered remains of Lynn's birthday party—torn wrappings, ribbons and one lonely balloon, a cellophane-covered box that had once held a miniature set of pots and pans.

I started skimming the headlines, looking sleepily for any interesting news. Lynn had enjoyed every minute of the party; best of all, she seemed to know what it all meant. For several weeks Louise had marked off each day on the calendar, pointing to April 16 and saying, "That's your birthday. April sixteenth. We'll have a birthday party." Then she sketched a birthday cake, with four candles. "You'll have a cake just like this! For you!" We showed her pictures from the previous year and slowly she grasped the idea.

Louise came out of the bedroom in her bathrobe and went to the kitchen to start breakfast. Absent-mindedly I skimmed the page in front of me. I turned to the next page and the heading in large print brought me to full consciousness.

DENTIST CHAMPIONS PROGRAM FOR DEAF

I started to read. "As a child, Jim Marsters struggled to keep up with his classmates. They could hear but he couldn't. Not a sound. So he taught himself to read their lips and he learned to speak. Eventually they ceased to think of him as being different."

"Listen to this!" I called to Louise, at the same time getting up and heading for the kitchen. "There's an article here about a deaf dentist in Pasadena who learned to speak. He can talk to his patients and understands them by lip reading." I sat down at the kitchen table and Louise poured me a cup of coffee.

At forty-five, Dr. Marsters was a successful orthodontist. In addition, he flew his own plane and was involved in community activities. Even without hearing, he said he could sense when his patients felt pain whether they said anything or not. As the current National Chairman of the Oral Deaf Adults Section of the Alexander Graham Bell Association, Jim Marsters was lending his support to a program in oral education for the deaf; he maintained that manualism and the use of sign language should only be a last resort. He used his own experience as the best argument in favor of oralism.

He had attended the Wright Oral School in New York City and had gone on to graduate from college. He wanted to become a dentist, and even though his college grades were excellent, the dental school admissions committee rejected him. He applied again and was admitted to the New York University School of Dentistry, finished the rigorous training and went on to specialize in orthodontia.

Jim Marsters summed up his success: "I knew that if I could not develop good oral ability, I would have to become part of a deaf community. And I realized that the deaf community is severely limited as to the opportunities open to it."

Louise cut the article from the paper as I shaved; at breakfast we talked about it and I reread aloud several things Dr. Marsters said about oral education. Going to school that morning, I felt a new surge of hope for Lynn, a new determination to persevere.

One afternoon in the middle of May I came across a short article about a voice teacher who had turned from training opera singers to helping deaf people improve the quality of their speech. She held that the deaf could learn to speak more easily if they used the diaphragm and chest appropriately. Instead of feeling the vibrations in the throat, they should feel the ones in the chest. Once they learned to feel these vibrations and control the diaphragm muscles, speech development improved dramatically.

It sounded plausible; I wondered why no one had tried it before.

"Look at Lynn's speech," I said to Louise after we both read the article. "She mouths lots of words but without any sound at all. The problem is to teach her to produce and control the sound. When she first learns a word, she says it with hardly any volume; even her best efforts still sound quite weak. And look how hard she tries. It's as if she's straining but just can't make the sound come out."

I decided to try this novel approach. After Lynn finished her bath, I sat down with her on the living room couch. I placed her on my lap and took her hand and held it flat against my chest.

"Blue. Blue. Blue." I used a word she could already speak, although not always clearly. Her eyes lit up with recognition as I spoke—she had felt the vibrations.

"Blue. Blue. Blue." I held her hand against her own chest as I spoke; she quickly caught on.

"Bluuu." The words came out softly. Had she said it correctly? I couldn't tell. I moved her hand back to my chest.

"Blue. Blue. Blue."

Back to her chest. This time I waited.

"Blue. *Blue*. BLUE!" I listened, astounded. She had spoken twice as loud as I had ever heard her before! And the word now sounded like *blue*. It would have sounded that way to anyone! It was almost too good to be true. I told myself to go slowly, not to get excited.

"*Blue! Blue! Blue!*" Clear and loud, the word rang out. Incredible! Now I was excited. Was this the breakthrough we had been waiting for?

"Louise! Come and listen to Lynn!" Louise came from the bedroom and sat down beside me; Lynn looked pleased, as if she knew something important had happened.

"Blue. Blue. Blue." I held her hand on my chest. Without any prompting she moved her hand back to her own chest and spoke.

"*Blue! Blue! Blue!*" Louise looked shocked. I could tell it was the clearest she had ever heard Lynn speak. Not even the speech therapist had been able to elicit this kind of volume and control.

That night after Bruce and Lynn had gone to bed we talked for a long time about Lynn's progress. We discussed speech vibrations, felt the ones in our throats, then compared them with the chest sensations. We tried to remain cautious in spite of a new surge of optimism.

The next day I worked on two other words Lynn could say: "Bruce" and "open." Within minutes the faltering voice, the strained vowels, the fading sound that had been characteristic of these words for weeks disappeared. With her hand on her chest Lynn spoke them loud and clear.

"It's the breakthrough we've been hoping for!" I told Louise. "This could change everything. She could be talking by four and a half or five!"

The breakthrough had come on a Thursday evening. By the weekend Lynn could speak her four or five words with the new-found fluency. I decided to go slow, not to push her, to limit the lessons to ten or fifteen minutes.

Monday afternoon I came home, eager to have a brief session

with Lynn before dinner. She met me at the door, and after several minutes of play I sat down for a review. I no longer had to put her hand on my chest; if I said a word she could lip-read it and then, by feeling her own chest, she could produce the better-quality sound.

"Blue. Blue. Blue." I said.

"Ggrrrrraaaow!" It came with great force, an animal-like noise I had never heard her make before.

"No. Now, try again." I shook my head and repeated "blue" several times. I held her hand to my chest as I spoke, then moved it back to hers and waited.

"Ggrrrrraaaow!" Perplexed, I tried again. Louise had heard the strange sounds and came in to observe. For the next twenty minutes, no matter how patiently I coaxed, Lynn did nothing but growl. The words she had said so clearly the day before refused to come forth. Was she teasing? It didn't seem like it from the expression on her face.

Several times that week we encouraged Lynn to use her voice. "Ggrrrraaaow! Ggrrrraaaow! Ggrrrraaaow!" Something strange *had* happened; she seemed incapable of speaking correctly.

On Friday night of that week, we took Bruce and Lynn out for dinner. The waitress brought four glasses of water and the silverware, then took our orders. While we waited Bruce and Lynn sipped their water and drew pictures on the paper placemats.

"Ggrrrraaaow!" She spoke without warning. Her voice sounded unnatural and twice as loud as any girl her size would make.

"Sssshh!" Louise had her finger across her own lips and scowled at Lynn, shaking her head. We noticed people looking our way.

"*Ggrrrraaaow!*" Now it came louder. Lynn saw that she had attracted the attention of other customers.

"No! No!" I shook my head vigorously.

"GGRRRRRAAAOW! GGRRRRRAAAOW! GGRRRR-RRAAAOW!" She threw her head back and grinned as she filled the small restaurant with this new sound she couldn't hear. We smiled helplessly as people looked at Lynn. Embarrassed, we did our best to distract her. Finally our food arrived and she stopped; we ate quickly and left before Lynn thought to repeat her performance.

On Saturday, Lynn began walking around the house growling loudly. All our efforts to stop her abnormal sounds proved futile. Even more discouraging, we couldn't coax her to say a single word correctly.

On Sunday she regressed to smacking her lips, "smmmmmk, smmmmmk," instead of making the "m" sound.

"Tom, what is she doing now?" Louise asked in consternation. For days Lynn walked around the house growling and smacking her lips like some strange animal. Discouraged, we discontinued all attempts to get her to speak for about three weeks. Slowly the growling and smacking disappeared, and with it the volume and clarity of her voice also disappeared. Lynn's speech therapist had never heard of this approach; she discounted its effectiveness. We never tried it again.

The end of the semester arrived and Lynn's teacher sent home the following report:

> Lynn enjoys the other children, and likes to communicate with people, adults or children. Her moods change quickly from great exuberance to complete refusal. Other than these periods of not cooperating, she is charming and delightful. She has an excellent sense of humor. Lynn is so effective with her personality appeal, her gestures, and her ability to lip-read that she is able to communicate with others without the use of language. She says "blue," "yellow," and "open," and can imitate with fair accuracy the vowel sounds u, o, and a. Lynn can shape some words even though there is little sound produced. Lynn is efficient in using her hearing aid although latest tests show she is profoundly deaf. She seems to hear gross sounds such as a drum and can raise her hand to indicate when she hears these.

Earlier that spring I had received a letter from a friend at American River College. They would be hiring four math teachers to start in the fall; if I sent my credentials he thought I would have a good chance. About the same time I received a notice from the National Science Foundation about a mathematics summer institute at the University of Oregon. And so I sent off two applications. We settled down to wait, uncertain of what our future held. I could stay on at Northview High School in Covina but I was eager to get back into college teaching.

At about the same time Lynn stopped growling, the good news arrived in the mail. The National Science Foundation accepted me for the summer institute and I landed the job at American River College in Sacramento. We packed a small trailer with enough belongings for the summer and headed north in early June.

Fifteen

"Tom!" Louise called anxiously from Lynn's bedroom. "Bruce and Lynn *both* have temperatures. Almost a hundred and one! We'd better find a doctor today." I glanced at my watch; class would begin in forty-five minutes. Bruce had run a slight temperature intermittently for more than two weeks, accompanied by a sore throat and hacking cough.

To get the name of a pediatrician, Louise called George Rodgers, an old friend from high school days. George and his wife, Fran, both attended graduate school at the University of Oregon and worked on the counseling staff. A few minutes later she came back into the bedroom. "We have an appointment for Bruce and Lynn at two—Dr. Friedman is his name. You'll have to help me take the kids to the doctor after lunch."

Riding my bike along the street to the university that Monday morning in late June, I couldn't think about computer programming or numerical-analysis exercises. We had arrived in Oregon only two weeks earlier and found an apartment; after that we took a quick trip to the coast, and a week later the NSF summer institute had started.

"I'm really worried, Tom," Louise said when I returned. "I've never seen Lynn this weak. But at least her temperature hasn't gone any higher."

I carried Lynn into Dr. Friedman's office and sat down in the reception room; Bruce and Louise walked over to the desk to check in. A few minutes later the nurse guided us to a small examination room. After I laid Lynn down on the high table and Bruce sat down on a chair, the nurse took their temperature. Dr. Friedman came in and started with Bruce.

"It looks like an old-fashioned sore throat," he said, "but we'd best take a throat culture and check for strep. He looks like he's on the mend. Make sure he gets extra rest. If the culture comes back positive, we'll call you and put him on antibiotics."

"She's deaf," I said when he began to examine Lynn. "She might need one of us to help her understand what you want to do." Dr. Friedman tried to assure Lynn with a smile. "You'll be all right," he said. "I just need to check your neck and stomach." Lynn looked apprehensively at Louise.

Dr. Friedman looked in Lynn's mouth. I expected him to take a throat culture but instead he asked the nurse to help him set Lynn upright on the table. Then he tried to have her bend forward and touch her head to her knee. She could only lean down a few inches before crying out in pain.

"This could be serious," he said, looking at both of us. "I want to look at a sample of her spinal fluid and that means a spinal tap. I'll have to take her down to another room." He spoke in a low, even tone.

I nodded and swallowed hard and looked at Louise. "Could one of us go with her?" I asked.

"I think you should both wait here," Dr. Friedman said. "I'm sure she'll be okay. It will only take a few minutes."

Dr. Friedman shook his head in a serious, authoritative manner, then gave instructions to the nurse to take Lynn down the hallway and prepare her for the spinal tap. I looked at Lynn as the nurse picked her up; she looked at us, her eyes filled with terror. We looked back in helpless silence. She mustered the last bit of strength in her feverish body and began crying, kicking and fighting. The nurse held her firmly, but gently, and started down the hallway.

Lynn's screams disappeared abruptly as we heard a door close. Neither of us spoke for a long minute; we both knew what the other was thinking. "Wasn't there some way we could have communicated with Lynn? Why didn't we think to bring a picture or something?" But we knew that none of her experience books could have prepared her for this.

"I wish he would have let us stay with her," Louise said.

Five minutes dragged by. Then ten. A door opened somewhere in the clinic. We heard Lynn crying. Louder. Footsteps approached. Dr. Friedman opened the door and gave Lynn gently to me; her crying turned to exhausted sobs as she clung limply to my shoulder.

"Her spinal fluid is cloudy," he said without emotion. He hesitated, as if groping for the right words. He looked at the floor, at Lynn, back to Louise and me.

"I'm afraid she has meningitis." Insistent, urgent, as if he wanted to make sure we comprehended, Dr. Friedman's words seemed to fill the small examination room and hang suspended in the air.

"Meningitis?" I asked in disbelief. I looked at Louise, then at Lynn, then back at Dr. Friedman. I suddenly felt weak; I searched for words.

"H-h-how serious will it be?" I stammered. "What are her chances for recovery?" I cradled Lynn into Louise's arms. She stopped whimpering. Her head rested on Louise's shoulder. Exhausted, her cheeks burned with a dry redness, her eyes appeared listless.

"Twenty years ago her chances for recovery would not have been very good." Dr. Friedman hesitated, then went on, "But we can start her immediately on antibiotics. I'll phone the hospital, it's just down the block. She'll have to go into isolation directly from here. I want you to take her down and go in the back entrance. I think she has a pretty good chance of pulling through, but the sooner we get her on some medicines, the better."

I took Lynn in my arms and held her as gently as possible. She felt tiny. Helpless. Her body was limp. I fought back the fears. We started down the hallway of the clinic. We passed the other patients, the nurses, the receptionist. We started up the sidewalk. I could see the back of the hospital across a large parking lot. We started to walk faster. The short distance seemed to stretch out for miles. Louise had her arm in mine; Bruce held tightly to her other hand.

Only ten days before, filled with her customary exuberance, Lynn had dashed back and forth on an Oregon beach; she chased the small receding waves, then ran to escape the next incoming wall of water. I could see her now, responding to the natural elements which spoke in a language she heard so clearly. The sand squeezed up between her curled toes. The moist wind threw ocean spray in her face. The salt clung to her lips. The tiny sea creatures wriggled in her hands. The fog had lifted by noon and she basked in the warm sun. And these voices she so easily understood asked nothing in return. No pressure to watch diminutive movements whose meaning forever escaped her. No request to make strange vibrations in her throat, sounds beyond her experience. No heads shaking when she didn't grasp the meaning of some silent word. And most of all, the elements seemed to understand her. The sand responded to her running feet, the air to her gestures. Even her "Aaahhaaaeeeiiiooo" was caught by the high cliffs and thrown back to the ocean without a frown or pleading expression to try again. Lynn had never been more alive, more at home.

We rounded a corner of the building and started through the parking lot. She whimpered softly in my arms. We went through the hospital door, the four of us clinging to each other. All Lynn's accomplishments seemed like nothing. Right now, when we needed to communicate with her the most, we could not. Our own daughter —and we hardly knew her! What if she never recovered? She could lip-read several hundred isolated words, but she couldn't speak her own name. She had never said "I'm tired," "I'm hungry" or "My tummy hurts." She had never said "I love you." She had never asked for a doll or stuffed teddy bear. She had never told us what she liked or wanted or who she played with.

Communication! That's what we had been denied. An uncontrollable anger welled up within me. We had been cheated—it wasn't fair! Why? Why? Why?

"Tom, what are we going to do?" Louise tugged urgently on

my arm. "Lynn won't understand what's happening. The nurses won't know what she wants. We can't just leave her alone!"

"We'll stay with her," I said. "There's no other way." I prepared myself to insist, no matter what the hospital rules.

A tall Catholic sister, her flowing white robes swishing along the polished floor, led the way to the isolation ward. I laid Lynn on a high bed. Another sister began adjusting a bottle of clear liquid that hung from a chrome stand attached to the side of the bed.

"She's deaf," I said. "She may not understand what you say to her."

The sister nodded, then began inserting the needle into Lynn's wrist. Lynn hardly flinched. They fastened white tape around her wrist to keep the needle in place, then tied Lynn's arm loosely but securely to the side railing of the bed. We watched as the sister adjusted the valve; drops of the intravenous solution began moving steadily through the tubing.

"Can we stay with her?" Louise asked anxiously.

"Yes. We have no visiting hours; you can stay as long as you like, day or night." Louise sighed, suddenly relieved. Lynn's eyes opened for a moment and she looked at us.

"You're in the hospital now. You'll be okay. We won't leave you." Louise spoke slowly; Lynn looked back blankly. Before the last words left Louise's lips, Lynn had closed her eyes again and settled into a restless semiconsciousness.

For an hour we stayed together by her bedside, looking at her, watching her tiny ribs rise and fall, praying silently that she would recover, dreading the awful possibilities.

For five days and nights we kept our vigil. We talked to Lynn whenever she stirred or opened her eyes. We held her hand, we stroked her forehead, we rubbed her back, we patted her. We tried to communicate, to let her know we were there even when her eyes were closed. Occasionally she would wake, look to see if one of us was still standing at her bedside, then doze off again into fitful sleep.

The nurses came in and out, checked the IV solution, examined the needle, took Lynn's temperature, recorded her pulse. We watched their calm faces, searching for the slightest hint of hope or concern. In two days they had punctured Lynn's wrists so many times that it became impossible to find a place to inject the needle, so the tape and tubing were fastened first to one ankle and later to the other. Lynn whimpered, fought back weakly, then settled again into her drowsy state.

Thursday morning I went to class, came home for a hurried lunch, then went to the hospital to take Louise's place. Dr. Friedman had told us the previous night that Lynn seemed to be holding her own. Her temperature had not gone higher. He had been cautiously optimistic. "She's still very sick," he said, as if to keep our hopes realistic.

Preoccupied with Lynn, I parked opposite the hospital and started across the street toward the front entrance. A man and two women were walking by the hospital about thirty feet in front of me. Suddenly I saw they were different. They gestured back and forth in rapid, animated movements, and I knew instantly that they were deaf. Their heads moved back and forth as the silent conversation changed from one person to another. I could see their faces. Their lips hardly moved, but the flow of changing facial expressions added meaning to the conversation that came from their hands. I stopped in my tracks. They were actually talking to each other!

I watched, spellbound. Not since that day in church when I was only five years old had I seen deaf adults communicate in this way. Only a few seconds had passed, but I could tell that this strange, mystical language was working.

And then I thought of Lynn.

Could *they* talk to her? I wanted to run up to them, to stop them. I wanted to shout out, "Wait! Can you talk to my daughter? She's sick. She could die! But she's deaf like you and we can't communicate with her! She can't understand us!"

I had stopped, immobilized, at the edge of the curb. Their hands and arms continued to fly. Could they use these gestures with Lynn? Could she even understand their strange language?

Could they tell her that we loved her? That we wouldn't leave her alone? Explain what was happening? Where she was? That Dr. Friedman was doing everything possible to help her?

Then it struck me. How could I ask them? These deaf adults probably could not lip-read or talk.

These were the kind of deaf people who used gestures. I watched as they rounded the corner and disappeared. Confused, anxious, helpless, and feeling as isolated from Lynn as I was from these strangers whose language I did not comprehend, I slowly crossed the street and made my way to her hospital room.

Lynn's temperature finally went down. She smiled now when we spoke to her. Louise held up pictures Lynn recognized and said the words she could lip-read. On Friday, Dr. Friedman came in and moved Lynn from her room; he wanted to do another spinal tap. I could hear Lynn crying and screaming weakly. I imagined the nurses turning her over, holding her down, Dr. Friedman inserting the needle.

"Her spinal fluid has cleared," Dr. Friedman told me when he returned. "Even though the medical lab at the State Health Department hasn't identified the exact infective agent, she has pretty well recovered, but it will take a few weeks to get her strength back."

Louise wrapped Lynn in a blanket on Saturday afternoon and carried her to the car; we drove home and put her at last into her own bed. We sensed her delight at being back in familiar surroundings. For the next week Lynn spent a good part of every day in bed. By the end of the week she wanted to go outside and play, and a few weeks later she had regained her strength completely. When George and Fran invited us to go on a short backpacking trip with their family, we decided to join them. We left Eugene at six o'clock in the morning, all nine of us packed into the Rodgers' Travelall.

Several hours later we reached the Willamette Summit, then George turned off onto a dirt road that took us deep into the Willamette National Forest.

We set out at a slow pace, single file, Lynn following close to Fran. Jim and Dan, one tall and slender, the other of average height but heavyset, seemed to dwarf Bruce. George led the way; Louise and I brought up the rear. After about half an hour of hiking, the three boys unexpectedly broke into song at the top of their lungs.

"Flea, flea fli flo
Eni mini deci meni ouwa . . ."

We all broke into laughter. Everyone except Lynn. She looked around at the rest of us, but she couldn't see anything to laugh at.

Every ten minutes we stopped for a brief rest; then a different person led the way. Lynn's turn came near a fork in the trail. She went to the front and marched along, never looking back, as if to show us all she could lead as well as anyone. But when we came to a fork, she went left instead of right.

"We go to the right!" George called out from near the end of the line and everyone stopped. Everyone except Lynn. She blithely walked on.

"Lynn! Wait, that's the wrong way!" Jim, who was second in line, called out. I waited a few seconds, hoping I wouldn't have to chase after her. Finally she glanced over her shoulder and saw us all standing almost ten yards behind her at the fork in the trail. Instantly recognizing her mistake, she smiled, looked embarrassed, laughed, then jabbed the air with her clenched fist in a gesture of mock disgust. She quickly joined us and led the way to the right.

The trail began to climb slightly; we came out over a rise and saw a small lake sparkling below us, surrounded by a dense cover of pine trees. We soon found a clearing where several trees lay crisscrossed, their upper trunks extending into the shallow water at the edge of the lake.

"This is where we stop for lunch," Dan said. We swung our packs to the ground and leaned them against the weatherbeaten trunks. Seated in an irregular circle at different heights on the fallen logs, we began devouring our lunch. I slapped at mosquitoes on my arm and face; then everyone laughed when Lynn slapped herself in exact imitation.

"It's so quiet up here," someone said, and we all stopped eating and talking to listen. The wind whistled through the trees overhead; the logs creaked as the water in the lake gently rose and fell. From far across the lake came the rat-a-tat-tat of a woodpecker.

Everyone remained still while Jim, cupping his hands and directing his voice to the high cliffs that climbed up from the opposite shore, shouted "Hello!" Within seconds his echo shouted back. Then Bruce cupped his hands and shouted "Bruce!" A broad grin broke out on his face as his echo came ringing back within a fraction of a second

"Didja hear it, Dad?"

"Bruce!" Again he cupped his hands and waited until the sound of his own voice came back.

Lynn, not to be outdone, stood up, cupped her hands to her mouth, lifted her shoulders slightly, tipped back her head and silently held this shouting position for several seconds. Then she dropped her hands to her side and grinned at everyone. While the others continued to test their voices against the sheer granite wall in the distance, Lynn lost interest and sat down on the log beside Louise.

We camped out overnight, then hiked back out to the Travelall. On the drive back to Eugene, Louise and I sat in the back. I looked at Bruce, Jim, Dan and Melinda, who was Bruce's age, crowded into the wide middle seat. Jim and Dan would begin junior and senior high school in the fall and they had become Bruce's heroes; he followed them everywhere. Lynn sat up front between George and Fran, completely unaware of the chorus of voices behind her. In another week we would have to leave Oregon and our friends.

We drove for an hour along the Willamette River Highway, then stopped to watch a roaring torrent of water that fell several hundred feet over Salt Creek Falls. We all had to shout in order to talk above the noise of falling water.

Back in the Travelall, Jim, Dan, Bruce and Melinda began to sing:

> "Flea, flea fli flo
> Eni mini deci meni ouwa
> Ouwa ouwa a meni
> Be billi oto bedoto
> Be deton dotan
> Shhhhhhhhhhhhh."

The four of them filled the Travelall with their voices, pouring out verse after verse as though each one had profound meaning. Every now and then they would stop, out of breath, and laugh, obviously taking great pleasure in sharing the rhythm, the cadence, the pitch, the rhyme and the chanting sounds of their own voices.

At first Lynn didn't know they were singing but soon became aware that something was happening in the seat behind her. She stood up, one arm over the back of the seat, the other on George's shoulder. She watched the silent comic opera; she moved her lips to try and imitate them. When the others laughed, she laughed. After watching for several miles, in a moment of silence after the four singers had finished an exceptionally long verse of a song, Lynn grinned at Bruce, took a deep breath and shouted "BRRRUUUUUU!" as loud as she could.

Sixteen

"Baby-sitter's here!" I called to Louise. Bruce ran through the living room to answer the doorbell. It was shortly after seven o'clock and the gray darkness of an early November evening had already settled over Sacramento. The parents' meeting at Starr King Exceptional School would start in twenty minutes.

"I hope you don't have too much trouble with Lynn tonight," Louise said to Pat Kerns, who was taking off her coat. "We won't be late; it's a meeting at the school. She should go to bed about nine o'clock, and if you have any trouble, Bruce can probably make her understand."

Reluctant to leave Lynn with someone she did not know, someone with whom she could not communicate, we felt lucky to have found sixteen-year-old Pat. She only lived a few houses down the street. "She's good with kids," her mother, Lois Kerns, had told Louise a few weeks after we moved into the neighborhood. "And she can always call me if there is a problem."

"Hi! Glad you both could come tonight." Fred Hockett, the principal of Starr King, stood near one of the doors to a large room that during the day had a partition down the middle to form two preschool classrooms. A gold tweed carpet gave warmth to the room. We sat down beside Mrs. Conklin, Lynn's teacher, and waited while several more people came in. Nearly all of the more than twenty parents were still strangers to us.

We had moved to Sacramento as much for the Starr King school as for my job at American River College. For Bruce, it hardly mattered where we moved. He could always count on a school and friends, but Lynn's future demanded careful planning and investigation. Whenever I had heard of a possible teaching position, I immediately wrote to inquire about local programs for educating deaf children.

Was the school committed to an oral approach? Did special classes for the deaf end at age six or eight? Would we face another search, another move in a few short years? What could we expect when Lynn reached high school age? Did the school system place deaf students in classes along with the hearing? At some later date we did not want to have to choose between sending Lynn away to a residential school or making still another move.

My letter to the Starr King school had brought good news from Mr. Hockett. "I feel our program is equal to any in the nation," he wrote. The school served one hundred children with speech and hearing handicaps. Their teachers had been trained at the John Tracy Clinic, Gallaudet University and the Clarke School for the Deaf. In high school, deaf children were integrated with the hearing. Most important, everyone at the school was deeply committed to using *only* the oral approach.

"I'd like to welcome you all," Dr. Mason, the school psychologist, said. "Tonight we thought it would be helpful to talk about discipline problems that you have with your deaf child. But before we break into small discussion groups, Barbara Simmons has an announcement that she wants to make." He nodded in her direction and sat down. An attractive woman in her early thirties with a resolute manner rose to her feet in the second row on the left-hand side. "A group of concerned parents from our school and some deaf people from the community are going to meet tomorrow night," she said. "We will be discussing total communication and talking about using sign language along with speech and lip reading. Some of us have become interested in ways to improve communication with our deaf children. You are all welcome to join us. We will meet at the Sutter Hospital auditorium on F Street at seven-thirty."

A strange stillness hung in the air. No one spoke. I could feel the tension grow as the implications of this brief announcement ran through the minds of everyone present. Dr. Mason started to rise, hesitated, then got up to let us know how to organize our discussions. "Not more than six to a group," he said quickly, avoiding any comment about Mrs. Simmons' announcement. "And one teacher to each group. We'll spend about thirty minutes in small groups, then get back together to compare notes."

Before we stood up, Mrs. Conklin leaned over to Louise and spoke in a low voice. "You both support the oralist philosophy, don't you?" When Louise nodded she continued, "Our school is an *oral* school and we want it to remain *oral*. I'd stay away from that group of parents who want to use a manual approach."

It seemed strange to us that these parents were interested in sign language. Why would they want to start that kind of thing with a four- or five-year-old? I thought to myself. Maybe their kids have other problems; maybe they just can't learn to lip-read and talk. I recalled the little girl in Lynn's class in Covina who could only understand a few words. We had heard of older children who failed to develop speech even here at Starr King. At the insistence of the only teacher on the staff who knew sign language, a total-communication class had been started at a nearby school for six twelve-year-olds who couldn't talk or lip-read well enough to communicate. But failure to speak at age twelve couldn't be compared with an inability to speak at age five.

Louise and I moved our chairs over to one side of the room where several people had pushed their chairs up to a small oval table. Mrs. Garvin, a preschool teacher, Barbara Simmons and several other parents joined us and we all introduced ourselves.

Mrs. Garvin started the discussion with a question. "Is anyone having discipline problems at home?"

I looked at the floor. A minute of silence finally ended when a woman across from Louise spoke. "It's hard to get my boy to obey—like going to bed. He's stubborn, but mostly he just doesn't seem to understand. I never had problems like this with my two hearing children."

After a short pause Mrs. Garvin said, "You know, I think we sometimes treat deaf children different because we *feel* they're different. We should treat them just like normal children. Expect them to obey. Insist that they obey. Your child doesn't have to know what you say to follow a simple command like 'go to bed.'"

"We have the same trouble with our daughter," I put in. "We try to act the way we did with our son; I suppose sometimes we feel Lynn just doesn't understand, so we give her the benefit of the doubt. We try to explain, but if she keeps refusing, we just have to resort to force."

"Is this a common problem with the rest of you?" Mrs. Garvin asked. Two more heads nodded.

Then a young woman, pulling her maroon coat more tightly about her, spoke. Her words came slowly and her eyes shifted here and there without looking at anyone. "You know, I find that it is very easy to come close to being brutal to my deaf boy." She hesitated for a long moment. "It's so different from our boy who isn't deaf. I just can't communicate with Jeff. I ask him to do something, like 'put your pajamas on now.' I pick up the pajamas and *show* him what I want done. I ask again. He balks. Then if this is the tenth time during the day I've had to go through this routine, I've had it! I'll grab him and force his pajamas on. Then he'll start kicking and twisting and biting and fighting like an animal. And when I spank him, if he's twisting and kicking, I'm liable to miss and hit him across the back or even on the face. I feel so bad, but what can I do?" She looked down at her hands, clenched white against the deep maroon of her coat. She was fighting back tears of remorse and anger.

Behind her I could see a row of hooks on the wall where Lynn and the others hung their coats each day. A sweater still dangled from one hook, a pair of black rain boots lay on the floor. I could hear the voices from the other groups scattered around the large classroom. At the same time it was as if we were looking through a window at ourselves, seeing with frightening clarity how we acted, observing the cause of our own increasingly frequent fights with Lynn. "It's time for your bath" would lead directly to a kicking, screaming struggle all the way into the tub. Once in it, she refused to get out; splashing water all over us, she clung to the faucet. When we motioned and called her to dinner, she came but refused to climb into her chair or eat. It happened almost every day over something, but her war of resistance was constantly interspersed by delightful periods of truce when she spontaneously cooperated.

The small group of parents and Mrs. Garvin discussed the problem from several angles; all the solutions offered seemed like ones we had heard before. The questions then shifted to lip reading, to speech therapy, to difficulties someone had keeping his daughter wearing her hearing aid.

Then, almost without thinking, I asked it. I heard myself saying the words that had haunted me for years. The question we had pushed out of our minds, avoided, as if we didn't *want* to find the answer. Even as I spoke, I wondered why we had not asked this question when Lynn's deafness was first confirmed.

"How many deaf children *actually* learn to talk clearly and lip-read everything you say?" I looked at Mrs. Garvin. "And how long does it *really* take?"

Mrs. Garvin remained silent for several seconds, then began hesitantly, "I'm not sure what the exact figures are. In the past the record has not been good for children born deaf because they were five or six or even seven years old before they started school. But now, with children beginning at age three and even earlier, I think we can expect good results. Maybe you have some statistics on this," she said, looking directly at Barbara Simmons.

"Well, the statistics are not too encouraging," Mrs. Simmons said, shaking her head. "The latest study indicates that only five or ten percent of all the children born deaf ever develop intelligible speech. It can take fifteen years and still be very difficult to understand them." A stillness had settled over our group as she spoke. Skeptical, I leaned forward in my chair.

"Nobody can learn to lip-read everything," she went on. "A skilled lip reader—and that's most often someone who learned to speak *before* going deaf—is lucky if he can understand one fourth of what is said."

There was a gasp from the young mother who had told us about spanking her son. "You *don't mean* that deaf children who start school as young as ours turn out that poorly, do you?" she asked, incredulous.

"Yes," Barbara Simmons said matter-of-factly. "That includes children starting before the age of one year." In the long uncomfortable silence that followed I thought to myself, Five or ten percent! How can that be? My thoughts raced back to the Jane Brooks School for the Deaf. I could see myself walking with Louise from one class to another, listening to the strange sounds of deafness, watching as second- and third-grade children struggled to gain control over their unused voices.

Finally, breaking the silence, I turned to Mrs. Garvin and asked, "Do you agree?" I could see I was not the only skeptic in the group; several others were frowning, shaking their heads in disbelief.

"I think Barbara Simmons is probably correct," Mrs. Garvin replied. "I'm not sure what the exact numbers are. I've taught deaf children for a long time and after their first year of preschool, at least by the time they're five, I can pretty well tell whether they're going to develop intelligible speech. Most will never make it.

"Then what do you do with the five-year-olds you're pretty sure won't make it?" I asked, still doubting what I had heard.

Mrs. Garvin looked down at the floor, then back at the group. "Well," she said slowly, "we can't be one hundred percent sure. We have to keep trying. When a child gets older, if they still can't communicate orally when they are in their teens, it's best to send that child to the state residential school."

Another strained silence ended when Dr. Mason asked the groups to break up and return to the rows of chairs in the front. The only thing I remember about the rest of that meeting was what Mr. Hockett, the principal, said when he reported on the discussion that had taken place in his group.

"We talked about temper tantrums and what to do when your child absolutely refuses to obey," he began. "Some of the parents in our group said that even spanking their child or sending him to his room did not bring cooperation. One parent suggested a solution that might help those of you who have similar difficulties.

"She had tried spanking. She had restricted her son's activities. She took away privileges. And sometimes, at her wit's end, she just gave in to what the child wanted. One day another temper tantrum occurred. She had reached her limit, so when her son completely refused to obey, in desperation she grabbed him and forcibly shoved him in the shower. Then she turned on the cold water, clothes and all. After half a minute she turned off the shower, pulled him out and started drying him off. His temper tantrum had ended! She helped him change clothes and for the rest of the day he was most cooperative."

All the way home I kept thinking about our discussion group. "Five or ten percent make it"... "I can pretty well tell by the time they're five whether they're going to develop intelligible speech." Could she tell right now if Lynn was going to make it? Had we overlooked some hidden sign? "She's a phenomenal lip reader." More than one of Lynn's teachers had described her that way. Was it possible that she *still* might not develop speech? How could anyone be sure at this age? Wasn't it worth it to keep trying?

Louise and I both wondered about the group of concerned parents who would meet at Sutter Hospital the next evening. Why would these people give up? Did most of them have older children? Had their children started too late?

At home I paid Pat Kerns and then walked her down to her house. Light streamed from windows along Finsbury Avenue, casting dark shadows across the lawns on each side of the street. Our house seemed especially quiet when I returned; Louise was sitting at the oak table in our small kitchen. Steam rose in two thin columns from the coffee she had poured. I sat down, took a sip, put my cup back down on the table and sat for a long moment in silence.

"Tom," Louise finally said, "I don't think our situation looks good. Lynn can't talk now and she might never talk. In fact, it seems to me that she has regressed since she started school this year!''

I sipped my coffee slowly, searching for words, reviewing the evidence, trying to sort out my own feelings. For the first time I realized that we had worked so hard on speech and lip reading that we had never fully entertained the possibility of *failure*. In a few months Lynn would celebrate her fifth birthday. She could not talk; the few words she spoke were intelligible only to us and a few close friends. She could only lip-read names of common objects and a few common verbs. What if all our efforts, what if all Lynn's valiant attempts actually did fail? What then? What were the alternatives? Clothed in the enigmatic and forbidden phrases like ''manual language,'' ''signs,'' ''finger spelling,'' ''residential school,'' ''deaf-and-dumb,'' the alternatives conjured up animalistic, nonhuman images in my mind. I feared to think of them. I didn't want to investigate them as a possibility for Lynn.

For three years we had accepted the axiom: *all deaf children can learn to lip-read and talk almost as well as their hearing peers.* This axiom was conditional, we knew that. It required an early start and a pure oral environment, but we had not denied Lynn either of these conditions. Now we had encountered contradictory evidence. Or maybe it was only hearsay. Surely, if 95 percent of deaf children *never* learned to talk well enough to communicate, those facts would have been reported in the *Journal of the Alexander Graham Bell Association.* I couldn't recall a single article or news item in the *Volta Review* that even hinted at such a possibility.

I got up from the table, poured more coffee into our cups and sat down. ''Well, what else can we do?'' I asked, feeling perturbed at Louise for her questions, at myself for entertaining doubts. ''We can't just give up and send her off to the residential school! If she's ever going to get an education, a good job, have a family of her own—she has to learn to live in a hearing world. That means we can't quit now! It's the day-to-day thing that's hard; I realize some days look like no progress. But I think Lynn's doing better than we think. Like the sleeping thing. Only a few months ago we thought she'd never learn.''

Louise nodded, though I sensed her discouragement even as I struggled with my own. Lynn *had* finally learned to sleep through the night in her own bed. For more than a year we had lived with her nightly visits, and the problem continued after we moved from Southern California to Sacramento. Several times a week Lynn would come to our room in the middle of the night, roll out a sleeping bag next to our bed and sleep there until morning.

''What can we do to help her sleep through?'' We had both asked the question on many nights but the answer eluded us. Finally, after she had become familiar with our new neighborhood and begun to enjoy school, we decided to make another attempt. We carried her back to bed, trying to explain what we wanted. On some nights she slept through in her own room and this shored up our hope that it could become a permanent nighttime routine. On those rare mornings when we awoke to find her sleeping bag empty, we raced to her bedside, and with lavish praise, tried to impress on her the importance of her accomplishment. But our enthusiasm remained a mystery to her.

Then we hit upon a plan. I went into Lynn's room one evening after she had fallen asleep and took her picture. When the print came back, Louise pasted it to a blank calendar she had ruled out on a large piece of red construction paper. Lynn laughed and pointed to the picture as we attached it to her bedroom wall. Then we began a bedtime ceremony of looking at the picture together, nodding our heads and pointing to Lynn.

''You can sleep in your own bed all night. You're a big girl now.'' A hint of understanding rose in her eyes.

''Louise! Lynn made it through the night!'' I woke with a start. It must have been a week after we had hung the calendar in her bedroom; we both went to see if she had awakened. Louise retrieved the box of gold stars from the top of the refrigerator and when Lynn opened her eyes, we were both standing next to her bed exuding approval.

"You slept in your own bed!" Louise exclaimed and gave Lynn a warm hug. We took her to the calendar and with great fanfare recorded the accomplishment. Louise gave her a gold star and pointed to the first square on the numberless calendar below the photograph of Lynn sleeping. Lynn couldn't have looked more pleased as she licked the star and pasted it in place. For the next twenty-seven days Lynn slept through the night in her own bed and woke each morning to add another gold star under her picture. When the calendar filled up, we left it hanging on her wall. We half expected a return to the old pattern, but night after night she stayed in her bed until the picture calendar grew old and was unceremoniously replaced by a picture Lynn had painted in school.

We had stumbled onto the solution which, in hindsight, appeared so simple. I wondered about the problems that still remained. We desperately needed to talk to Lynn in words she could understand. To have her communicate in words *we* could understand. We longed for a common language to handle the common routines of dressing, taking a bath, cleaning up her room, coming in, going out, waiting in the car, going back to find her coat, taking turns in children's games, and a hundred others. Would we have to find a different solution for each of these while we waited for her tongue to be loosened?

One evening a few days after Thanksgiving, Louise came across a notice in the local paper. A group which called themselves the Concerned Parents of Starr King Exceptional School had presented a proposal to the San Juan Board of Education. They asked for a class in which the teacher used sign language in addition to speech, because their children were not learning to speak and lip-read at a rate which allowed adequate communication at home. The article pointed out that the Starr King school did not teach sign language to deaf children, nor allow them to use it at the school.

"Do you suppose they are the same group of parents who announced that meeting at Sutter Hospital a couple of weeks ago?'' I asked after Louise read the article. ''I still can't understand why they want to use sign language with such young children. We probably have as much trouble communicating with Lynn as they do with their kids. I don't know. The next couple of years are crucial. I don't want to ruin Lynn's chances of learning to talk by admitting failure now when she just might start talking in the next year or two.''

Three days later Lynn came home from school with several mimeographed notices. One was on the table with the new *Volta Review*, which had arrived in the mail. The large blue printing which spread out across the entire page of the notice caught my attention.

ORALISM VS. MANUALISM

ALL PARENTS OF STARR KING EXCEPTIONAL SCHOOL ARE IN-
VITED TO AN IMPORTANT MEETING TOMORROW NIGHT WHERE
WE WILL DISCUSS THE CONTROVERSY OVER ORALISM AND MAN-
UALISM AND HOW IT WILL AFFECT THE SCHOOL.

TIME: 7:30

ALL PARENTS URGED TO ATTEND.

I picked up the *Volta Review* and sat down to browse through it. It was the December 1969 issue. The table of contents listed an article on special education in Sweden, another on the mental health of deaf children. I turned the page and quickly scanned an advertisement. ''Electronic Futures, Inc. A wireless auditory training system.'' I turned another page.

Book reviews. The first title caught my attention. *The Influence of Finger Spelling on the Development of Language Communication and Educational Achievement in Deaf Children*, by Steven P. Quigley, Ph.D. The review was written by the director of Tucker-Maxon Oral School.

Dr. Quigley had studied two hundred students in six public residential schools to determine which method worked best: a pure oral approach or an oral approach that also used finger spelling. According to Quigley, his study showed that the use of finger spelling improved school performance and communicative skills among deaf children.

However, the reviewer disagreed. Carefully and systematically he pointed out that Dr. Quigley had made a number of questionable assumptions. The superior performance by children using finger spelling might also be attributable to the fact that at a residential school, whatever approach used can be monitored and controlled more easily. The control groups who used a pure oral approach had not lived in such an environment.

Clearly, the study didn't stand up under careful scrutiny. It appeared that Dr. Quigley wanted to prove that finger spelling worked better than a pure oral approach. I was glad someone could refute these kinds of claims and wondered if the group of Concerned Parents at Starr King ever read the *Volta Review*.

The next evening when I left home alone to go to the parents' meeting, I picked up the December *Volta Review*. I wasn't prepared to speak up at the meeting, but if the debate over the oral and manual approach should become heated, I could at least cite these arguments against the use of finger spelling for young children.

I pulled into the driveway of Starr King Exceptional School; more than the usual number of cars were parked in the asphalt-covered lot. I decided to sit near the back; if the meeting became uninteresting I could slip out early and go home.

Seventeen

I left the car and walked quickly up a roadway that ran parallel to a long classroom. It led to the Special Education offices and the classrooms on the Starr King campus. The lights from several office windows cast yellow streaks and dark shadows across the grass and covered circular drive, where each morning the buses discharged their load of handicapped children.

More than a dozen rows of brown metal chairs had been unfolded and arranged in the middle of a large meeting room that functioned during the day as lunchroom and gymnasium. Already more than half had been taken and people were moving into vacant rows. Lunch tables lined the back wall and in one corner a trampoline stood folded up near a pile of tumbling mats.

Several groups of parents and teachers had collected near the front of the room and stood talking. I recognized a few faces but, as yet, I did not know anyone on a first-name basis. Lynn's teacher had taken a seat in the third row; Mr. Hockett moved among the groups, welcoming parents to the meeting with a broad smile and handshakes. Wishing Louise had come with me, I made a beeline for the tables against the back wall which would give me a good view of the room. I looked casually at my watch as I sat on the edge of a corner table near the rear exit. Seven twenty-five. The meeting would begin in five minutes.

Then I saw them! Their hands darting in and out, fingers pointing, twisting, jabbing the air with lightning strokes. At least a dozen of them had taken chairs together, several rows in front of me, slightly off to one side. One woman, her chair turned around to face the others, wove patterns in the air with her hands as she spoke each word silently. A curious feeling came over me, as if I were in a foreign country, unable to speak the native language. Judging by the glances of curiosity from parents around the room, I knew that others felt this same mood of apprehension. The huddled groups engaged in conversation looked as if they were discussing the small band of deaf people. Obviously not parents or teachers, they seemed like intruders.

As if by common agreement, the hands of the deaf people fell silent. They turned to watch a large middle-aged man at the end of the row. A conspicuous plastic receiver protruded from one ear, the gray cord disappearing inside his shirt collar. He spoke with both hands to the woman who interpreted, his nimble fingers curling, knitting, jabbing and pointing in the small space before his chest, occasionally touching his head or chin. I could catch expressions of interest here and there on half-turned faces, smiles, nods. His hands stopped and fell silent into his lap. All eyes shifted to the interpreter; people nodded in agreement as she said something with her hands and mouthed the words. When she finished, the man with the hearing aid burst into a loud crackling laughter that sounded peculiarly "deaf." Everywhere around the multipurpose room, heads turned to look; the other deaf visitors smiled or laughed quietly, then continued their silent conversation, unaware of the attention briefly turned their way.

"Will everyone please take a seat now?" Mr. Hockett had gone to the front. Slowly the conversation died down. People in the back moved into the empty rows; someone went for more chairs, which squeaked loudly as they were unfolded.

"We're glad so many of you joined us tonight. This is an important meeting for all of us." He shifted from one foot to another, waiting for the talking to end. "As you all know, Starr King Exceptional School has always been a *pure* oral school. In fact, for the last fourteen years, the San Juan Unified School District has always had a policy to maintain a pure oral environment in the special-education programs for the hearing-impaired."

I listened to Mr. Hockett, but my eyes kept shifting back to the woman who continued to interpret for the deaf visitors. The designs created by her hands flowed with incredible speed.

"We think that Starr King has one of the best programs in the United States. Most parents are pleased with the progress that their children have made here. It is my impression from talking with many of you that most parents want their children to have an oral education.

"A few parents, the ones who call themselves Concerned Parents, have gone to the board about starting classes using manual communication. However, many feel that our school should remain a *pure* oral school. The deaf people who learn the manual language do not have the same advantages in a hearing world. They can only obtain poor jobs. They live in the deaf ghetto. They miss out on many things that hearing people enjoy. Tonight we are here to discuss this request made to the board."

The interpreter's gestures involved both hands, sweeping, integrated patterns that moved in a kind of silent musical rhythm. Then, in the midst of these patterns, she would stop and make tiny jerking movements with the fingers of one hand. I noticed other parents glancing uncomfortably in the direction of the deaf, then studiously trying to ignore this new phenomenon that had invaded our parent group meeting.

"These *concerned* parents"—Mr. Hockett looked quickly at several parents sitting with the deaf visitors—"their proposal to the Board of Education asks for teachers to instruct their children in sign language. Mrs. Simmons will read that request so you will all be aware of what they want in our program. Then I think we can discuss it. It does involve *all* the children in our district."

Barbara Simmons walked to the front of the room. She began to read from a sheaf of papers in her hands:

We are the parents of bilingual hearing-impaired children. Our children are not only using the *spoken* language but the language of *signs*.

We are here not as parents with a quarrel with any teacher,

214

administrator, or any other parents. Instead, we respect those who possess differing views and we would hope that they would grant us the right to differ.

There will be those who will say that our children should be kept at Starr King but stop their use of signs. As our children become more proficient in the use of signs and are better able to communicate with their friends, it will become increasingly difficult to stop the signs without having to use some of the methods that a few teachers have mentioned. Besides the usual slapping of hands, there is the use of nylon stockings to tie the children's hands behind their back, and some oral schools use bags in which they place the offenders' hands and then tie it. Even though the teachers were not to instigate such action, our children will be made to feel that they are inferior by their peer group. Many of the oral parents have drilled into their children that to sign is bad. We can understand why these parents have done this. But it will not make our children feel welcome in that type of school environment.

She read the requests for special classes, folded the papers together and returned to her seat. The requests she made all sounded reasonable. And even though she had asked for classes using sign language, she had also emphasized they still wanted oral language for their children.

Mr. Hughes, the PTA president, went to the front of the group. All whispering had ceased, although I noticed one deaf woman gesturing to a man sitting next to her.

"We are concerned parents too!" Mr. Hughes gripped the edge of the table and looked directly at the small group of parents sitting with the deaf people. His tense voice filled the large room. "I don't think it was right for you to make your request to the Board of Education without notifying the rest of us so that we could tell them of *our* concerns. We have deaf children too!"

Heads nodded around the room. The woman interpreting for the deaf visitors seemed unmoved by the comment, her fingers picked up speed as she changed the spoken words into signs.

215

"We believe that our deaf children have the right to learn their *mother tongue*! Sign language is not even a language!" With each sentence Mr. Hughes's voice crept to a higher pitch. "It's just a primitive form of gesturing! I don't know why they even call it sign *language*! If you teach deaf children those gestures, they will never learn to talk. They will never learn anything! You can't teach them to read and write using that sort of thing!" The interpreter maintained a steady rhythm, painting Mr. Hughes's words in the air. It did seem that some of her movements had grown more exaggerated, as if to match the deep feelings conveyed by his words.

Mr. Hughes paused, looked down, then went on in a quieter tone, "I'll never forget"—he shook his head slowly—"an experience I had some years ago. I was a life-insurance salesman. I went to this one house and knocked on the door; the lady let me come in. A young man in his early twenties was sitting there. It became very apparent to me that something was wrong with him.

" 'Is your son deaf?' I finally asked.

" 'Oh, yes. He's been deaf since birth.'

" 'Can he talk?'

" 'No, he can't talk.'

"That young man would try to talk with his mother, but he could only make the most grotesque sounds you ever heard. It sounded like an animal! Then he would move his hands trying to communicate, gesturing, pointing, as if he wanted something. His mother would go get it. They seemed to partially understand each other, but it was really awful." He paused for a moment. "It was the gestures that had kept him from learning how to talk. And I just determined right there that my daughter should learn how to speak. We would never use those gestures that had prevented this deaf kid from learning to talk.

"And another thing..." He glanced in the direction of the deaf visitors. "If we have a manual class for some kids at Starr King, even if they go to another school, our kids will see them signing on the bus and begin to sign themselves. It will spread and we will no longer have a pure oral school. The rest of us are happy with it as it is. If you want your children to learn to sign instead of talk, why don't you send them to the state residential school?''

Mr. Hughes stopped for a moment, then suggested we open the meeting to discussion with other parents. Eager hands went up all over the room except for the silent group of deaf visitors.

''I don't want my child exposed to these gestures,'' said one woman.

''If some parents have given up, that's their business, but I think we should keep Starr King a pure oral school,'' added a young-looking gray-haired man with glasses.

''My boy is four years old. I'll admit that communication at home isn't always easy. But he *does* lip-read. Someday I'm sure he'll start talking. I think we have to be patient. I'm just glad the teachers and the administration at Starr King are so willing to work with us to teach our kids to talk.'' A slight woman in a blue coat, she went on to praise the school as one of the best she had known.

The deaf visitors watched the woman interpreter change the various comments into signs; they looked first to the parent or teacher who spoke, then back to her rapidly changing hands. More than one person talked about the John Tracy Clinic, the research it had done on deaf kids, and that if sign language worked, surely those people would know about it.

I began to feel that nearly all the opinions weighed against the concerned parents and their request for change. Then a woman in her late thirties got to her feet. Her blond hair fell close against her narrow, attractive face. She waited until recognized, then started hesitantly, ''I'd like to say something about our daughter, Debbie. She's probably older than most of your children. For ten years we have hoped that she would talk, patiently struggling to communicate as best we could. Debbie's almost twelve now. And most of that time we wondered what was wrong, if maybe she was retarded.

''We were told again and again: 'Keep trying. You must have patience. Debbie can lip-read and someday she'll talk.' I'm afraid we *were* patient. Too patient. We waited too many years before we gave up! Thank God for Mr. Wilson, that he taught at Starr King. He has deaf parents and he can sign and he understands deaf children better than anyone else. Last summer he started a class for six of the deaf children here at Starr King, children everyone considered failures. Debbie was one of those failures!'' Her eyes dropped to the floor momentarily; hardly anyone or anything moved in the entire room except for the hands of the interpreter.

"Well, he started a class at Cameron Ranch School using sign language along with speech. What a difference it has made with our daughter! Now my husband and I are learning sign language too, and for the first time we can communicate with Debbie. She can talk to us with her hands. What's more, for the first time she's learning things in school.

"I think these parents have made a very reasonable request. They just want a class at a different school with a teacher who can add signs to speech. These parents want to start *now*, while their children are young. I wish we had started when we first discovered our daughter was deaf.''

When she sat down I could see her husband lean over and whisper something to her. For a long minute no one said anything.

Then Mr. Hughes asked if anyone else wished to speak. A woman in a green pants suit stood up, an angry expression on her face. Her voice cracked with emotion. "We have *two* deaf children.'' She paused, as if to allow the enormity of their problem to sink in. "We lived in a small town in Iowa, where they had almost nothing for handicapped children in the schools. We decided that if our children were to get an education, we would have to move; so we started looking at programs all over the country. We wanted a pure oral program, one where they could learn to speak and lip-read.

"We located some good schools, ones that provided excellent oral classes, but they almost always had classes in signs for the older children who had failed. We knew that if we sent our children to those schools, they would pick up signs from these other children. It could have kept them from ever learning to talk. Finally we settled on Starr King because it had a first-rate oral program. My husband had to quit a good job; we moved to Sacramento; he had to search for another job and take a cut in pay. But it was worth it!

"One of our children has some speech and we manage to communicate. The other one can't say a word yet and maybe will need signs someday. But we feel we must give our one child the chance to become oral, to allow him to live in a hearing world. That's why we came to this school!"

Her voice had become louder and louder as she spoke. "Now, *we* had to give up a lot to put our children in Starr King, to have a pure oral school. If a few parents have decided to have their children learn sign language, that is *their* choice. But why can't they move to another location? Why can't they find a school that already uses signs? I don't think it's right for them to try to change a program that other parents believe in and have made great sacrifices to make it available to their children."

I felt sorry for the woman as she sat down. I kept thinking about her one deaf child who could *not* speak. How would these two deaf brothers communicate with each other?

No one else from the Concerned Parents group had spoken. Couldn't they defend their request to the Board of Education? Why didn't anyone argue for adding sign language to the oral method? The sentiment at the meeting was obviously strongly in favor of the pure oral approach. Although I agreed, I had begun to feel that some of those who defended Starr King's present program overstated the dangers of having one class that used sign language in addition to speech. Then a new hand went up: the deaf man with the hearing aid. Mr. Hughes pointed in his direction, he stood up and faced the audience while still in full view of the other deaf visitors. Everyone watched expectantly.

"I would like to say something," he began in a loud voice that had a noticeable accent. If he had not signed or worn a hearing aid, I would have assumed he was a foreigner. Yet his words came clear and unmistakable. "Some of the things I've been hearing tonight are *ridiculous*!'' He shook his head, looked around the room, and at the same time moved his hands in rhythm with his words.

''You people don't know what you're talking about! I *am* deaf! My hearing aid does *not* help me. I wear it for only one reason: it makes people talk slower and then I can lip-read more of what they say. I would *prefer* to communicate with everyone in signs but, of course, that's not possible. Even though I have speech and can lip-read some people, on my job I always rely on writing to make sure I am understood and that I understand what others say.

''Now, I want to ask all of you one question. Is there anybody here who can't understand me?'' He looked all around the room, slowly moving his eyes from one row to the next. A strange silence hung over the audience, as if transfixed by hearing this man speak. Not a single hand went up.

''Do you know why I can talk? Because I was *not born* deaf! I could hear until I was six years old. Then I went deaf. I didn't have to go through a long period of learning to make each little sound that I could *not* hear. Most of your children will never have that advantage and they will *never* talk as well as I do even if they spend all their life working on it.

''Now, I want to say one other thing. Sign language has not ruined my speech. Before I learned sign language, I had a difficult time understanding what people said. Tonight I followed every word that was spoken because this hearing person interpreted for me in sign language.'' He pointed toward the woman. As he spoke, his hands continued their rapid pace of movements.

''There's been an attack made on sign language tonight. That it's not even a language! I don't think this gentleman who spoke knows anything about sign language. Do you know a single sign? It's a perfectly good language and I've been able to understand everything that was said—not because I lip-read, but because this interpreter has used *sign language* to tell me what's going on. And that young man you referred to who couldn't talk, who could only point and try to make his mother understand what he wanted—

if his parents had known sign language, if he had known sign language, that could never have happened. He was that way *because* of your pure-oralist approach. He had grown up without *any* means of communication!

"If your children knew sign language, they could easily grasp what you or their teachers wanted to communicate. Of course, you would have to learn sign language first. But is that too much to ask of parents with deaf children and professionals who work with the deaf? Most of your children who are deaf will need sign language to help them get an education. And sign language will help their speech too. And it won't put them in the 'deaf ghetto,' wherever that is." He looked in Mr. Hockett's direction, then added, "I don't know where the deaf ghetto is, but if I live in it, that's okay by me. I drive a car, I have a pretty good job, I live in an expensive house. If that's living in the deaf ghetto, then it's the deaf ghetto!" With that, he sat down amid the silent approving expressions from the other deaf visitors.

I was deeply moved. His words rang in my ears: "Your children need sign language." This stranger had lived with deafness. Other parents were talking now, but I heard none of them. I looked down at the copy of the *Volta Review* I had brought to the meeting, folded it up and stuck it in my coat pocket. I no longer knew what to make of the article that criticized Dr. Quigley's research on using both oral and manual approaches. I had seen deaf people signing, talking, participating on an equal basis with the hearing world *because* of sign language, not in spite of it.

I looked around the room at the teachers. They had special training in the education of the deaf, but none were deaf. I looked at the principal. He had talked about Starr King having one of the best programs in the United States, and of the deaf who use manual language ending up in the deaf ghetto, but what, really, did he know of other deaf programs, of deaf ghettos? Not one adult at Lynn's school knew how to communicate with these deaf people in their language. None of them, so far as I knew, were deaf. I thought about Louise and me. We had no deaf friends.

We knew nothing about the day-to-day lives of honest-to-God deaf adults.

What had happened? Why had our lives been so insulated from deaf adults? We had never heard the kind of things this deaf man said. The only deaf adults we knew of we read about in the *Volta Review*. The Oral Deaf Adults. But surely there were thousands and thousands of others who graduated from state residential schools—the ones who had tried to learn to speak and had failed. Had we been fooled into thinking that most deaf people learned to lip-read and speak so well that they became socially invisible, that they somehow melted into the larger hearing world and became one of "us"? Could it be true that 90 percent of the deaf did not develop intelligible speech? The deaf who had come tonight were certainly not Oral Deaf Adults. They lived by the language of signs, even though some could talk.

I knew I had to find out more.

The meeting ended and I made my way through the milling crowd of parents to Barbara Simmons at the front.

"Hi, my name is Tom Spradley." I had waited until she finished signing to one of the deaf visitors. "You might remember me from the discussion group a couple weeks ago?"

"Sure. You have a little girl. In kindergarten, isn't she?"

"Yes. Lynn. She's profoundly deaf." Trying to sound neutral, I went on, "Your comments tonight were quite interesting. You seem to have a whole different slant on deafness and the education of deaf children. It's one I've never read about or heard of before."

"Well, yes. I guess not everyone agrees with it." She smiled and let her eyes sweep over the dispersing crowd of parents who had broken into many small groups, some huddled in serious talk about the discussion that had ended.

"Where can I get more information about the kind of thing you were talking about?"

"Would you like to bring your family and come over to our house next week? You could meet some of our deaf friends. You could learn a lot from them. And I can also give you copies of some current research articles about deaf children and deaf adults.''

Even as I accepted Barbara's invitation, wrote down her address and made my way out of the meeting room, I had second thoughts. Had I given her the *wrong* impression? Did we really want to get involved with this sign-language thing, even to spend the time finding out about it? And who were her "deaf friends"? What would they be like? Would they pressure us to start Lynn using gestures the way they did? Would we become involved in the controversy that had developed at Starr King?

That night when I arrived home Louise and I talked for several hours. I recounted the meeting in detail, describing the deaf visitors, the reactions of Mr. Hughes and several other parents, my impressions of the interpreter, and what the deaf man had said.

"Tom, I think we have to go very carefully." Louise had listened perceptively to my report of the evening. "Lynn may not be making the fast progress we thought she would, but we've got her whole future to think about." Then, in a voice that seemed to drift back to the past, Louise asked in a sad tone, "Do you remember that deaf man in Oklahoma, the one I met in the supermarket?" I nodded, and we both knew instantly each other's thoughts. We had to make sure Lynn's future didn't turn out like that.

It had happened a few weeks before we left Norman. I had driven Louise to the Safeway market a few blocks from our apartment on a scorching day when the humidity left everything damp and sticky.

I waited in the car; Louise had only a few grocery items to pick up. Lynn, always eager to go shopping, went along and climbed into the seat in the market basket. They started down the first aisle together, Lynn pointed to the bright packages and looked for other children, Louise was preoccupied with her list of things to buy.

Without warning, a large man in a threadbare sports coat loomed up in front of her basket, silently blocking the way. He pushed a card in front of Louise; it was pinned to a tiny handmade doll. The card said: "*I am deaf. Would you make a contribution?*" Louise stared at the card, glanced down at Lynn, back at the man, then began searching through her purse. All she could find was her checkbook.

"I'm *really* sorry! I don't have any money! My daughter is deaf too." She spoke slowly, her voice quivering, hoping the man could read her lips. "How did you become deaf?"

Nervously the deaf man shifted from one foot to the other. He looked blankly at Louise through thick glasses. He wore a faded sweat shirt; beads of perspiration stood out on his forehead, wrinkled in confusion. Then he slowly reached into his pocket and took out a dirty pad of paper and a short stubby pencil. He started scribbling something, then handed it to Louise.

"*Deaf me. Chicken pox. Not hear.*"

"*I'm sorry*," Louise scribbled hurriedly. "*My daughter was born deaf. I had German measles.*" She handed the note pad back to the man, who stared at it for several seconds. A woman with a bandana around her head pushed a shopping basket past and looked curiously at the two of them trying to communicate. A smile spread across the man's face, then he began writing again, this time more eagerly: "*I deaf too.*" He pointed at Lynn, then at his ears. "*I go to Sulphur, the state school for deaf.*"

"*I'm sorry. I don't have any money*," Louise had written back, then awkwardly moved off down the aisle as she watched him take this doll and hold it out to another shopper. She finished quickly, went to the express lane and wrote a check for the amount of purchase. As she lifted Lynn out of the basket and started to pick up the bag of groceries, she saw the man shuffling out the door into the parking lot.

I could tell by Louise's hurried walk that something was wrong. She came directly to my window. Fighting back the tears, she spoke in urgent, anxious tones. "Tom, quick! Give me a dollar bill. Quick!" I reached for my wallet. "It's for a deaf man." I handed her the money and opened the door to help Lynn into the back seat. Louise turned and ran across the parking lot to an old Chevrolet, the front bumper missing, the right fender rusted and crumpled. I could see two men sitting in the car. Louise went to the passenger side and pushed the dollar bill inside to the man she had met. "No, you keep the doll, sell it to somebody else," she said when he held it out to her. Then she turned and walked quickly back to the car.

For days after that we talked about this deaf man. Where had he come from? What kind of education had he received at the state school in Sulphur? Already, at three and a half, Lynn seemed to have progressed further than this adult. He confirmed everything we had heard about the state residential schools. He couldn't speak! That bothered us the most. How different from the Oral Deaf Adults we had read about. How different from Carolyn Graves at the Jane Brooks oral school in Chickasha. We felt a deep sadness for this man, and at the same time, a sense of hope for Lynn.

But tonight I had seen another deaf man. I had heard him speak. Yet this man had also used sign language at the same time. It had been deeply unsettling. Perhaps he was a special case. He had lost his hearing at age six, after learning to talk. Perhaps children like Lynn who had been born deaf required more insulation from sign language. We needed more information. More facts.

Several roads fanned out in front of us. All seemed to hold great risks for Lynn. We fell asleep long after midnight, anxious and troubled about the future.

Eighteen

Lynn dashed up the walk ahead of us and had already pushed the doorbell when we reached the porch. I felt uneasy. Louise and I both wondered about the deaf people we would meet tonight. Bruce, always eager to make new friends, looked forward to playing with the Simmons' youngest son, a boy about his age.

"Come in! We've been expecting you!" Barbara Simmons smiled warmly and took our coats. Lynn held on to Louise; we followed Barbara into a small but cozy living room. A faint odor of smoke came from the glowing coals in the fireplace. A Christmas manger scene, complete with hand-carved sheep and donkeys, decorated the mantel above the fireplace.

A man and a woman rose to their feet as we entered; I recognized the man as the deaf person who had spoken out at the PTA meeting.

"I'd like you to meet Jim and Alice Hudson." I stepped forward and held out my hand. Barbara spoke so Jim and Alice could see her lips; at the same time, her hands introduced us in sign language.

"Hello!" Jim's voice was clear, though it had an unmistakable "deaf" quality. "We're glad you all could come tonight."

"And this is Diane, our four-year-old," Barbara said. A dark-haired girl wearing jeans and a light-yellow sweater had just come in from the kitchen. Lynn smiled sheepishly at Diane but held tightly to Louise's hand. Both girls attended preschool sessions at Starr King, but because they were in different classes, they had only seen each other on two or three other occasions.

We met Mike Simmons, a soft-spoken man who smiled almost continuously. I liked him immediately. Barbara and Mike were a few years older than Louise and I. Louise and I sat down on the couch; Jim and Alice went back to their chairs. Jim caught Diane's eye, said something to her in sign language and she came running. He tickled her on the stomach and she dashed back across the room to Lynn.

Barbara excused herself to go to the kitchen for a moment; Mike left with Lynn and Diane to get them started playing in another room. Alone with Jim and Alice I felt uncomfortable, at a loss for words. Without thinking, I reached out and pushed aside a magazine on the coffee table; another magazine caught my attention: *The Deaf American,* large white letters printed against a beige background. November 1969. Beneath the picture of a distinguished-looking man in academic cap and gown were the words "Fourth Gallaudet University President: Dr. Edward Clifton Merrill, Jr."

"That's a magazine published by the deaf," Jim said as he read my expression of interest. "I don't suppose schools like Starr King even know about it. There are a lot of things in there you will never see in the *Volta Review*!" He smiled in a way that left me unsure of what his words implied.

"I really appreciated what you said at the school meeting last week," I said, feeling more relaxed. He and Alice watched my face intently. "I guess I was surprised, just like the other parents, to see a deaf person like yourself using signs when you also have such good speech." Now Jim and Alice looked at each other, then back at me with a puzzled expression. I knew they hadn't understood.

"Next week?" Jim asked and his deaf-sounding voice forcefully reminded me he could not hear. I glanced at Louise, then back at Jim and Alice. Feeling at a complete loss, like the hundreds of times I had tried to make Lynn understand, I tried again, more slowly.

"I - liked - what - you - said - at - the - school - meeting - last - week. I - was - surprised - to - see - a - deaf - person -who - talked - so - well - also - using - signs." I looked directly at Jim as I spoke.

"Oh! The meeting last week!" Alice said in a soft, squeaky voice. She began talking to Jim in sign language, at the same time mouthing the words "the meeting last week." Louise and I watched as Jim broke into a smile of recognition followed by the crackling laughter that had caught everyone's attention at the meeting. "Yes, that was some meeting, wasn't it?"

I still couldn't tell how much he had caught or if Alice had interpreted everything I had said. The tension of partial understanding hung in the air between us, relieved a few seconds later when Barbara Simmons walked back into the room.

"Tom was just talking about the school meeting last week," Jim said to Barbara and gestured simultaneously. "I'm not exactly sure what he said." Jim looked back at me and smiled as if to say, "We're used to having trouble understanding what hearing people say." Just then Lynn and Diane came running through the room pointing and gesturing to each other in their own private language. Mike returned, threw a log on the fire, then pulled up a straight chair and sat down.

"I really appreciated what Jim had to say at the school meeting last week," I repeated, looking this time at Barbara, and instantly her hands went into motion. "I was as surprised as everyone else to see that you, a deaf person, used gestures but you also had good speech." Barbara's fingers flicked off the words, her hands alternating between broad sweeping gestures and tight intricate patterns.

I began to relax; shifting away from Barbara, I spoke directly to Jim, yet I knew my words would only become comprehensible as they came off Barbara's hands. It all happened in a matter of seconds and a broad smile came on Jim's face. "Thanks. I just couldn't let the kinds of things that those other parents were saying about sign language and about deafness get by without saying something. They didn't know a thing about sign language. I guess I'm probably the first deaf person over the age of fifteen that most of them have ever seen!" As Jim spoke to me his rough hands smoothly twisted and turned in delicate patterns so his wife could understand what he said. "I'm sorry I didn't get what you said the first time. I have trouble reading lips. *Signs* make the words crystal-clear.''

The way he said ''signs'' struck me. It was as if, for him, *signs* were like words or sounds. Somehow, actually seeing this deaf person *speak* and *sign* at the same time showed us possibilities we had ruled out. For the first time we saw how important *signs* were to people like Jim and Alice. It *was* another language.

''You've probably been told that Lynn will be able to understand everything that people say to her.'' With a look of sadness Jim shook his head slowly. ''It's not that easy. Alice and I had both learned to speak before we went deaf; once you've heard and spoken English, it's that much easier to lip-read and speak. Lynn will have a difficult time mastering these skills.''

''Lynn is really a good lip reader,'' Louise said. ''She can understand many of the things we say to her, it's just that she can't talk yet, she can't always make herself understood.''

Jim and Alice looked back and forth from Louise to Barbara's hands. It was as if Louise and I were outsiders. Barbara and Mike Simmons could easily communicate with Jim and Alice. They all knew sign language; we watched, but except for their speaking, we could not understand what their hands said. And we couldn't make ourselves understood. I had the curious feeling that *we* were the ones who didn't know how to ''talk.'' We were as ''deaf'' to Jim and Alice's language as they were to ours. In this small group, they were obviously no more handicapped in communicating than Louise and I, perhaps even less. I had always thought that *deafness* was the handicap. Could it be, instead, their minority status? Deaf Americans dominated by a larger hearing society?

''Your daughter will be okay,'' Jim signed and spoke. ''You're worrying too much about her speech. *Communication* is what's important. You shouldn't worry about *how* to communicate. She is never going to get a good education by having to guess every word that comes off a teacher's lips. You can see how hard that is for us. Your daughter really needs *you* to *sign* so she will understand what you're saying.''

I felt uneasy almost defensive. I wanted to change the subject, to have time to think to assimilate what I'd seen and heard. I turned to Barbara and asked about Diane and when she and Mike had decided to start signing.

"Sign language has meant a big difference for us," Barbara began. Then, for the next fifteen minutes, she and Mike told us about their experience. Like us, they had been advised by professionals to provide Diane with a good oral environment. They had started working to teach lip-reading skills and speech. Hours and hours of lessons. Then speech therapy. Preschool classes. By the time Diane was three, they still had almost no communication except for pointing or drawing pictures or using experience books.

"I was at my wit's end," said Barbara, who continued signing for Jim and Alice's benefit. "I talked to various teachers and speech therapists. 'You can never tell,' they kept saying. 'Wait until she's older, she'll be talking.' Finally I went to the pastor of our church, who suggested that I go talk to the minister in another Lutheran church, in downtown Sacramento. They have a minister to the deaf who comes once a month and speaks in sign language to deaf people who live in the community.

"So I drove there the very next Sunday. I went up to the minister after church and told him about Diane. 'We can't communicate at all with her,' I told him. 'Look,' he said to me, 'I don't know anything about educating deaf children, but there are some deaf people here and they don't have any problems communicating. Let me introduce you to them.' And that's when I met Alice!"

She finished signing her last sentence, finger-spelling Alice's name. Alice broke into laughter; we could tell that she and Jim had recalled their early encounter with the Simmonses. We learned how Jim and Alice had begun to teach Mike and Barbara to sign.

"Would you like coffee or tea?" Barbara stood up and started toward the kitchen. Louise and Alice offered to help and the three of them left.

Mike Simmons had sat quietly through much of the conversation. Now he looked at the clock on the wall, and as Diane and Lynn came running through, he caught Diane's eye. She stopped and watched his hands and face intently.

"I think it's time for you to get your pajamas on," he said slowly in much the same way we talked to Lynn—except that he added signs at the same time. Not once did he pantomime taking off clothes or imitate putting on pajamas. At one point he tapped his watch with his fingers, which I thought must mean "time."

"No!" Diane shook her head and sat down on the floor to watch our conversation. Mike and Jim and I talked for a few minutes, then Mike turned back to Diane. "Are you going to get your pajamas on now or not?" he asked, at the same time painting his question in the air. Diane's expression changed to one of deep thought. Then her hands moved alternately up and down in front of her in a quick gesture.

Mike and Jim broke into peals of laughter, first looking at each other, then back at Diane. A surge of isolation swept over me. What had she said? Why were they laughing? Was this how Lynn felt when Bruce and Louise and I laughed over some funny experience recounted at home? I looked at Diane, who smiled demurely, aware that she had been the source of something that made these two grownups laugh. Puzzled, I turned to Mike.

"What did she say?"

" 'Perhaps.' "

I was astonished. Diane had understood her father instantly. Her face had not clouded over with confusion. And her reply! It hardly mattered that it came in *sign* rather than *speech*. "Perhaps!" Her father had asked a simple question, one that implied a command. Disdaining a simple yes or no, she had signed with an ambiguous delaying tactic.

"Maybe!"

"Perhaps!"

"I don't want to tell you right now!"

I could see Lynn sitting on the floor beside Diane. She could barely utter five words. She didn't even have such an abstract concept as "perhaps"! She couldn't have understood the question! Yes, she could read our lips, but mostly objects, concrete things in the here and now. Ball. Shoe. Cow. Train. Bird. Things she had memorized. And specific actions that I had repeated hundreds and hundreds of times. Running. Jumping. Falling down.

"Lynn can go with you to your room and you can play for a few minutes after you get your pajamas on," Mike Simmons signed to Diane, speaking at the same time. Obviously pleased that getting ready for bed didn't mean she could no longer play with Lynn, Diane jumped up, tapped Lynn on the shoulder and signed something that Lynn could not understand, and together they went off to Diane's bedroom. In a few minutes, clad in her pajamas, Diane brought Lynn back into the living room.

The ladies had returned with coffee and chocolate cake. I wanted to interrupt everyone, to say, "Louise, you should have seen Mike and Diane signing! She understood! She signed back!" Instead I sat quietly, sipped my coffee and tried to absorb the implications of what I had seen.

"Your daughter might not talk for a long time," Jim said thoughtfully after everyone had started eating. He laid down his fork so he could sign. "How long are you willing to wait for her to learn to talk? She's almost five now, isn't she? Are you willing to wait until she's seven or eight or ten or even fifteen?"

"Well, Lynn *is* an exceptionally good lip reader," I said. "She can already say a number of words."

"Learning to talk depends on so many things," Barbara said. "Not only *how* deaf a child is, but also the type of hearing loss and whether neurological damage has occurred. Many kids, especially if they have a profound hearing loss, never learn well enough for anybody outside the family to understand them. And often even their families can't understand them."

"Don't forget right now!" Jim said, a sense of urgency pervading his voice. "Can Lynn tell you what happened at school today? Can she say the names of her friends? Can she say her own name? Can she talk with you about the sky? The mountains? Has she ever asked you a question? Does she want to know who made the stars? She *could* talk to you about all these things right now with sign language!"

I nodded weakly. I could not answer. All I could do was ask myself other, more pressing questions: Why hadn't someone asked us these questions before? Why hadn't we asked them of ourselves? Was our concern about Lynn's speech blinding us to something more important—communication? Were we realistic in thinking that without speech at the age of four and a half, Lynn would suddenly start talking at five or six or even ten?

And what if she suddenly did start putting her small vocabulary, the few hundred words she could lip-read, into speech? What kind of communication would it be to go around naming objects and common actions? Or had she actually learned prepositions, articles, conjunctions and tenses that would all flow out in normal sentences when she started to talk? Would she go on struggling to learn one new word at a time, year after year, while normal children used their language to handle concepts, to reason, to debate, to tell humorous stories and to think about their futures? What would this tedious battle for speech do to her mind and personality? What had it already done?

I looked into the fire as the conversation turned to other topics. I thought of that hospital in Eugene, Oregon, when I carried Lynn through the back door, down the hallway to the isolation ward. I thought of her lying there day after day not knowing What was happening. If only we had been able to sign then. Would Lynn have understood as easily as Diane did?

"Is it difficult to learn sign language?" I asked, without addressing my question to anyone in particular. Barbara Simmons had assumed the role of interpreter and quickly signed whenever Louise or I spoke.

"It takes a long time to become proficient," Jim said. "But if you started now while Lynn is young, you'd have plenty of time to learn. And you could learn enough in a few months to communicate with Lynn surprisingly well. Mike and Barbara have only been learning sign language for about a year now."

The conversation shifted to Jim's work as a specifications writer for the State of California. When there was a lull in the talking and signing, I looked at my watch and nodded to Louise. It was getting late. Lynn and Bruce had to go to school in the morning.

"How do you say 'Thank you' in signs?" Louise asked Mike Simmons as I started to get up.

"Like this," he said, demonstrating the movements slowly so we could observe. He touched his chin with his fingers, his hand open and flat. He held them there only for an instant, then moved his hand downward and forward.

"Thank you," we signed in unison to Jim and Alice. They both smiled approvingly. Then they showed us several other words.

"You" seemed logical and easy. The index finger of one hand pointing at another person. "Me"—Alice simply pointed to herself.

We learned words like "I," in which Mike made a fist with only his little finger raised and then held it against his chest.

"Love" became hands crossed at the wrists and held over the heart.

"Name" was more complex. The first two fingers of each hand formed the shape of a gun and then the two fingers of the right hand tapped gently across the side of the first two fingers of the left hand.

It felt strange to move our hands in these new patterns. I had trouble remembering "Thank you" by the time we had tried the third or fourth word. It was a difficult new language!

"Don't worry about Lynn, she'll turn out fine," Jim said, smiling, as Mike went to retrieve our coats. "You have a beautiful daughter. You can really enjoy her now if you start adding signs to your speech." We started for the door, thanking Mike and Barbara for the evening.

Then Alice handed me a large envelope. "Here are some articles that you might like to read, and also a finger-spelling chart if you decide you want to start learning how to spell words on your hands. You're both welcome to visit our sign-language class at the Lutheran church on Oakland Avenue any Tuesday afternoon."

We drove down the dark street in silence. Without speaking, we both knew instinctively that we had come to a crossroad in Lynn's life, in our lives.

"Those people are all right," Louise said simply. "We've never heard things like that from Lynn's teacher. I don't think it would hurt trying signs with Lynn for a few months."

We arrived home, hurried Bruce and Lynn into bed, then sat down in the living room and opened the large brown envelope that Alice Hudson had given us.

"I'm exhausted!" Louise exclaimed, taking the finger-spelling card with printed hand shapes for each letter of the alphabet. "I just don't know what to think about all this. If we do start finger spelling and signing with Lynn, we could have trouble getting her into schools in the future."

"They couldn't keep her out just because she used signs," I said. "And we don't even know for sure if she can learn them. Or how long it will take." We both knew that some children at Starr King had deaf parents who communicated in American Sign Language, but those children were forbidden to use this visual language while at school.

Louise began practicing the alphabet, saying the letters softly to herself, trying to mold her hand into the pictured shapes. I picked up the first article. "The Failure of the Education of the Deaf," by McCay Vernon, Ph.D., a reprint from the *Illinois Association of the Deaf Bulletin*. For the next hour I devoured the information contained in these new articles.

"Does this look right?" Louise interrupted from time to time; I examined the chart, trying to figure out the curious hand position of some letter. And then, as I came across some new fact of idea, I read it to Louise.

"Listen to this! It says here that ninety-five percent of deaf persons in the U.S. marry other deaf persons. And the ones who marry hearing are almost all hard-of-hearing or have become deaf later in life."

"Stop and think, Tom," Louise interrupted me. "How many deaf adults have we ever met besides Carolyn Graves? We've known Lynn was deaf for almost four years and tonight was the *first* time we've really talked with deaf people! And someday Lynn is going to be a deaf adult."

Louise went back to the finger-spelling chart and I continued reading. I was filled with a new sense of discovery. All these years of trying to get Lynn to become like us, and we knew next to nothing about the world which would become hers!

Louise went to check on Lynn, and when she returned I read another paragraph to her.

> Most young people today who are deaf were born with their hearing loss or acquired it early in life before they were old enough to have learned to talk or to use language. Under these circumstances, normal speech cannot be developed. Sometimes intelligible speech can be acquired, but in many cases the prelingually deafened client will not be able to talk in a way that is understandable to employers and the general public. If we will remember the trouble we may have had speaking a foreign language which we could not hear, and if we will then imagine the difficulty we would experience in learning to articulate a foreign language if we could not hear our own voice, it is easy to understand why many capable deaf persons lack the ability to speak intelligibly.

"That makes so much sense!" Louise exclaimed. "We've been pushing Lynn to do the impossible!"

"And this article is loaded with footnotes to research studies that back up what he says." As I read on, it became clear that the hundreds of hours we had spent on the John Tracy Clinic lessons, always hoping that someday we could communicate orally with Lynn, had serious implications we hadn't thought about.

"Vernon, the man who wrote this article, is at the Michael Reese Hospital and Medical Center in Chicago," I told Louise. "Listen to this:

> As a psychologist, most of the mentally ill children and adults I see are those who lack real communication with their parents. In most cases, oralism does not make possible

the kind of communication that is required between parent and child. The reader who wants to verify this has but to go to some classes for older deaf—not hard of hearing—children in schools in or around his neighborhood. Observe the speech, lip-reading skill, and written language of the deaf youth in these schools and you will see that they are grossly inadequate to equip these young deaf persons to discuss such issues as religion, ethics, marriage, sex, a career selection, etc. It is my view that every parent of a deaf child should learn the language of signs and finger spelling as soon as his child's deafness is discovered. Parents should use this communication system along with oral speech from then on or until and if other methods permit fluent communication.

It was after midnight, but I couldn't put down the material we had received. We both felt the excitement of discovery, a new sense of relief, but still a mixture of doubts and even anger. It seemed as if everything we had believed, the things we had worked for, our hopes and dreams for Lynn, had all begun to crumble. Why hadn't we seen these studies earlier? We had never even heard of *The Deaf American*, a national magazine for the deaf, the original source of some of the articles Alice had given us. It appeared that the John Tracy Clinic had told us only one side of the story. Had we simply ignored the evidence because we still wanted so badly for Lynn not to be "deaf"?

"Let me read you one more thing," I said to Louise. "It's from an article called 'Dumb Children,' and it's reprinted from *The New Republic*, August 1969.

There are between half and three-quarters of a million deaf people in the country—deaf in the sense they can't understand ordinary speech, with or without a hearing aid—and the number is increasing. A recent German measles outbreak (rubella) produced about 20,000 deaf babies, now reaching school age.

Deaf children are being taught to read lips and imitate

speech, but this is immensely difficult for children who never have heard sounds. Nevertheless, many teachers of the deaf disparage sign language, though this is the natural way to communicate among the deaf. Consequently, the youngsters by the time they're 12 may have learned only to make a sort of "ba" sound.

The world of the deaf is still very much controlled by the doctrinaire philanthropies, teachers and doctors who swirl around the Alexander Graham Bell Association for the Deaf. The Association was begun by the inventor, who taught his deaf wife how to read lips, and it is devoted to the idea of propagandizing lip reading and imitative speech. The Association has 7,000 members and an impressive board of directors including J. Edgar Hoover and the head of the AT & T. Of the 7,000 members, only 250 are deaf. The Association answers the queries from frustrated parents of deaf children who are asking for help, and it publishes the *Volta Review*, one of the few magazines for the deaf.

The *Volta Review* is a siren song to the parents of the deaf, telling them just what they want to hear: deaf children can live happily in the hearing world if they only learn to read lips and speak. And in many instances, high-powered hearing aids can help them. The pages of the *Review* are chock full of splendid-looking hearing aids. "As they hear... so shall they speak," says a come-on for Jay I. Warren, Inc., hearing aids. A little boy, looking like an astronaut with his headphones and battery pack strapped to his chest, stands before a machine with a delighted look on his face. "Now the thrill of hearing can become a reality for many aurally handicapped children," the ad says.

Two years ago Herbert Kohl, the author, made a study called "Language and Education of the Deaf," for the Center for Urban Education. Kohl observed how sign language really was the common language among the deaf, and how difficult it was to master lip reading. He urged the use of sign language as a first language, and lip reading as a second language. His study sent the Bell Association up the wall. The *Volta Review* attacked him for possessing inferior credentials. The National Association of the Deaf, which backs the simultaneous method, and is at loggerheads with the Bell Association, asked to buy an ad in the *Volta Review* telling where one might get a reprint of the Kohl study. George Fellondorf, executive director of the Association and editor of the *Review*, refused to print the advertisement.

I stopped reading and looked at Louise in disbelief.

"That hardly seems possible!" She slumped down and rested her head against the back of the couch. Running through both of our minds were the dozens and dozens of testimonials we had read in the *Volta Review* about Oral Deaf Adults whom we had never met. Louise shook her head slowly. It was too much to believe that we had been the victims of propaganda. We had made too great an effort to give up now. Maybe a breakthrough waited just around the corner. But what if it didn't? Maybe trying signs for a few months would not ruin Lynn's chances for learning to speak.

"Let's go to bed," I finally said, unable to absorb any more, unable to sort things out in my own mind. "We've got to do a lot more research. We can't believe what anyone tells us anymore. We need to talk with more deaf people."

I lay awake for a long time, staring into the blackness, listening to the clock and thinking about the future. In the midst of all my bewilderment I also felt a new surge of hope, almost excitement about the possibilities for Lynn. We have to take a chance with signs, I thought to myself. I kept seeing a four-year-old deaf girl, a child like Lynn, a girl who could not talk, her hands moving up and down in front of her.

"Perhaps."

I kept hearing Jim Hudson say, "You don't need to worry. You've got a beautiful daughter. She can learn to sign."

Diane's hands had become a voice that could reach across the empty spaces to the hearts and minds of Mom and Dad. If only

Lynn's hands could talk like that. The details of the evening kept repeating themselves over and over in my mind. Sleep would not come. Beside me Louise tossed and turned restlessly. I could see by the luminous dial of the clock on the dresser that it was ten minutes after two.

Finally I turned on the bed light and we sat up. Half asleep, Louise had been trying to form the shapes of the alphabet with her hands. But now they were not just shapes. They were *words*. We silently prayed they would somehow unlock for us Lynn's five years of silence —and unlock for her the secrets of the silent universe we had created.

If only she could learn to sign! We talked of all Lynn's bottled-up feelings, frustrations, ideas, wants and hopes. All the things she had wanted to say but couldn't. We talked about the formality that had crept into our relationship with Lynn, turning us from Mommy and Daddy into teachers of an impossible language that always stayed half concealed inside our mouths.

"Tomorrow." Louise said with a new urgency in her voice. "We must start tomorrow." She reached for the finger-spelling card that she had laid on the bedside table.

"Can you remember any of the signs we learned tonight?" I asked.

"You." Louise pointed to an imaginary person in front of her. I imitated her movement.

"Me." At the same time we said the word aloud and each pointed to ourselves.

"I." Louise made a fist with her right hand, extended her little finger, then held her hand close to her chest. I practiced it after her.

"Love." We could never forget that one. Both fists clenched, crossed wrists over the heart.

We went over each letter in the alphabet, struggling to shape our hands to make them look like the picture. An hour passed. We spelled Lynn's name, forcing the unused muscles to move from one letter to another. Then Bruce's name. Mother. Father. We didn't seem to be able to remember the shape of a letter for more than three or four minutes, then we had to look back at the card. We lost track of time. We tried to remember more signs. We talked again of Jim and Alice, about Diane and Barbara and Mike. We recalled again how quickly Lynn had learned our homemade signs for "all gone" and "come" before she could lip-read a single word. Finally, sometime in the early hours of the morning, we switched off the light. We had turned the page to a new chapter in our lives. Exhausted, we slept fitfully for a few short hours.

Nineteen

"Aaahhhiieeo! Aaahhiieeo!"

I struggled to wake up.

"Aaahhhiieeo!" Lynn tugged at the bedspread, then climbed up on the bed between Louise and me. I rubbed my eyes and looked at the clock. It was ten after seven! We had forgotten to set the alarm.

"Bruce!" I called. "It's late! Are you up?" A muffled sound came from his bedroom down the hall. I turned over and looked at Lynn, snuggled up close to Louise. Lynn's bright eyes and pleased smile told us she felt special at having found us asleep in bed.

Louise sat up sleepily, propped a pillow behind her back and placed Lynn on top of the covers, Lynn's legs straddling hers so that they faced each other.

"I love you," she said slowly to Lynn. Simultaneously Louise's hands glided through the signs we had learned the night before. I had already forgotten them. Right hand in a fist close to her body, little finger extended, then both hands forming tight fists that crossed at the wrists over her heart; she ended by pointing at Lynn with the index finger of her right hand. Without hesitating for an instant, she reached out and pulled Lynn close in a warm embrace.

"I - love - you." Louise signed the words again, saying them at the same time, then held Lynn close for a long time, kissed her, then let her sit back. A puzzled expression came over Lynn's face. Was this a new game that Mommy had invented? What did it mean? She looked at me, then back at Louise. What was she

242

supposed to do? She watched as Louise signed again, followed by a hug and kiss.

We had called and whispered and spoken "I love you" at least a million times during Lynn's short life. She had seen those fleeting words on our lips again and again, but we had not been able to devise a test to see if she understood "love" the way we had done for words like "run" or "ball." Someday she would *say* "I love you." Then we would know she had learned the meaning of those words on our lips. For now the five words she could speak didn't include these three.

I sat up, reached over, pulled Lynn toward me and wrapped my arms around her tiny body in a bear hug. I buried my face in her neck, then kissed her and sat her back on the bedspread.

"I love you," I said while awkwardly making the same signs Louise had used. Now Lynn's quizzical expression grew more vivid; she looked back at Louise, then to me. I hugged her once more, then spoke slowly in both languages.

'I''—my right hand formed a fist, little finger extended, held close against my chest for half a second—"love"—I crossed my wrists in a deliberate action, fists tight, held them for a brief moment over my heart—"you"—I dropped my left hand and pointed at Lynn with the index finger of my right hand.

Lynn, looking both curious and embarrassed, poked me in the stomach and then pulled the bedspread over her face. What were we doing? This *was* a new game. It would take time for her to figure it out. I hugged her again. She then jumped down and ran off to get dressed for school.

"It's going to take time," I said as we got out of bed. "Lets not get our hopes up. Just remember how long it took her to lip-read 'ball.' And it's taken five years just to learn to say five words."

"I know," Louise said. "But we've got to keep trying. One thing we know: all our talking hasn't worked yet." She had pulled on her robe and headed for the kitchen to make breakfast.

"Your bus will be here in just a minute," Louise said to Lynn after a hurried breakfast. She helped her fasten the hearing-aid harness, then walked her to the front door. I picked up the articles we had brought home the night before and put them in my brief-case.

"I - love - you." Louise stooped down to Lynn's level at the door. She signed the simple words as she spoke. Lynn watched, with interest but without understanding. Another hug. A kiss. One more time through the three simple words: "I - love - you." They seemed to come more smoothly now off Louise's hands.

Lynn grinned at me. "I - love - you" I signed from across the room; then she turned and dashed out the door and down the walk just as the bus came. Waiting for the driver to open the door, Lynn looked back at Louise standing in the doorway.

"I - love - you," Louise signed quickly. Lynn could not pos-sibly have seen the words on her lips but the graphic hand move-ments shouted the message. Lynn waved, then climbed aboard the bus.

I left for school filled with a sense of excitement. A new adventure had begun. Take it slow, I kept saying to myself. It may take months and months before Lynn understands what you're doing. Remember, you haven't gestured to her for several years.

All morning Louise worked on finger spelling. Shortly after three o'clock the yellow bus arrived. "I - love - you" Louise signed from the doorway as Lynn stepped off the bus and raced up the walk into her arms. After a long hug Louise signed again, "I love you." Then they went into the kitchen together to bake cookies.

I arrived home at four-thirty. I found Lynn in her bedroom working on a green Christmas tree in a coloring book.

"I - love - you," I said, signing the words, which seemed more natural now. I knelt down beside her on the floor and gave her a warm hug and kiss. She seemed to pay no more attention to my hands than she had to those same words on my lips for the past few years.

"What are you and Mom doing?" Bruce asked a few minutes later. He had noticed our gestures.

"We're going to try sign language with Lynn," I said. "We think it might help her communicate. We'll all have to learn it."

At dinner that night we signed a simple prayer, the only thing we could say with our limited vocabulary:

"Thank you - food." We said the words in unison. While Bruce copied our signs Lynn watched as our three hands moved from our chins, down to the table, then we brought the fingers of our right hands, tightly held together, up in front of our mouths for "food." Lynn smiled in amusement but made no attempt to copy what we had done.

Both Bruce and Lynn went to bed at eight o'clock that night; they had been up late the night before. We were tired and planned to go to bed early ourselves. I sat down on Bruce's bed after he had brushed his teeth and crawled in. Louise went in to get Lynn settled for the night.

"How deep can you go in the ocean with a scuba tank?" Bruce asked me.

"I don't know. I think about a hundred feet. The pressure gets pretty bad after that."

"Well, how do they explore the bottom of the ocean when it's a mile deep?"

I started to explain.

"Tom! Bruce! Come quick!"

Bruce threw back the covers. I jumped up. In an instant we were in Lynn's room.

"Watch!" Louise said, tears streaming down her face. "She said it two times!" Lynn, legs crossed in front of her, sat at the head of her bed. Louise, sitting on the edge, turned back to Lynn.

"I - love - you," her voice came through the tears as she signed. She hugged Lynn, then sat back and waited.

Lynn, beaming, held up two tiny fists, crossed them tightly against her heart, then pointed knowingly at Louise. Without hesitating, she reached out and hugged Louise tightly. The room blurred; fighting back tears, I picked up Lynn, pulled her close in a long embrace, then set her back on the edge of her bed.

"I - love - you," I signed slowly, my voice quivering as I spoke. I dropped my hands and waited.

"Love you," Lynn signed clearly, confidently, then reached out to hug me. I looked at Louise. There were tears in our eyes.

Bruce hugged his little sister. "I love you," he signed perfectly, a broad smile on his face.

"Love you," Lynn signed back, this time in a more definite exaggerated rhythm.

She had found her voice!

A few minutes later in the kitchen Louise spoke first, trying to control the excitement in her voice. "Tom, it's working! I can hardly believe it."

"And it seems so easy for her," I said.

For several hours we talked about sign language, about lip reading, about the hours and hours we had spent trying to help Lynn use her residual hearing. We reread the articles Alice had given us. We practiced the few signs we knew. We memorized the finger-spelling alphabet. "L-y-n-n." "B-r-u-c-e." We each spelled their names, checking the shape of our hands against the pictures. Long after midnight we went to bed, tired but filled with an exhilarating sense of hope.

"We'd best go slow and not push her," I said to Louise just before we fell asleep. "Let's not forget what happened when her voice improved so fast by feeling our chest vibrations."

"Yes, but I think this will be different."

At breakfast the next morning Lynn watched as we signed "Thank you - food." Bruce joined in and we tried to treat it casually. More than once we each said to Lynn "I love you," using our voices and hands simultaneously. "Love you," she signed back, her eyes twinkling with understanding.

"What are some other signs?" Bruce asked us after breakfast. We showed him how to sign "mother" and "father." His eyes grew wide with possibilities when Louise showed him the finger-spelling card.

"Can I take this to school with me?" he asked. By dinner that evening he had mastered the alphabet.

"How shall we sign 'Bruce' and 'Lynn'?" Louise asked after we had signed our prayer and started to eat.

"I know a good one for me," Bruce exclaimed. Jim and Alice had explained how the deaf use special combinations of hand shapes, positions and movements to create their own unique sign names. "Like this." With his hand flat, thumb curled in against the palm, he formed the letter "b," then tapped it against the side of his head in the same position used for "father."

"That's great!" I said.

"Bruce." Louise tapped the side of her head and said his name at the same time. With her other hand she pointed to Bruce so Lynn saw what she meant. I repeated it, Lynn watching with a curious expression on her face.

"L-y-n-n." I finger-spelled her name. We decided not to create a sign-name yet; she had learned to print those letters and we wanted her to connect the two.

"L-y-n-n." Louise pointed at Lynn as soon as the last letter came off her fingers. Bruce took his turn, then repeated his own name and pointed at himself. Lynn grinned at our strange antics, as if she liked these new hand games. She made no attempt to imitate us.

At dinner the next evening we reviewed our family names. "Mother," I signed. Then I looked directly at Bruce with a questioning expression as I pointed to one person after another. Bruce caught on instantly.

"Mother," he signed and pointed to Louise.

"L-y-n-n." I looked at Bruce again. He pointed quickly to Lynn, then finger-spelled her name. Lynn's curiosity changed now to intense interest; she watched our every move.

"Bruce." I looked at Bruce, but before my hand had left my face Lynn cried out.

"Aaahhhiiieeeeooo!" She strained forward in her chair, pointing again and again to her brother.

"Yes! Yes! That's right!" Louise and I joined her and pointed to Bruce. We tapped the B-shaped hand at the side of our heads again. Lynn continued pointing at Bruce, then tapped the side of her head with her open hand and said, "Bruuu." We all clapped and laughed.

"That's incredible!" I looked at Louise. "We've only been using sign language for three days and she's already catching on. She said Bruce's name in signs and speech at the same time!" I pushed my empty plate forward and leaned on the table. I had the strange feeling that we were watching the birth of Lynn's native language.

"Father," Louise signed, now looking at Lynn with a question on her face. Delighted to be included, unaware that each word she spoke with her hands held out enormous hope for us, Lynn responded instantly.

"Father," she signed, then pointed directly at me.

"Mother," I signed. She read it, signed and pointed at Louise.

"L-y-n-n." It took an instant for her to recognize her name, then she laughed out loud. Dramatically, with great pride, her hand flew out and her index finger jabbed against her chest. At last, she knew her own name.

Of all the injuries that oralism had inflicted on Lynn, the most insidious had been to rob her of a name. We had unwittingly told her, "You are not a person until you can see 'Lynn' on our lips, until you can say 'Lynn' with your voice. We will accept no substitutes." Lacking a name and a language to give it life, she could not say, "I *am* someone. I am *Lynn*." Without an accepted symbol for herself, her capacity for self-awareness and self-control had failed to take root and grow. She could not experience that universal feeling that says, "I can control the things around me by learning their names."

At breakfast the next morning we began with our simple prayer. "Thank you - food."

As if she had waited too long to join us, Lynn's hand followed the rest of us. She touched her chin with the tips of her fingers, then moved them gracefully through the rest of the phrase. She had watched us speak those words more than a thousand times in the last three years. We had signed them fewer than ten times in three days.

248

Although we continued signing at every opportunity during the day, it seemed that mealtimes quickly became the opportunity for Lynn to learn new words. That night at dinner I signed the word for "name." Two fingers extended on each hand, then a quick tapping motion of the right fingers across the edge of the left ones.

"Name?" I pointed at Bruce, raised my eyebrows and looked around for someone to sign.

"Bruce," Louise signed.

"Name?" I pointed to myself.

"Father," Bruce answered, speaking and signing at the same time.

"Name?" Louise asked this time, pointing to Lynn, whose bright hazel eyes seemed filled with understanding.

"L-y-n-n," I finger-spelled as everyone watched.

"Name?" I asked, pointing to Louise. Then we all looked questioningly at Lynn.

"Mother." Her tiny hand spread out fanlike, thumb resting on her chin.

"Name?" I signed, pointing this time to Lynn's glass of milk. I squeezed each hand alternately as though milking a cow. I pointed again and Bruce answered with his hands.

"Name?" I asked, pointing again to Lynn's milk.

"Milk." She squeezed the air with both hands in alternating movements.

Louise brought in a plate of cookies for dessert and we all practiced the sign, cutting an imaginary cookie in the palm of our left hands. Lynn followed, growing more animated. She shifted to a kneeling position in her chair, her eyes darting from Bruce to Louise to me so as not to miss a single word. Then suddenly she shifted from answering our questions to asking her own.

"Name? Name? Name?" She tapped her two fingers from each hand together repeatedly, then pointed to the salt shaker. None of us could mistake what she wanted to know but none of us could answer. In the whole world there was nothing else we could name! Slowly I finger-spelled s-a-l-t, but Lynn made no attempt to copy me.

"Name? Name? Name?" Her hands moved up and down more insistently, her eyebrows raised slightly higher. She pointed at her plate.

"How do we tell her we don't know?" I asked Louise and Bruce, feeling more helpless than ever.

"Name? Name? Name?" Lynn held up her spoon.

"Mother. Father. Bruce. L-y-n-n. Cookie. Milk. Food." I signed all the things I had names for, pointing as I went. Finally I pointed to the plate and the spoon, shrugged my shoulders and shook my head.

"We've got to learn more signs!" Louise exclaimed. She really wants to know!"

"Name? Name? Name?" Lynn had finally tasted the forbidden fruit of sign language and with it came the realization that the infinite variety of things in her world had *names*. Not just fleeting, half-hidden motions of tongue and lips. At last she had discovered that objects had names she could capture, control, understand and *sign*.

"I love you." "Thank you— food." "L-y-n-n." "Bruce." "Mother." "Father." "Cookie." "Milk." "Name."

Thirteen words in less than a week. Almost three times as many as she had learned to speak in five years. We were totally unprepared for the speed with which Lynn now began to use signs spontaneously. The very next day the bus dropped Lynn off after school; she ran up the driveway and burst through the front door. She beamed with ideas as she found Louise.

One week later the three of them came home from their first class in this new language.

"Cookie!" With lightning speed she twisted her right hand repeatedly in the palm of her left.

"Milk!" Both tiny hands pumped vigorously up and down in the familiar milking motions.

"Cookie! Milk!" She fairly shouted again.

Louise watched in disbelief. She didn't have to guess what

Lynn wanted. She didn't need to point or plead. She didn't have to search through cupboards and drawers. She didn't have to run through the house holding up first one thing, then another. She didn't have to struggle to interpret garbled sounds. Lynn's hands spoke with unmistakable clarity.

"Where cookie?" Louise asked, looking around the kitchen as she signed "where" so Lynn would understand this new word that Louise had recalled seeing Alice sign. Lynn pointed to the cupboard; Louise set the tin of cookies on the table.

"Where milk?" she signed. Lynn laughed, obviously delighted with her new ability to understand Mommy's questions so easily.

"Aaahhheeeiiee!" she cried and ran to the refrigerator, then stopped, spun around and signed "milk" before opening it.

When I came home from school that afternoon Louise was ecstatic. The thrill of finally *talking* with Lynn. To someone who had never experienced the barrier of silence, to someone who had never watched the simplest everyday situations turn into tantrums, to someone who had never known how a four-year-old's wants could become major obstacles to human contact, asking for cookies and milk might seem a trivial improvement in communication. But we knew differently.

Teachers, speech therapists, audiologists and principals could ignore the need for communication. They didn't crawl out of bed every morning to a deaf daughter or son. At three o'clock they closed up shop and went home. They never were awakened in the dead of night, longing to know what their child wanted but unable to find out.

When a deaf child struggles week after week to form an "m" sound, then reverts to "smmmk," professionals can blame it on some inherent weakness in deaf children. When a deaf child finally masters her brother's name, "Bruuu," but then for months and months doesn't say anything else, professionals can counsel patience, they can tell you, "Your daughter is *withholding* speech." They can ask you to lower your expectations; "someday the words will come pouring out."

But now the words came in a flood from Lynn's hands instead of her mouth. But that didn't matter any longer.

"She talked!" Louise said. "She asked me questions! She answered me! Tom, she's learning so fast I don't know what we're going to do."

"Why don't you take Bruce and Lynn and go to the Tuesday sign class at the Lutheran church?" I suggested.

One week later the three of them came home from their first class in this new language.

"I don't know if I'll ever go back!" Louise looked discouraged. "I can't remember any of the signs. I'm the only one in the class who doesn't know *anything*. The teacher's totally deaf and can't talk. He showed us a sign and when I tried to make it, it came out backwards! We all had to sign the words of a sentence in front of the others and my hands just froze. It all went so fast I don't think I can remember any of the signs we learned."

"I remember them!" Bruce interrupted. He had learned many of the same words in a separate class.

" 'Butter' is like this." He made a spreading movement with two fingers on the open palm of his left hand.

" 'Bread.' " His right hand made two quick cutting gestures across the back of his left hand. Louise and I watched and copied while Bruce rattled off ten more signs. Later that evening we practiced, asking Bruce to show us again, to tell us if we were getting it right.

Several weeks later I joined Louise and the small group of parents in the sign-language class.

"T-o-m, my h-u-s-b-a-n-d," Louise introduced me to Ernie, a young man with brown hair and a broad, friendly smile. He said something to me with his hands that I could not understand.

"He heard that you teach at a college and wants to know what subject," another member of the class said.

"M-a-t-h," I finger-spelled, feeling all thumbs.

Ernie looked pleased and signed, "Now you must become a student again!"

The class was conducted in silence. Ernie pointed to a list of words he had printed on a sheet of poster paper.

"Dream." He made the sign slowly. We followed in unison. Louise tried to jot down a description to help us later at home.

"Here." Another gesture.

"Tomorrow." Ernie's thumb came up to his cheek, then moved forward and down. On and on we went, repeating old words, learning new ones, becoming confused, hoping we could remember.

Later that night we reviewed the words, watched Bruce show us ones we had forgotten, and said the words over and over again as we practiced the signs.

"Should our hands be vertical or horizontal?" I asked Louise, trying to recall Ernie's hands.

"I don't know," she answered.

"On this sign, did our fingers point up or down or backwards?" Neither of us could remember. We found ourselves struggling to remember positions, movements, shapes, none of which had been named. The details slipped away; we had no mental pigeonholes to place these new images.

"If sign language is so difficult for us," Louise said after an hour of practice, "think what lip reading and speech are like for Lynn. She has to learn where to place her tongue, her teeth and her lips. She has to remember how to shape her mouth and when to vibrate her vocal cords. And then she has to coordinate all these things with just the right amount of breath."

"And she can only see a tiny bit of all that," I added. "We can at least see how our hands move and where to place them."

As the weeks passed and we raced to keep up with Lynn's desire for more signs, we slowly crawled out of our hearing world and tried to imagine what the universe we had created looked like to Lynn. We had placed the entire responsibility for successful communication on the shoulders of a three-year-old. The one member of our family with the least ability to accept such a responsibility. The schools had done the same. Oh, yes, we had believed that our task was the difficult one, that we had sacrificed. How painstakingly we had worked to provide Lynn with a "pure oral environment." We even felt sorry for ourselves, for all the effort and sacrifice demanded of us.

But oralism, instead of asking us to sacrifice and work for Lynn, actually demanded that Lynn sacrifice and work for us. We had told her, "You must become like the hearing." Like a preamble to her whole life, we might well have engraved the words in stone that our actions spoke during those first years: WE FORBID YOU TO LEARN YOUR NATIVE LANGUAGE.

We had unwittingly prohibited Lynn from learning *her* native language because it was so different from *our* native language. Lynn had quickly copied our natural gestures at only one year of age. She had even invented her own signs and then used them to communicate, to tell us what she wanted, what she needed, even to tease and play. "All gone," "come," "up," "hot," "no." She had smiled brightly, her eyes gleaming when she used these signs; she seemed to say, "I'm alive, I'm normal, only my language is different. But look how easily I can learn it and how I enjoy using it!" But we hadn't heard. Instead we started courses and went to clinics and listened to professionals; by our actions we had said, "You are not to communicate effortlessly like all those deaf people who have escaped from the control of hearing parents and teachers. You must give up your childhood. You must sacrifice your early education. You must experience terrible frustrations. You must live incommunicado for five or ten or maybe fifteen years. *You must become normal!*"

Normal. That word had haunted us from the moment we learned of Lynn's deafness. "You want your child to be normal, don't you?" It had driven us to talk, talk, talk. Now we began to ask a different question.

"What is normal?" From Lynn's perspective, nothing had been normal. Least of all the kind of communication skills we had expected her to learn. *A deaf child's idea of normal cannot possibly coincide with a hearing parent's idea of normal.*

By denying her deafness and treating her as if she were normal, we actually made her feel different. Even in the most ordinary family activities, by talking as if she could hear when she could not, we created for her the profound feeling that she was on the outside, a stranger to what was going on. Only after we began to sign regularly did we realize how the pretense of normality had appeared to Lynn. For the first time in her life she did not merely sit at the table watching our mysterious lips, seeing us laugh and smile for unknown reasons. She began to share the day's activities.

"What you play school?" I asked one evening, using the best English I could with my small vocabulary. It was several months since Lynn had begun to sign.

"Swing. Ball. Story."

Each of us learned to sign whenever we spoke and Lynn "listened" raptly, her eyes on the rest of us. That evening we had sat down to eat without Bruce; we did not know why he was late. Soon he came in looking guilty, mud all over his pants and shoes.

"Bruce," I exclaimed without signing, "where have you been? Why are you so late?"

"Eeeeaahhhhiieeooo!" Lynn screamed before Bruce could answer, and began signing with sharp, demanding movements.

"What talk about? What talk about?"

I suddenly realized how she felt, how she must have felt for years when we talked. "Bruce dirty. Shoes dirty. What happened?" I signed quickly to Lynn, and her questioning look immediately faded. From that time on, Lynn seldom allowed anyone to speak without signing. If she saw someone talking on the telephone, she immediately demanded, "What talk about? What talk about?" One teacher at Starr King had advised us, "Deaf children must learn that they cannot always expect to know what other people are talking about." Lynn refused to learn this! She had been left out for too long.

In April, Lynn blew out five candles on her cake and our hands sang "Happy Birthday" to her. For the first time she understood the words. Although her native sign-language ability was only approaching that of a two-year-old, she had showed remarkable progress in a few short months. It all happened so quickly and we were so filled with the excitement of learning a new language together that we hardly thought about Starr King and Lynn's days at school.

"Are you signing to Lynn at home?" Lynn's teacher asked a few weeks after Lynn's birthday.

"Yes," Louise said matter-of-factly. We saw no need to hide it.

"Well! I won't stand for it in *my* class!" She bristled with scorn, angry and hurt at this indication that we had departed from the oralist faith.

We ignored the issue for several weeks. Only a few children at Starr King were learning to sign and we didn't think Lynn would sign at school. On a recent visit to Lynn's class we noticed a curious thing: a kind of homemade sign language had developed without anyone being aware of it. But somehow this slipshod use of gestures did not carry the same stigma as the systematic use of a sign language that belonged to the deaf. The teacher was preparing the children for recess.

"Now it's time to go out and play," she said. Blank faces looked at her.

"It's time to go out and play," she said again, but this time she stood up and pointed toward the door. The children quickly grasped the meaning of this oft-repeated gesture and started to get up, watching the teacher at the same time.

"Wait at the door until I dismiss you," she said. Simultaneously, without realizing it, her hand opened and the palm turned outward in a gesture for "stop." Heads nodded and the children made their way to the door.

"Where is your jacket, Eric?" the teacher asked. Eric's face tightened and his brow lowered.

"Coat. Coat." The teacher spoke slowly, emphasizing the word. Eric watched her lips but his look of consternation remained.

"Where is your coat?" She repeated, but now her palm turned upward in a homemade gesture she unwittingly used whenever she asked "where?" Understanding flashed across Eric's face and he pointed at his coat hanging nearby.

"Well, go and put it on," the teacher said and pointed to his jacket. All smiles, he raced to the coat rack and pulled his jacket from the hook.

We watched as the children lined up at the door, impatient to race to the playground. One boy, tall and muscular for his age, worked his way forward and took over the lead position at the door. Two smaller boys were jockeying for the second position in line when the leader touched his own shoulder, then pointed to one of the two boys, who returned the gesture. They repeated the gesture two or three times in rapid succession. "You and I are friends; we'll stick together," they seemed to say. The other boy retreated to the end of the line. But as he went, he returned and flicked his finger as though shooting a paper spit wad toward the two boys at the front of the line. We knew this sign from our classes; it meant "I hate you." The two boys at the front of the line flicked their fingers back, then they touched their own shoulders and pointed to each other. The entire exchange lasted only a few seconds.

"I don't know why they touch their shoulders like that," the teacher said to us as she opened the door for the children to go out. "It couldn't mean anything. They just like to mimic each other."

We didn't think anyone would notice if Lynn signed in school, but one afternoon the phone rang; it was Mrs. Blanchard, the mother of a boy in Lynn's class who was also learning signs.

"I visited school today and I thought you should know what is going on. Lynn was punished for using a few signs in class."

We felt angry, but helpless. The children had watched the teacher tell the story of "The Three Bears." With stuffed animals and a doll to illustrate the tale, they seemed to follow.

"Eric, where is Baby Bear?" the teacher asked. Eric sat in confused silence.

"Lynn, where is Mama Bear?" Lynn looked around but did not point or otherwise answer.

"Can someone show me Papa Bear?" Again, questioning looks, silence. It had not occurred to the teacher that those three words—baby, mama, papa—all appeared identical on her lips. Then Lynn jumped to her feet, pointing to the middle-sized bear.

"Mama Bear!" she had signed excitedly. The teacher scolded her and made her sit on her hands during the whole next lesson.

Louise and I discussed this new situation that night. From our deaf friends we had heard stories of such punishment for using signs. "They would never do anything like that at Starr King," we had said confidently. We couldn't allow Lynn to endure this kind of treatment. From the oralist point of view, it made sense. All the time spent on talk, talk, talk about daily activities, the auditory-training games, the rhythm excercises, the restrictions on using gestures—it was all part of the necessary struggle to help deaf children become "normal."

But for us, the path to success now began to look like failure. We visited the high school deaf program where a sixteen-year-old boy from our oral school could not say or write his own name. A teacher confided that this boy, she felt sure, was retarded. No one had tried to break into his world of silence with signs. We saw another deaf high school student, a girl who struggled successfully among hearing peers. She had gone through the oral program but she also learned signs. Her deaf parents had communicated with her in Sign from the start. We wondered why the school did not provide an interpreter so she wouldn't have to guess at what went on in her classes.

Soon we discovered that signs dramatically improved Lynn's lip-reading ability. Within a few days after finger-spelling her own name, she could lip-read the minuscule movement of our tongue when we said "Lynn" without finger-spelling. She would learn a new sign, then with a little practice she could lip-read it, and soon mouthed these new words and even attempted to speak them. While the benefits of signing and speaking at the same time were now obvious to us, we realized that her teacher's attitude toward signing would make it uncomfortable for Lynn to stay at Starr King. We would have to find some other alternative.

But what choices did we have? Locate another school? Not in Sacramento. Everything went by the oral system. Send Lynn away to the state residential school? She wasn't old enough for us to consider that, and even at the residential school the lower grades were taught by the oral method. Move to a new community? I knew only two schools in the entire state of California that used signs in elementary school classrooms. We knew of some states where laws actually forbid the teaching of sign language to deaf children in public schools. I did not want to uproot the family, try to find a new job, go through all the adjustments of a move.

But there were other questions. What about Lynn's deaf friends at Starr King? Some, like children in Oklahoma and Covina schools who had been paraded before us as an example of successful oralism, were only hard-of-hearing. Without the profound loss that rubella had given Lynn, these children could benefit more from hearing aids. They would learn to communicate orally, even though many would miss out forever on the subtleties of spoken English.

But many of the children at Starr King had severe and profound hearing losses. Of these, 80 to 90 percent would probably never communicate adequately if limited to speech and lip reading. Like Lynn, they would only hear gross, distorted sounds, even with the best hearing aids.

With the other parents who had begun to learn sign language we requested a summer school class using sign language and the addition of a class using signs in the fall. Slowly the sign barrier in our school district began to crumble.

It must have seemed incredible to Lynn that summer as she went off to school with five or six other children. For the first time she had a teacher who actually signed! Slowly the world of adults who had only moved their mouths was changing for her. By the end of the first week she could finger-spell the names of all her classmates. Each day she gave us a report of her day at school.

"Chuck sick," she said, "stay home."

"Eric vacation."

"Ice cream tomorrow."

And that fall she joined five other children at another school in a class that used sign language and speech. Total communication in the San Juan Unified School District had its first kindergarten class, carefully separated so as not to contaminate the pure oral environment of Starr King.

From Starr King Exceptional School, from the John Tracy Clinic, from speech therapists, from the *Volta Review* and from professionals of all kinds, we had received a single, unequivocal message: LANGUAGE IS EQUIVALENT TO SPEECH. When Lynn began signing we realized that language could *not* be equated with speech. Language resides deep within the mind; it is the rules and symbols for creating sentences, giving life to ideas. Language finds expression in *speech*; it also can find expression in *sign*.

Lynn was fast becoming bilingual, but not by a rote memory approach. Instead of imitating adults, children learn their native language by a spontaneous process. They listen or watch native speakers or signers. Then they form their own *child grammar* for speaking, saying things that often sound strange to adults. Slowly they modify this early grammar until their speech, or their signs, conform more and more closely to the rules; they can then interpret new sentences seen or heard for the first time.

At first we tried to teach Lynn signs in the same way we had attempted to teach her lip reading and speech. Memorization. Show her a sign. Ask a question. See if she remembered. But now Lynn began having trouble *imitating* our two- and three-word sign sentences. Instead of repeating the obvious string of signs we had used, she would literally play with dozens of variations.

"Thank you for the food." We signed the simple prayer at each meal.

"Thank food," Lynn signed. "Food for thank." "Thank you the for." "Food, thank you."

"Why doesn't she follow our example?" one of us would ask. We worried that something might be wrong, that she couldn't seem to put words together in the sentence order of English. Unknown to us, she *was* following our signing examples, in the way all children learn language.

Slowly we grew less formal in our instructions. We simply signed at every opportunity. Then we noticed Lynn's phrases began to grow, to take on order.

"Thank you for the food."

"Thank you for the milk."

"Thank you for the meat."

One day late in the fall we sat down to eat and she looked up with a grin. "Thank you for my food and for my school." The words fell off her fingers with a confident rhythmic smoothness. Nine words! A sentence we had not seen before. A sentence we had never taught her. Spontaneously. For ten months we had haltingly and brokenly used the natural language of the deaf in our home. From these fragment examples Lynn had discovered the grammar we knew. She had begun to make Sign her own language.

In the weeks and months after Lynn began to sign, we noticed that our acceptance of her went through stages. The first step had been to give up the oralist dream of making her like us. Next, we began to help her to acquire her native language. It meant we had to learn Lynn's language ourselves. The difficult but enjoyable task of learning Sign had been a new level of acceptance. It seemed to tell Lynn, "We no longer feel your deafness is bad."

But accepting Lynn meant more than communicating in her language, more than hoping that someday she might learn ours and become bilingual. It meant a personal involvement in that world which would surely become hers in the future—the world of deaf people. We couldn't have taken that step without Bill and Bunny White. They took us by the hand and led us slowly but surely into the world of the deaf. We would always feel like outsiders in that world, where Lynn, our own daughter, would always be an insider. But Bill and Bunny helped us build a bridge of understanding that so often separates hearing parents from their deaf children.

I first met Bill and Bunny White in December of 1970 when I wanted to telephone a deaf couple in Oakland whom we had met during the previous summer. We wanted to invite them and their two deaf children to a Christmas party. I knew they had a TTY—the teletypewriter/telephones used by a relatively few deaf people—and the TTY nearest our house was the one owned by Bill and Bunny White.

We had wondered why other deaf people did not have TTYs. It turns out that few are available. They come by donation from Western Union, telephone companies and other organizations, but it still requires several hundred dollars' investment to install and convert them to residential usage. And even with a TTY, a deaf person can only phone another deaf person who happens to have a TTY. Who else can be phoned? Not the fire department. Not the police station. Not the hospital. Not a mechanic or drugstore. Not even the telephone company. The telephone, a spinoff from Alexander Graham Bell's attempt to amplify sound for the benefit of the deaf, had up until now forced the deaf into even more isolation. Bill White used his TTY to keep in touch with the other officers of the California Association of the Deaf throughout the state.

I drove over to his house on a cold Sunday afternoon. I knocked at the door and waited, wondering what I would sign. "Hi. My name is Tom Spradley. I came to see if I might make a phone call on your TTY." The signs came awkwardly, but I managed to explain my situation.

Bill, a gracious individual in his early fifties, smiled and spoke in a clear, easily understood voice. "Sure! Come in." His speech surprised me. Later we discovered that both Bunny and Bill had been deafened by meningitis as young teen-agers, long after learning to speak. They sounded so similar to hearing speakers that one might suspect they were not deaf. They both signed constantly as they spoke to each other. For half an hour before I made the phone call they plied me with questions. How long had I been signing? Who was my teacher? Was my daughter born deaf? Where did I learn that sign? Did my daughter understand it?

I made my phone call, typing out the message on the tele-typewriter, waited for the answer to come back, then went home to tell Louise about the Whites. "We'd like to meet your daughter sometime," Bunny had said when I left.

In the weeks that followed, our friendship with Bill and Bunny grew. I remember the first time we introduced Lynn to the Whites. She watched our signs, then looked inquisitive, at the same time not completely sure of these strangers. We said nothing about their deafness. They smiled and Lynn took a step toward Bunny White.

"I'm deaf too." Bunny did not sign the individual words but used the idiom of Sign. The index finger of her left hand touched her ear, then the corner of her mouth in the sign for "deaf." At the same time her right hand, in the shape of a Y, moved back and forth between her and Lynn; she held the expression "same as me" and the sign for "deaf" in the air for several seconds. Her warm smile seemed to say, "And there is nothing wrong with being deaf!" A look of disbelief spread over Lynn's face. She turned to Louise with large, questioning eyes.

"Deaf like *me*?" she signed, her right index finger thrust with extra force against her chest. Louise smiled and nodded.

"Deaf too?" Lynn pointed quizzically at Bill White, then looked back at Bunny, who answered her question.

"Yes," she signed, and we all laughed. "He became deaf when he was a few years older than Bruce."

From that moment on, Lynn seemed drawn by a powerful magnet to Bill and Bunny. If they came by unexpectedly, Lynn would drop everything to shower them with questions and recount what she had done at school. She hung on their every sign, picking up new expressions on each visit. Her face would shine with a new radiance, and the look in her eyes seemed to shout the discovery which never grew old: "Deaf like me! Deaf like me!"

"Deaf" was another word that oralism had concealed from

Lynn. "Don't tell her she is deaf. Don't treat her like a deaf person, or she will begin to act deaf." How often we had heard those instructions or read them in the *Volta Review*. But once sign communication began to flow between us, we decided to end our secrecy. At first we simply used the sign for "deaf" casually. Lynn picked it up, then slowly, as the difference between hearing and deaf dawned, she bombarded us with questions. "Why am I deaf?" "Is Bruce deaf?" "When I grow up, will I hear like you and Daddy?" Sometimes she became angry, stamping her feet and signing with deep emotion, "I don't want to be deaf! I want to hear!"

We answered her openly, explaining in signs: "You are deaf. No one can change that. But we love you. It's okay to be deaf."

We knew that Lynn would need more than our words and love. At first we found it painful to admit that we could not give Lynn all she needed to live in a hearing world. She needed the example of people like herself who had faced the same problems she would and solved them. Even at the age of six, Lynn had begun to see the world from the distinct perspective of her deafness. We could not entirely share that perspective. Bill and Bunny and other deaf friends could. Slowly we accepted the fact that only deaf people could provide some things Lynn would need, helping her through some of the important stages of childhood, pointing the way to a meaningful life.

Bunny and Bill had met while students at Gallaudet University. They married, and before finishing college, Bill had entered the printing profession. In their own family, Bill and Bunny had experienced the opposite of what we had known. While they were profoundly deaf themselves, their children grew up with perfect hearing. All of the children began to speak before they were a year old, but their first words had come from their fingers as well as their lips. They became bilingual, fluent in Sign and speech. At the age of fifty, Bill was completing a long-delayed B.A. degree in psychology at California State University, Sacramento.

One rainy February night two months before her sixth birthday, a little more than one year after her birth of natural language,

Lynn took a last gulp of milk, then caught my attention with a scream and a wave of her hand that said, "Watch, I have an idea!"

"We go see Mrs. White!" She signed each word distinctly, an eager anticipation written all over her face. "Put coat on." Her signs flowed smoothly into a brief pantomime as she lifted an imaginary garment onto her shoulders.

"Open door," she signed, then a look of surprise covered her face at what she saw outside.

"Rain! Get umbrella!" Her signs came emphatically. Bruce and Louise and I all listened with our eyes in rapt silence. An imaginary umbrella went up over her head. She centered it to keep the rain off. For the next minute with mime, invented signs and the limited signs she had learned, we followed the pictures her tiny hands painted so clearly in the air. Walking through the rain. Folding up the umbrella. Getting into the car. Turning on the ignition. The windshield wiper swishing back and forth on the glass in front of her. Driving to the Whites'.

"Stop. Red light," she signed, then waited for a brief moment. "Green, we can go." Up a slight incline. Across a bridge. "Bridge," she signed, gliding without interruption into a turn. Two more turns. Another stop. Off with the ignition. Opening the door. Running to the Whites' house, shielding her head from the rain.

"Knock. Knock. Knock." She struck the palm of her hand, using the traditional sign. A pause, waiting, expecting. A door opening. Only a few seconds had passed but it hardly seemed we were still sitting at the table.

"Surprise!" Lynn signed to Bunny White, then ran to give her a hug. She stopped, very pleased with herself, then looked at the rest of us as if to say, "Well? What are we waiting for?"

Twenty

It was February 1974.

The whine of jet engines grew louder as our Boeing 737 taxied down the runway of Hollywood-Burbank Airport. The roar increased and vibrations shook our seats as the plane picked up speed.

I smiled at Bruce in front of us, hunched forward next to the window. He sat alone in the first row of three seats which faced the back of the plane, creating a small booth for our family. Bruce returned an excited grin and turned back to watch the runway lights, dim in the late-afternoon sun, rush by at 180 miles an hour.

Eight-year-old Lynn sat on my left, her face pressed against the oval window as if to record every vibration that the smooth cement airstrip sent shivering through the plane. Louise, next to me in the aisle seat, took my hand. The wheels left the runway, the nose of the plane tilted upward, the ground fell away rapidly beneath us. At about three hundred feet the silver wing outside Lynn's window came up as the craft commenced a slow arc that would point us toward San Francisco and Sacramento, four hundred miles to the north. Louise caught Lynn's eye with a slight wave of her hand.

"Are you scared?" she asked silently, signing the question with spontaneous gliding motions. Bruce watched the conversation from his seat by the other window in front of Lynn.

"No!" Lynn snapped her tiny thumb and two opposing fingers together with extra force to emphasize how she felt, then turned to watch the cars and buildings grow small beneath us.

More than four years had passed since that night in December

1969 when Lynn had first signed "love you," but it seemed like a decade. When she signed she *mouthed* each word; she still could not speak most words distinctly enough for anyone except Louise, Bruce or me to understand. And Sign had become a second language for the rest of us, one we would go on learning the rest of our lives.

A short distance from the airport's western boundary lay Valhalla Cemetery. I looked past Lynn as the plane banked again; far below I could see row upon row of tiny grave markers, the lines broken only by a twisting narrow road that wound like a black ribbon through patches of green lawn and trees. I leaned forward and touched Lynn's knee.

"That's where Grandma was buried today." The words came off my hands at the same time that I spoke them. I pointed out the window to the landscape below.

"Down there?" Lynn signed back. I nodded a simultaneous "yes" with my head and right fist. Her eyes widened, then grew misty.

"Really!" she said in her clearest voice, her index finger moving forward from her lips in a graceful arc, the effortless sign seeming to coax the word off her tongue. She pressed her nose against the window again as we passed directly over the spot where, an hour before, we had stood beside the gray wreath-covered coffin with family and friends. It now appeared like a postage stamp inside a ring of miniature flowers.

"Look! There's the cemetery," I told Louise. She leaned over to catch a fleeting glimpse. The last rays of the afternoon sun filtered through a row of tall trees; like an honor guard the long shadows stood motionless along the western edge of the cemetery.

The scene vanished quickly, as if someone had tripped the shutter on a camera. The sun glinted off the left wing as it came up to meet the horizon a hundred miles out in the Pacific Ocean. I looked at Lynn, her face still glued to the window.

I recalled the first time Mom broke through the barrier of silence that had stood between her and Lynn. In a hesitant, self-conscious way, Mom had put her fists together and rolled them forward into the shape of a bowl; she crossed the first and second fingers of her right hand and moved them forward from her chin, then finished by pointing a single finger at Lynn: "How are you?"

Lynn's face had beamed with profound pleasure and not a little surprise. Grandma could sign! Instantly her hand came up, thumb to her chest, and tiny fingers had fluttered out her reply: "Fine."

"Grandma sign! Grandma sign!" she had said to Louise and me several times during that weekend visit, moving her hands in the exaggerated manner that filled her signs with emotion. Communication with Grandma gave Lynn a profound sense of acceptance.

"Is Grandma deaf?" she had asked once.

"No, she's learned to sign so she can talk to you."

Lynn sat silent for a long time after Louise said that, as if searching for some way to tell Grandma "Thank you." Mom, in her sixties, had started sign-language classes and attended religiously. Painful arthritis in her hands and arms had made it more difficult than we knew. Slowly, as she gained confidence and skill, she seemed to draw as much satisfaction from communicating with Lynn in signs as when she spoke with one of her other twenty grandchildren.

"Faaahthaa." Lynn's nasal voice brought me back to the present.

"What?" I struck a finger across my open left hand.

Lynn turned away, stared out the window for a few seconds. When she looked back sadness filled her eyes. "Is Grandma still dead?" Her hands swept out the question in an even, thoughtful manner.

"Yes," I answered reluctantly, my right hand closing in a fist that rocked slowly back and forth.

"Why Grandma die?" The expression on her face asked the question as clearly as the words that slid from her hands. It reached out to meet the same question that remained unanswered in all our minds.

"We will all die someday," I signed. She sat motionless, looking at the empty seats next to Bruce.

"I will *miss* Grandma," she said finally, the signs tumbling sadly off her hands, her index finger stabbing and twisting into her chin to underscore the deep disappointment expressed in that small word "miss."

I groped for words to help her understand, to share in her loss, to communicate my own grief. For Lynn, Grandma's hands had become forever silent, leaving her one less hearing person with whom she could communicate easily in her language, without the strain of guessing at words from silent lips.

"A long time ago," I explained, "when I was a small boy and my grandfather died, Grandma told me he went to live with God."

Lynn nodded, then after several moments she signed again.

"Can God sign?" She held the last word suspended in front of her for several seconds, her hands moving slowly in alternating fashion, down, out and up, with long gliding movements as if to say, "If God does sign, He would do it like this!" I started to speak, but before my hands could reply, Lynn answered her own question, emphatically nodding her head to add, "Yes, of course He can."

We looked out at the darkening sky and the thousands of lights that had started to come on far below. Then, as if to change the subject, she turned and asked, "How far S.F.?" Her left hand, in the tight fist of an "s," circled in a small loop, then moved smoothly into an "f."

"About three hundred m-i-l-e-s," I replied. "We should arrive there in about half an hour."

Bruce, who had watched our conversation without comment, finally spoke. "Will we change planes in S.F.?" he asked, signing at the same time for Lynn's benefit.

"No," Louise signed, then said, "We only stop to let people off or to take on new passengers."

The "No Smoking" sign over each row of seats had blinked off and I could now feel the plane begin to level off as we reached our cruising altitude. Bruce and Lynn both turned back to their windows and the twinkling lights that spread out in every direction across the California countryside. Louise and I adjusted our seat backs to a reclining position.

Lynn tugged at my arm. "Airplane, does this airplane have a name?" she asked, chopping together two fingers on each hand with extra force to emphasize her last sign.

"B-o-e-i-n-g 7-2-7," I finger-spelled.

"Will I go to school tomorrow?" she asked, changing the subject.

"Yes, in the morning." I thought about Starr King Exceptional School and the changes that had occurred during the last two years. The long restriction against using sign language had finally lifted; deaf children could now talk to one another in their native language without fear of reprisals. Teachers had started to learn sign language, and no longer did Lynn have to go to another school in order to sign.

The plane began to shake slightly. I looked up. The captain announced we would pass through some turbulent air for a few minutes, nothing serious. Then the shakiness turned to a bumpy, jerking motion.

"What's that?" Lynn asked, looking around.

"Choppy air," I signed. "The pilot said we will pass through it soon." She grinned, then turned back to her window to enjoy the stronger vibrations.

Our plane landed at the Sacramento airport after darkness had settled over the valley. We drove home and soon were all asleep.

"Is Grandma still dead?" Lynn asked the next evening after dinner. We talked again about death, about life after death, about my mom and the events of the last few days.

"Can we go see Mrs. White?" Lynn asked after a long, thoughtful silence. It was as if she wanted to make sure her "other grandma" was still alive, waiting to sign to her. As we piled into the car and drove to Bill and Bunny White's house, a mile away, I felt a new appreciation for our deaf friends.

"My grandma died," Lynn signed to Bunny soon after we went into their living room. "She went to be with God. She can't come back." While Bill and I talked, I couldn't help eavesdropping out of the corner of my eye.

"Do you want me to be your grandma?" Bunny asked, her soft hands signing with graceful movements. Without answering, Lynn reached out and gave her a long hug.

Eighteen months later, in August 1975, we went camping. We loaded our red tent-trailer and headed out of town on Highway 50. It must have reached 100 degrees in the shade that day, but as we climbed into the Sierras the temperature seemed to drop another degree with each curve of the mountain road. For three days we camped on the west shore of Lake Tahoe, enjoying our last short vacation before school began. We planned to leave on Friday to arrive home before the Labor Day weekend traffic began to jam the highways and overflow into the campgrounds.

"Are we going home now?" Lynn signed as she and Bruce helped load the trailer.

"Yes," Bruce signed back. "But we're going to stop and meet Bill and Bunny at a casino." He used a sign Lynn had invented, pulling back and forth on a slot-machine lever. Nothing could have pleased her more! She raced over to Louise, signing so fast neither of us could understand. She wanted to verify what Bruce had told her.

"Yes. Yes. Yes," Louise said, "At the Sahara Tahoe. We'll have dinner with them." From then on, Lynn kept hurrying all of us to finish packing and get on the road.

In the huge banquet room of the hotel, we sat at a table for six and signed and talked and laughed for two hours over dinner. Aware of the curious glances from people around us, I no longer felt conspicuous. Lynn recounted in wide sweeping gestures the events of our camping trip for Bunny and Bill. Bruce filled in the details here and there, signing and talking as if he were deaf himself. We finished dinner and decided to look around the Sahara Tahoe, perhaps walk through the large casino before heading home.

At one end of a cavernous lobby sat a bank of electronic games, a place where parents left their children while they played the slot machines and roulette tables or drank in one of the many bars. On our way to the game area I stopped at a row of slot machines in a small alcove. I changed two quarters in a wall machine; then, explaining to Lynn and Bruce that people usually lost more money than they earned by gambling, I started disposing of my ten nickels. Everyone crowded around to watch. The first nickel brought an orange, a pear and plum dancing up in the little windows. Lynn signed the names of each, then I deposited the second nickel without any better success. On the third try, nickels came jingling out of the machine; I decided not to push my luck any further.

We meandered over to the children's game center, not wanting to end our brief visit with the Whites. I gave Lynn a quarter and pointed to the change machine so she could get some nickels. Eagerly she dashed forward, pushed the quarter into the slot, turned the knob and started jumping up and down excitedly.

"I won! I won!" she signed, half in jest and half believing that somehow *five* nickels must have more value than *one* quarter. We left Bruce and Lynn racing cars on a TV screen and walked back to the large, brightly lit casino. We stood near the entrance talking casually and watching the bustle of activity. Five minutes had passed when Lynn appeared and began tugging at my arm.

"Two deaf boys!" she signed, pointing urgently back toward the children's games, beckoning me to follow her.

"I'll be over at the games with Lynn," I said quietly to Louise. She and Bill and Bunny had become engrossed in the outcome of a nearby roulette game.

About a dozen boys and girls, ranging in age from seven to fourteen, were playing games or watching others play. Bruce had joined a group of six or seven; eyes glued to a large television screen on which four brightly colored blips of light moved, they shouted encouragement to two boys who sat opposite the screen on chairs fitted with steering wheels. It was impossible to tell which of the boys might be deaf. Lynn tugged on my hand and pointed to a freckle-faced boy who stood several inches taller than Lynn and must have been a year older.

"Can he sign?" I asked her.

"No. Never learned Sign." Now the boy saw Lynn standing with me and came running over to us.

"My father." Lynn signed the words and mouthed them clearly at the same time. Then she pointed matter-of-factly at me. The boy smiled but said nothing.

"What is your name?" I spoke slowly and distinctly, signing at the same time. His face went into a series of contorted expressions of perplexity, embarrassment and what seemed like an effort to speak.

"Ooooohoooaaadddnnaahhh!" His mouth moved with exaggerated lip movements. A hollow, nasal sound, more like the cry of an animal than the voice of a human, filled the air and brought curious looks from the other children and some passers-by.

"Can you understand signs?" I asked, trying to speak more distinctly and moving my hands more slowly.

"Aaaahhhaaeeeinnnnnh!"

I felt a tight, empty feeling in the pit of my stomach, a great sense of helplessness such as I had not felt in four years. He reached out, apparently to shake my hand; when I responded, he clasped my hand in both of his and began pulling as if to lead me away from the game area, shaking my hand up and down and from side to side. I could feel the stares from people nearby.

"Ffaaaerrrr! Ffaaaeerrr! Ffaaaeerrr!" His loud, unnatural sounds made me feel more conspicuous than ever as he kept pulling and making louder noises, pointing in the direction he wanted me to go.

I pulled him back toward me and pointed to Bruce, who had taken over one of the steering wheels at the racing game. The deaf boy now dropped my hand and ran to Bruce, grabbing his arm to get his attention. Excitedly he imitated Bruce's actions, turning an imaginary steering wheel back and forth in short, jerky motions, his eyes darting from Bruce to me and back again. He seemed to be trying to tell me that he could play the game too. Bruce lost the race, gave his place to another boy, then came to where Lynn and I stood, followed by the deaf boy.

"Can he sign or talk?" I asked Bruce.

"I think he was trying to say 'father,' " Bruce replied, signing so Lynn could understand him. "No. He doesn't know signs. He sure makes a lot of gestures, though."

The deaf boy watched us, then made an awkward, pointing movement, followed by moving his arm up and down. It had no meaning to any of us. He repeated the gesture, then began pumping his arm back and forth, up and down, over and over again, as if somehow the repetitions would make us understand. An angry, futile expression filled his freckled face. I looked at Bruce, at Lynn, shaking my head in helpless questioning. The empty feeling in the pit of my stomach grew more intense. As the deaf boy gestured, his face twitched and grimaced in seemingly random expressions.

I glanced up for an instant and another boy, about Bruce's age, caught my eye. He had been watching from about ten feet away.

"You deaf?" he signed, much to my surprise.

"No," I signed back as he approached. "My daughter is deaf." I pointed at Lynn, who was still trying to figure out how to communicate with this strange anomaly, a deaf boy who couldn't sign or talk or make himself understood.

"I talked to her." The older of the two boys smiled as he signed. "I'm deaf too."

"Do you know this boy?" I asked, pointing to the freckle-faced boy, who was still trying to say something to Bruce.

"No. It's really sad. He goes to an oral school. I went to one and couldn't communicate either." He signed fluently in the idiom of American Sign Language.

Louise, Bill and Bunny joined us just then and we all introduced ourselves to the older deaf boy. He seemed delighted and almost overcome to find so many adults and children signing in this place. John, we learned, was twelve. He attended the State School for the Deaf at Riverside in California. He talked about his schools and teachers, recalling how he couldn't communicate at all when he had started at the state school when he was eight.

"Do you know Mr. Schmidt, a teacher at your school?" Bill asked.

"Yes! He's my print-shop teacher!" John's eyes lit up as he signed with excited, quick movements.

"He's an old friend of mine. We went to college together at Gallaudet." For five minutes we talked, mostly Bill and John, and as their hands flew, often using expressions in Sign that I did not understand, I sensed an immediate bond, a profound sense that this fifty-four-year-old man and the twelve-year-old boy who had met only minutes before had known each other all their lives. It was as if their facial expressions and bodily movements became part of the language of signs that flowed from their hands, as if the very act of communication in Sign said something more than the words that came off their fingers.

The deaf boy without a name stood quietly watching Bill and John. Then Bill turned to him and signed, speaking at the same time. "What's your name?"

For an instant it seemed as if the entire hotel, the noise of children playing games, the clanging slot machines off in the distance, the laughter coming from the casino had all evaporated. There we stood, surrounded by deafness. Bill and Bunny, parents of hearing children. Louise and I, slowly learning the language of deafness. Lynn, deaf from birth, signing fluently. John, a twelve-year-old, like Bruce in so many ways, except he couldn't hear. Yet both could sign. But all eyes were on the boy without a name.

Silence. A look of painful embarrassment spread across his uncomprehending face. A lump formed in my throat. I wanted to do something, do anything, but we all seemed frozen in silence to the red-and-gold commercial carpeting. Concealed under his shirt, two bulges protruded where expensive hearing aids pressed against his body, held tight by an unseen harness. Wires ran up his neck to ear-mold receivers which fit tightly in each ear.

With volcanic force the memories that had begun to fade erupted inside of me. Hearing aids. Auditory trainers. Jumping! Running! Falling down! Banging on pans! Hoping. Lynn, pointing, grimacing, crying, screaming in tantrums born of frustration. Dashing for experience books. Pointing. Questioning. Page after page of pictures. "What do you want?" Hour after hour of repetition. Ball. Shoe. Spoon. The sad face of a black grandmother: "When will our Sally talk?" "You must be patient." "Everyone has *some* residual hearing." Someday. Someday. Someday Lynn will talk.

A great surge of anger flooded over me. And a mixture of sorrow and hopelessness for this tow-headed, freckle-faced boy who didn't have a name!

Why? Why?

Deafness in itself was handicap enough. But deafness without language!

I reached out and the deaf boy took my hand. He shook it again in an overstated manner, as if to say, "*Please* understand me." Then he pointed to a group of six people standing nearby.

"That must be his parents," I signed to the others and we walked toward them in silence.

John had run ahead, and by the way one of the men put his arm on John's shoulder I knew it must be his father.

"Hi." I introduced myself, speaking and signing, nodding at John. "We were just talking to John. My daughter"—I nodded at Lynn, who had taken Louise's hand—"she's deaf too." In the next few seconds we learned that John's parents, quite by accident, had just met the parents and grandparents of the other deaf boy. They told us his name was Mark.

"We decided to send John to the Riverside School for the Deaf about four years ago." John's father spoke hesitantly, as if he needed to explain why his son went to a residential school. "We're very happy with his progress, but we do miss not having him at home. But *John* is much happier now that he has friends he can communicate with." Both of John's parents looked down at their son, a wistful expression on their faces. John's mother spoke, and Louise began interpreting her words into Sign so that Bill and Bunny and Lynn and John could understand.

"We just haven't had time to learn sign language," she said. "We can finger-spell very slowly when John doesn't understand us. He has become a pretty good lip reader since going to the state school." John, standing with his father's arm resting loosely on his shoulder, never took his eyes off Louise's face and hands. Mark's parents and grandparents listened politely: the father shifted nervously and looked toward the front of the hotel.

"We really must be going," John's mother added quickly. "It was nice to meet all of you."

They walked away and Mark's father shifted, as if to leave also, but his wife and Mark's grandparents made no move. "Where are you folks from?" Louise asked, breaking the tension that had arisen when John and his parents left.

"We're from Los Angeles," Mark's mother said, smiling in a friendly but guarded manner.

"Mark went to the John Tracy Clinic School for four years," she said. "Three years ago we moved to be near a new oral school."

Then Bill spoke. His words came in the clearly discernible tones of a deaf man, but he spoke with compassion and frankness. "I had an enjoyable visit with John. No problem communicating with him. But I can't communicate with your boy at all. Have you ever considered learning sign language?"

Mark's mother lowered her eyes; her upper lip quivered slightly, her face flushed, she fought back the tears. Her voice cracked as she spoke. "I've thought of learning signs," she admitted. "I've even looked into classes, but there is so much pressure on us. All our friends at school are oral. They keep encouraging us to be patient, to keep trying. I have prayed for the Lord to give us direction. Did it take you long to learn to sign?" She looked at Louise.

"Well, I'm still learning after five years, but we were able to communicate with Lynn very quickly."

"Mark is *not* dumb." The silver-haired grandmother had entered the conversation. Her voice was soft, but intense. "He is really a very intelligent boy. But *we* can't communicate with him at all. We have encouraged them to try sign language too. I think he really needs it."

We visited for a few minutes more. We promised to send them information on schools and sign-language classes in Southern California. We said good-bye. As they walked toward the front of the hotel Mark waved to us, a silent empty look on his face, completely unaware of what had taken place.

Heavy-hearted, we walked past the games where other children now played. We walked past the slot machines that invited people to believe, to hope with a nickel, a dime, a dollar. We walked past the open doorway to the casino, filled with people playing other games of chance. We made our way to the parking lot, chatting about Mark and John and the thousands of parents who even now were being lured by the promises of oralism.

"Good night," we said as we left the Whites. We turned and started for our car. Lynn, who had seemed especially thoughtful, suddenly turned back to Bunny and Bill and signed them a question.

"Is Mark deaf like me?" Her hands dropped silently to her side and a look of understanding spread across her face. Before either of them could answer, she turned to follow us.

Epilogue

Lynn Spradley

I was 7 years old when my father started writing *Deaf like Me*. I remember my dad sitting all day at his typewriter. There were papers all over his desk. Sometimes he got angry, pulled a paper out of the typewriter and threw it at the wastebasket. I wanted to know what he was doing. We were still learning to communicate, but he managed to explain that he was writing a story about our family back when I was still a baby. That didn't seem important to me then.

I was 11 years old and in the fifth grade when my father and Uncle Jim finished writing *Deaf Like Me*. That same year I also learned about the California School for the Deaf, Berkeley, from a school friend. We called it just Berkeley; all the kids knew what that meant. It was a residential school 100 miles from my home in Sacramento. There were more than 500 deaf kids there, and some of the teachers and counselors were deaf. They had their own football team and clubs and dances. And everyone could sign!

I wanted to go to Berkeley. My parents didn't want me to go away to school. They wanted me to stay at home and attend a mainstream class at a nearby school. But I wanted more friends and teachers I could communicate with easily. English and math were hard for me to understand, and when I came home I didn't have any friends my age who were deaf. My brother, Bruce, had lots of friends. Sometimes I got frustrated and angry or lost my temper.

Then my school hired Linda Raymond, a graduate of Gallaudet University, to direct the deaf program. Linda was deaf, and she understood how I felt. She helped me convince my parents that I should go to Berkeley.

I entered the sixth grade at the Berkeley school in September 1977 when I was 12 years old. Hedy Stern was my new teacher. She and her husband had both graduated from Gallaudet University. Hedy made us work very hard, but we loved her. She could make us understand anything with her dramatic signs and expressive face. I thought mainstreaming must be *boring* compared to this!

One evening in April 1978 Hedy drove her van to a Walden's bookstore. She was pregnant and wanted to buy a baby book. But the title *Deaf Like Me* caught her eye. It was on the same shelf with the baby books. She picked it up and was surprised because the story was about me. She paid for the book and went home and started reading it. She was so excited she forgot about the baby book. She even forgot to wash the dinner dishes!

The next day Hedy had a surprise for me and my classmates. She showed us a new book. I read the title and saw my father's and Uncle Jim's names across the bottom. I was shocked and excited. My classmates were very curious. When Hedy explained that the book was about me, they wanted to know why someone had not written a book about them. Then they acted very proud that we were in the same class together. I was proud too.

Deaf Like Me was too difficult for us to read on our own yet. So Hedy read a chapter every night at home. The next day she told us what happened and read parts of the story from the book. We all sat very still and watched her. If someone interrupted, we got angry. We didn't want her to stop. This was our story, not just mine. Our favorite part (it had happened to all of us!) was about me waiting for the yellow school bus every weekend. Of course it never came. The kids all laughed at this. I was embarrassed, but I had to laugh too.

Some of my classmates remembered going to schools like mine where they were not allowed to sign. We thought that was stupid. We felt lucky we had learned to sign and could discuss things so easily. We agreed that *Deaf Like Me* would help people understand how it feels to grow up deaf. They could understand that deaf people are not dumb. Deaf kids are just as smart as hearing kids. With sign language deaf kids can do anything.

I learned a lot from the story. Many things had happened to me that I didn't remember. I didn't know that my parents were sad, scared, and confused when they discovered I was deaf. Now I understand how they felt. They wanted me to be normal. They didn't know how to communicate with me. And people who were supposed to help them told them things about deaf kids that were not true. I'm so glad my parents learned how to sign!

I'm 19 years old now (January 1985). In June I will graduate from the new California School for the Deaf, Fremont (that's where the Berkeley school moved in 1980). I remember, when I entered the Berkeley school, that I had a lot of trouble learning to share a room with three other kids in a huge dormitory. Now I share a campus apartment with several other girls. We plan our meals and shop for food together. Our counselors have taught us important independent living skills. I'm hoping to begin full-time work after graduation.

The California School for the Deaf is a great school. The teachers and staff are wonderful. I've made many friends, and I'll miss them. I'll never forget the experiences I've had there. Neither will my teachers!

Last month I was happy to be home for a two-week vacation. My mom and I had fun Christmas shopping together. My brother was home. He is a sailmaker; a few years ago he taught me how to windsurf. We are good friends. We share many secrets.

One cold, foggy afternoon after Christmas I took *Deaf Like Me* out of the bookcase. Pookee, my cat, was sleeping nearby on the warm bricks under the woodstove. I thought about the first time I saw the book in Hedy's class. I saw Uncle Jim's name under my dad's on the cover. I felt sad that he was dead, but I also felt good that we would always have the story he helped my dad write. I opened the book and read the part about waiting for the school bus. I laughed to myself. I hope you did too.

Acknowledgments

This new softcover edition would not have happened without the enthusiasm and persistence of Jim Stentzel at Gallaudet University Press. He and I began discussing the idea in 1983; now it is a reality, thanks to his efforts and the cooperation of Martha Levin at Random House. Lynn also offers special thanks to Jim for his editorial guidance on the epilogue.

Many people contributed to the research and writing of this book. Most important, without the extensive collaboration of Louise Spradley, this book would not have been possible. At every stage of research and writing she provided intimate and perceptive details that we had overlooked or had failed to appreciate. She read each draft of the manuscript and made many suggestions for improvements. Her influence has left its imprint on every page.

Barbara Spradley was a constant source of encouragement. She listened carefully to endless discussions of the manuscript, offered many valuable insights, and helped solve many of the problems in writing.

In 1975 Macalester College in St. Paul, Minnesota, provided Jim with a sabbatical leave during which he was able to do more intensive study of language acquisitions and deafness. He visited Gallaudet University, the national college for the deaf in Washington, D.C. At Gallaudet's Linguistics Research Laboratory he conferred with Bill Stokoe, who shared freely his ideas and enthusiasm for the project.

We owe a special debt of appreciation to Bill and Bunny White. Deaf since their early teens, they read and commented on each chapter. Their understanding of the world of deaf children and adults profoundly influenced us. Without them, the experiences described in this book, as well as the writing itself, would have been far different.

Fran Worthen provided insights into Lynn's aspirations and feelings that only their unique friendship could produce. David Fontana, who heard much of this story firsthand, then listened again as we wrote it, provided humor, reflection and perspective when most needed. Susan Lescher's excitement for the manuscript and deep belief in the story helped us through a time of doubt and delay. Bob Loomis guided us through a final revision with his skillful editing and encouragement.

We wish to express our thanks to the following people who read and commented on part or all of the manuscript: Joe Spradley, Joanne Spradley, Deborah Spradley, Laura Spradley, Priscilla Spradley, Richard Currier, Jessica Myers, Mary Lou Burket, Janet Olson and Barbara Bennitt. The following people typed the manuscript and also offered support by their warm interest in the story: Deborah Spradley, Romaine Cohen and Corrine Dickey.

About the Authors

JAMES P. SPRADLEY (1933-1982) was an urban anthropologist and a writer. Born in Baker, Oregon, he grew up in Los Angeles. He received his Ph.D. in anthropology from the University of Washington. He wrote the autobiography of a Kwakiutl Indian chief in British Columbia, *Guests Never Leave Hungry*. He studied skid-row drunks in Seattle and described their lives in and out of jail in *You Owe Yourself A 'Drunk*. With another anthropologist he wrote *The Cocktail Waitress*, a study of female roles in a midwestern college bar. His final work, *The Work-Stress Connection*, coauthored with another university professor, described the phases of, and offered solutions to, job burnout. Once an assistant professor of psychiatry and anthropology at the University of Washington Medical School, he was DeWitt Wallace Professor of Anthropology at Macalester College, St. Paul, Minnesota, at the time of his death. He is survived by his wife, Barbara, and their three daughters.

THOMAS S. SPRADLEY, Lynn's father, is a native of Los Angeles where he attended the state university. He holds a master's degree in mathematics from the University of Oklahoma. In 1980 he received an honorary doctor of humane letters degree from Gallaudet University. Currently he teaches mathematics at American River College in Sacramento, California, where he lives with his wife, Louise.

Other Books of Interest
from
Gallaudet University Press

Kid-Friendly Parenting with Deaf and Hard of Hearing Children: A Treasury of Activities
Toward Better Behavior, by Daria Medwid and Denise Chapman Weston
Sound advice and scores of play activities for parents to use with their deaf or hard of hearing
children from ages 3 to 12 to foster positive behavior changes. Written by child and family
therapists experienced working with deaf people, this guide helps parents set limits and avoid
power struggles.
320 pages, paperback, ISBN 1-56368-031-9

The Signing Family: What Every Parent Should Know about Sign Communication, by
David A. Stewart and Barbara Luetke-Stahlman
Two well-qualified educators of the deaf present to parents a rationale for choosing to sign with
their deaf children. Describes in even-handed terms the major signing options available, from
American Sign Language, to Signed English, Signing Exact English, and examines laws and
ways to work with the school system.
192 pages, paperback, ISBN 1-56368-069-6

The Silent Garden: Raising Your Deaf Child, by Paul W. Ogden
This completely rewritten classic presents parents of deaf children with more crucial information
on the options available today, including making the immediate choices about communication
and education. Technological alternatives are described, including when and when not to
consider cochlear implants, plus valuable insights from case studies and interviews with parents.
304 pages, paperback, ISBN 1-56368-058-0

Speak To Me!, by Marcia Calhoun Forecki
The author describes openly, and with humor, her experiences with her son, Charlie, whom she
discovered was deaf when he was 18 months old.
154 pages, paperback, ISBN 0-930323-40-8

You and Your Deaf Child: A Self-Help Guide for Parents of Deaf and Hard of Hearing
Children, by John W. Adams
This completely revised second edition of the best-selling self-instructional book provides
information for parents to cope with feelings about their child's hearing loss. It offers help on
family communication methods, family unity, child development, and an introduction to the Deaf
community, with worksheets and charts to help parents practice techniques.
224 pages, paperback, ISBN 1-56368-060-2

For more information on these and other books on being deaf, the Deaf community, and sign
language textbooks, write for a free catalog:

Gallaudet University Press
800 Florida Avenue, NE
Washington, DC 20002-3695

To order, call toll-free 1-800-621-2736 V, 1-888-630-9347 TTY, 1-800-621-8476 Fax
Or order on the internet: http://gupress@gallaudet.edu